Re-membering Culture

Erasure and Renewal in Hmong American Education

BIC NGO

UNIVERSITY OF MINNESOTA PRESS
MINNEAPOLIS • LONDON

Portions of the introduction were published in a different form in Bic Ngo and Thong Vang, "Re-membering Pedagogy: Reclaiming Hmong Heritage and Belonging within a Theater Program," *Diaspora, Indigenous, and Minority Education* (2024): 1–14; and in "Hmong Culture Club as a Place of Belonging: The Cultivation of Hmong Students' Cultural and Political Identities," *Journal of Southeast Asian American Education and Advancement* 10, no. 2 (2015). Portions of chapters 1 and 6 were published in a different form in "Culture Consciousness among Hmong Immigrant Leaders: Beyond the Dichotomy of Cultural Essentialism and Cultural Hybridity," *American Educational Research Journal* 50 (2013): 958–90; and in "The Costs of 'Living the Dream' for Hmong Immigrants: The Impact of Subtractive Schooling on Family and Community," *Educational Studies* 53 (2017): 450–67. A portion of chapter 4 was published in a different form in Bic Ngo and Jill Leet-Otley, "Discourses about Gender among Hmong American Policymakers: Conflicting Views about Gender, Culture, and Hmong Youth," *Journal of Language, Identity, and Education* 10 (2011): 99–118.

Published by the University of Minnesota Press
111 Third Avenue South, Suite 290
Minneapolis, MN 55401-2520
http://www.upress.umn.edu

ISBN 978-1-5179-1074-7 (hc)
ISBN 978-1-5179-1075-4 (pb)

A Cataloging-in-Publication record for this book is available from the Library of Congress.

Printed in the United States of America on acid-free paper

UMP BmB 2024

Re-membering Culture

for Chris, Isko, and Mia

Contents

Introduction

> Yea, yea the war, USA has had many, many allies over the years, none of them but your community of locusts have expected to come here for a free ride after a police action. Come here and demand EVERYTHING. I doubt the 28-year-old mother with 10 children fought in the war. It ended 29 years ago.!!!!!!!!!!!!!! . . . I cannot afford to pay for your 12 children per family. I can hardly afford to take care of my own two. BUT SEE I only have two because I don't expect any one else to support them. But your culture does. Immigrants that have come here in the past have wanted to assimilate and learn to speak English, not you. You want all the western charity AND still be able to practice your backward way of life.
>
> —Anonymous letter to Hmong American organization, 2006

> I made a promise our wars will no longer be secret. We will no longer suffer in silence.
>
> —Zurg Xiong, Hmong American activist, 2021

Yellow flyer in hand, Hmong Culture Club secretary Paul Vue[1] announced to club members an opportunity to attend a Hmong culture day celebration at a local state college. While he detailed in English the variety of activities, such as a talent show and a dance, that were part of the event, the treasurer, Tom Lor, interpreted in Hmong for two newcomers, girls who had recently arrived from Wat Tham Krabok refugee camp. Tom Lor struggled to come up with Hmong words for "student," "talent show," and "dancing" and sought help from Mr. Moua and Ms. Lor. The other club members laughed at his trouble—and laughed considerably more when Mr. Moua interpreted "dancing" with the Hmong words for "shake body." Tom Lor shrugged, laughed, and then proclaimed, "We speak Hmonglish here!"

When students like Tom Lor struggle to speak Hmong and declare "We speak Hmonglish," they simultaneously demonstrate the hybridity of the immigrant second generation and the consequence of subtractive acculturation. Tom Lor, Paul Vue, and other Hmong students at Dayton High School turned to the school's Hmong Culture Club in an effort to curb the destruction of Hmong culture and identity. For the Hmong diaspora in the United States, the impending loss of Hmong language, culture, and heritage are part of the structured forgetting of U.S. school and society that esteems whiteness and Western knowledge systems. Although education research has long focused on culture to explain and support the academic achievement of students from minoritized communities, an analytic is needed that foregrounds the necessity of everyday endeavors to disrupt white cultural hegemony's erasure of immigrant culture.

This book is a reckoning of culture. Its analysis of Hmong American education considers the ways in which culture is deployed to enact and reject oppression. It proceeds from the understanding that the United States was and continues to be an empire wrought by white supremacy.[2] Hmong in the United States are refugees to colonized Western space and imperial center. The Hmong diaspora is part and parcel of the U.S. empire's disenfranchisement, displacement, and fragmentation of peoples globally. School[3] is a project of coloniality that advances the cultural logics of Western knowledge systems to the detriment of an array of ontologies and epistemologies. This premise significantly shifts the focus of culture in education from inclusion, competency, respect, and celebration to an analysis of culture that attends to the exigencies of recovery, renewal, and remembering due to the violences of empire building. Dr. Martin Luther King Jr. ascertained the essence of U.S. imperialism when he suggested the Vietnam conflict reflects "the Western arrogance of feeling that it has everything to teach others and nothing to learn from them."[4] As if predicting Iraq, Afghanistan, Syria, and Somalia, among others, Reverend King maintained that "the war in Vietnam is but a symptom of a far deeper malady within the American spirit" that has dire ramifications for other countries "beyond Vietnam."[5]

In addition to militarism in Vietnam, the United States waged a secret war in Laos to advance its Cold War foreign policy to control the spread of communism.[6] The war in Laos was a secret because the 1962 International Agreement on the Neutrality of Laos signed by the United States, the Soviet Union, Vietnam, China, and nine other countries prohibited military intervention in Laos.[7] In the proxy war between the United States and the Soviet Union, the Cold War superpowers and their allies pretended that the war in Laos was solely a civil war between the Royal Lao Government and communist Pathet Lao, and the United States, the Soviet Union, and their respective allies were simply providing them with advisors and material support.[8] The "charade of neutralization"[9] included "American military and CIA personnel in Laos [who] were 'sheep-dipped,' resigning their commissions, removing all military dress and insignia, adopting civilian clothing and 'cover identity.'"[10]

The CIA recruited and trained Hmong and other indigenous groups in the mountains of Laos as proxy soldiers for the United States. Under the command of General Vang Pao (a major in the Royal Lao Army at the time) the primarily Hmong special guerrilla unit or secret army fought on behalf of the United States by providing intelligence, flying bombing missions,[11] engaging in armed combat, and rescuing U.S. pilots, among other duties.[12] Other Hmong assisted as aid workers, nurses, U.S. embassy workers, and Royal Lao Police.[13] When the United States agreed to a cease-fire with the signing of the Paris Peace Accords on January 27, 1973, and withdrew its military presence and aid from Laos, more than 120,000 Hmong became refugees in their homeland.[14] In 1975, with the fall of Saigon and the Lao monarchy, the communist Pathet Lao vowed retribution against Hmong soldiers and their family members for assisting the United States.[15] While General Vang Pao and approximately three thousand other Hmong military personnel and their families were evacuated by the United States, hundreds of thousands of Hmong refugees were abandoned, left to flee political persecution and ethnic cleansing on their own.[16]

As a "malady within the American spirit,"[17] cultural imperialism in Southeast Asia involved militarism in Vietnam, Laos, and Cambodia across four decades that destroyed lives and land with artillery, bombs, and poisons; left families broken, with orphans and widows; and forced the migration of over two million people.[18] Scholars of critical refugee studies suggest that Asian refugees, such as the Hmong diaspora in the United States, are "subjects of sutured histories of settler colonialism, militarism, and displacement" whose "subjectivity has to be understood within the more expansive context of overlapping imperialist wars in and occupation of Asian countries."[19] Such an analytic is critical because U.S. storytelling fabricates the neediness of Southeast Asian refugees that compel U.S. care and rescue and masks the principal role of its imperialism in the production of refugees.[20]

U.S. militarism and narratives of refugee rescue continue to reverberate in the contemporary social, cultural, political, and economic lifeworlds of Hmong Americans. The cycle of Hmong displacement is exacerbated by the erasure of Hmong involvement in Laos on behalf of the United States within narratives of the U.S. war in Southeast Asia as the Vietnam War.[21] Indeed, the Hmong diaspora in the U.S. imperial center continue to experience "the everydayness and ongoing-ness of war and displacement."[22] Over a decade after the evacuation of General Vang Pao and the arrival of Hmong allies in the United States, the ongoing wars of Hmong refugees in La Crosse, Wisconsin, included remarks like this: "People tell them their *[sic]* taking jobs away from Americans" and "People in parks, Quillins Foodhouse (customers) tell them to go back to their country"—as well as stories like, "[A] Hmong woman was walking to her house from a doctors appointment at Lutheran Hospital white man walking toward her on sidewalk said 'you have black hair you eat dog. If you eat dog go back to your country.'"[23] Rather than a local anomaly, the Wisconsin Historical Society noted, "These racist comments and actions are not unique to La Crosse and are representative of the experiences of many Hmong refugees."[24]

The anti-Hmong hate, xenophobia, and violence have continued across three generations. Anti-Hmong hate escalated into Hmong hunter Chai Soua Yang's killing of six white hunters in self-defense in the Wisconsin woods.[25] Soon after, bumper stickers appeared in Wisconsin and Minnesota advocating anti-Hmong violence, including "Save a Deer Kill a Hmong" and "Save a Hunter Shoot a Mung."[26] Cha Vang, a thirty-year-old father of five, was killed by James Nichols, a twenty-eight-year-old white man, who shot and stabbed Vang five times in an encounter while they were hunting in Wisconsin.[27] Sao Lue Vang, a sixty-four-year-old veteran who fought on behalf of the United States in the secret war, was severely beaten, tied up, and placed in a pickup truck by Kevin Elberg, a thirty-nine-year-old white man in Pepin, Wisconsin, because he accidentally walked beyond a public property line into Elberg's private property while hunting.[28]

The violences against Hmong Americans occur not only at the hands of ordinary citizens but also at the hands of the law enforcement officers who have sworn to protect and serve them. Minneapolis police officer Jason Andersen shot nineteen-year-old Fong Lee eight times while he was running away, killing him outside an elementary school.[29] Surveillance video showed Lee was not carrying a gun, even though a gun was found three feet from his body. Police reports indicated the gun was stolen in 2004, recovered by police, and was in police possession until it was found at the scene of the shooting.[30] Less than eight months after Minneapolis police officers murdered George Floyd, Minneapolis police responded to a 911 call about gunfire inside a house. When they arrived, they engaged in a confrontation with fifty-two-year-old Chiasher Fong Vue, who came out of the house with a rifle. Police officers fired fifty-nine shots and killed Vue on his own porch.[31] Hmong farmer Soobleej Kaub Hawj, a thirty-five-year-old father of three, was killed by four Siskiyou County officers at a checkpoint outside Big Springs, California, during the Lava Fire as he attempted to enter an evacuated area to protect his property because the local fire department neglected the subdivision, which was populated primarily by Hmong farmers.[32] During the confrontation, he pointed a gun at an officer, and they responded with over sixty shots.[33] Officers from the Saint Paul Police Department responded to a 911 call at an apartment complex about a man threatening people with a knife after he was kicked out of a party in the community room.[34] They shot and killed sixty-five-year-old Yia Xiong, who did not follow their orders to drop a traditional Hmong knife because of his extreme hearing loss and a language barrier.[35]

Beyond police violence, assaults on Hmong American lives take place in their everyday existence. A Hmong mother and daughter's Black Friday shopping excursion in Appleton, Wisconsin, turned into a confrontation when a white woman heard the daughter speaking to her mother in Hmong and berated them by saying, "If you live here in America, speak the language."[36] Bee Kevin Xiong, a Saint Paul, Minnesota, father of three who was running for city council, received a racist voice mail from another resident, who ranted, "You are Hmong, and I don't understand who you people think you can take the state of Minnesota over like this. We would never vote for you. You all do everything to have the Hmongs come over in the city of Saint Paul."[37] A Hmong family in Junction City, Wisconsin, was a recipient of gunfire from their eighty-year-old neighbor, Henry Kaminski, who told the police officer that "he felt there were too many Hmong people in the area."[38] In Siskiyou County, California, Hmong farmers were targeted by ordinances that prohibited water delivery and the selling of well water without a permit to inhabitants of the Mount Shasta Vista subdivision, home to primarily Hmong farming families. The edicts forced them to choose between using water for the needs of their household (e.g., bathing, cooking, and drinking), livestock, or income-producing crop.[39]

These news accounts bear witness to the ongoing disenfranchisement of the Hmong diaspora in the United States. The stories refute master narratives of rescue by and refuge in the United States, a nation of immigrants known for its beneficence in welcoming the "tired," the "poor," and the "huddled masses yearning to breathe free."[40] Instead, the United States is "a country of refugees" shaped by operations of its own imperialism, where Hmong and other refugees were forced into migration and continue to be assaulted by (settler) colonialist structures.[41] Indeed, as Nigerian author Chimamanda Ngozi Adichie affirmed, "Stories matter. Many stories matter. Stories have been used to dispossess and to malign, but stories can also be used to empower and to humanize. Stories can break the dignity of a people, but stories can also repair that broken dignity."[42] As the epigraphs suggest, multiple stories exist about Hmong American lives. As a product of the U.S. master narrative of "rescue and liberation,"[43] the first epigraph condemns Hmong families for resisting assimilation, prolonging Hmong knowledge systems, and requiring that the United States pay its debt, even after three decades. In contrast, the second epigraph[44] gestures toward stories of continual war, the silences of cultural imperialism, and the need to *re-member* the past as a means toward the recovery of Hmong culture, community, and dignity.

RE-MEMBERING CULTURE

Ngũgĩ wa Thiong'o suggested that colonialism in Africa resulted in the dismemberment of Africa, where Africans on the continent and in the diaspora are subjected to (ongoing) divisions from land, body, and mind.[45] More than dispossession from land, colonialism induces amnesia through the severing of "the colonial subject's memory from [the] individual and collective body" and replaces it with European memory through practices of naming, language, religion, and education.[46] Dismemberment projects of colonialism produce individuals who are "detached or uprooted from their ancestral heritage by devaluing their originality and instead centralizing Western knowledge and beliefs in their cultural systems."[47] The disconnection of colonial subjects from their ancestral heritage, knowledge, and cultural systems advances identity erasure. As wa Thiong'o put it, "Dismembered from the land, from labor, from power and from memory, the result is destruction of the base from which people launch themselves into the world."[48]

As a critical intervention to the coloniality of diasporas, *re-membering* refers to both memory and membership. Re-membering involves the recovering of memory of the past (e.g., language, heritage, epistemology) as well as the reclaiming of (ethnic/indigenous group) belonging and connectedness from that which was fragmented.[49] Re-membering may be part of individuals' being if their ethnic worldview perceives them "as an extension of ancestors" and if they believe that "one belongs first before existing."[50] Put another way, re-membering facilitates a reconnection of colonized individuals with their being.[51] Practices of re-membering withstand and deny the cultural imperialist and settler colonial demand to forget.

Stuart Hall maintained that as subjects of colonialism, "not only were we [African individuals] constructed as different and other within the categories of knowledge of the West by those regimes. They had the power to make us see and experience ourselves as 'Other.'"[52] While colonialism might have ended because of independence from colonial rule, "the categories of knowledge of the West" continue to define and structure the everyday. As Maldonado-Torres suggested, "coloniality survives colonialism" because beyond the structures of colonial administrations, colonial power "define[d] culture, labor, intersubjective relations, and knowledge production well beyond the strict limits of colonial administrations."[53] Consequently, "as modern subjects we breath coloniality all the time and everyday" because of the entrenchment of Western knowledge systems.[54] Current dismemberment projects of coloniality include the privileging of Western ontology and epistemology "in books, in the criteria for academic performance, in cultural patterns, in common sense, in the self-image of peoples, in aspirations of self, and so many other aspects of our modern experience."[55]

The literature on re-membering in education emphasized the use of past experiences for the present purposes of curriculum and pedagogy.[56] For example, Dillard suggested, "Re-membering refers to the process of bringing to mind a particular event, feeling, or action from one's past experiences and the process of actually putting those memories back together in the present ('re-membering')."[57] To re-member within pedagogy requires reflection, "a process of thinking upon such remembrances of the past in order to seriously consider them, and to consider their meaning in present circumstances."[58] In a different way, King and Swartz theorized re-membering as "as an approach to recovering historical content" that involves "reconnecting knowledge of the past that has been silenced or distorted."[59]

Further, re-membering within an Afrocentric praxis of teaching for freedom "combines 're-membered' (democratized) historical content with emancipatory pedagogy that has been 're-membered' or put back together with African worldview and the cosmologies, philosophies, and cultural concepts and practices of African and Diasporan Peoples."[60] Re-membering for King and Swartz thus underscores recovering (African) historical knowledge, epistemologies, and ontologies for liberatory pedagogy.

In *Re-membering Culture,* I draw on theorizing by Ngũgĩ wa Thiong'o to understand *re-membering* as concerned with both the recovery of memory of cultural heritage (e.g., language, customs, ontology, epistemology) and cultural membership (i.e., ethnic/indigenous group belonging and connectedness).[61] My engagement of re-membering also includes the concepts of (re)storytelling, resurgence, and refusal to better elucidate the facets of re-membering that reflect the sociopolitical consciousness of Hmong Americans to the continual dispossession and dismemberment of Hmong culture and identity. First, re-membering entails *(re)storytelling.* Because "the power to narrate or to block other narratives from forming or emerging is very important to culture and imperialism, and constitutes one of the main connections between them,"[62] re-membering necessitates the proliferation of alternate stories. In the face of hegemonic stories that discount and denigrate histories, experiences, and lives, "the cure is storytelling" or "counterstorytelling."[63] Notably, storytelling is not simply a response to the stories of hegemonic culture; it is also an expression of the experiences and practices of survivance.[64] This is critical because limiting storytelling to only responses to dominant stories continues to center hegemonic narratives.[65] Groups faced with cultural and ideological domination have long engaged storytelling—through songs, letters, parables, ballads, chronicles, and narratives—for their survival and liberation.[66] For peoples who have been silenced, devalued, and othered, (re)storytelling is part of "psychic self-preservation" and a "counter-reality" that creates shared meanings, bonds, solidarity, and collectivity in ways that challenge the dismembering, authorized stories of hegemonic culture.[67] Shie-Wei Fan suggested that the "enduring value of narratives in general, and counterstories in particular, inheres in their potential to affect their listeners precisely by engendering seemingly irreconcilable perceptions of societal attitudes."[68] (Re)storytelling thus disrupts satisfaction with the current world as it stands by nurturing sociopolitical self-recovery and a different view of the world for those within hegemonic culture.[69]

Education scholarship related to (re)storytelling is primarily grounded in critical race theory's conception of counterstorytelling as an analytic framework.[70] This robust research focuses on educational lives and experiences impacted by race and racism as a challenge to deficit discourses and the neutral meritocracy of educational institutions. (Re)storytelling in education research especially functions to articulate, first, the stories of scholars in their educational and professional pathways,[71] and second, the stories of students, teachers, and families in navigating schools.[72] An example of the first type of storytelling includes Urrieta and Villenas' *testimonio,* where they cocreated a story of their racialized experiences within the academy as graduate students, teacher educators, and scholars.[73] Their story drew on mutual dialogue and testifying as well as a twenty-year corpus of re-memberings that included personal stories documented in their publications, interviews others recorded of them, email records of their experiences with microaggressions, and reflexive writing that included poems, journal entries, and personal notes. An example of the second type of storytelling includes Cho's study of Asian American teacher candidates' experiences of racism and linguicism.[74] Counterstorytelling provided preservice teachers with a way to understand, analyze, and document pejorative racial and linguistic discourses about their social and academic identities. Their storytelling allowed them to mitigate deficit discourses by legitimizing first-language narratives.

Second, re-membering enacts cultural *resurgence.* Jeff Corntassel maintained, "If colonization is a disconnecting force, then resurgence is about reconnecting with homelands, cultures, and communities."[75] As a self-affirmative and self-transformative process, cultural resurgence shifts away from the (settler) colonial state toward a positive stance of self-recognition.[76] Coulthard specified cultural resurgence is a "politics that is less oriented around attaining an affirmative form of recognition from the settler-state and society" than a recommitment to culture and tradition that provides a "radical alternative" to the colonial structures of domination.[77] The affirmation of group belonging, commitments, and relationships are continuously renewed through "everyday acts of resurgence" that take place within individual and communal practices: "prayer, speaking [the] language, honoring [. . .] ancestors," among others.[78] Daily acts of resurgence to reclaim, restore, and regenerate cultural practices that have been dismembered by projects of coloniality are essential for sustaining group membership or "peoplehood."[79]

Educational research on resurgence especially underscores relationships and collectivity, where cultural resurgence centers family and community.[80] Sumida Huaman suggested small indigenous schools are spaces of cultural resurgence, where the purpose of schools becomes an "Indigenous knowledge sanctuary" instead of an assimilationist project.[81] Indigenous school leaders and community members contribute to school as "agents of remembrance" of cultural practices, languages, and difficult histories; practitioners of place pedagogy; and navigators of Indigenous and Western knowledge systems. Corntassel and Hardbarger's explication of land-based pedagogies identified "resurgence" as part of daily life relationships of the Cherokee family and community where parents, community members, and elders passed on life skills, cultural knowledge, and language.[82] The scholars stressed that "remembering is a key part of resurgence"[83] and "foundational to such remembrance are the multi-faceted importance and functions of community and our interdependence through relationships of dependency."[84] Tzou and colleagues spotlighted the importance of families in their learning design work.[85] In particular, story making with robots where Native "families coconstructed story, meaning, and identity" was theorized as "reflect[ing] Indigenous knowledge systems in everyday ways of knowing and being."[86] Remembering, making, and retelling stories are part of family making that are part of daily acts of renewal and resurgence.

Last, I suggest re-membering involves a *refusal* of Western cultural logics. Audra Simpson theorized, "'Refusal' rather than recognition is an option for producing and maintaining alternative structures of thought, politics and traditions away from and in critical relationship to states."[87] Instead of engaging in a liberal recognition politics that presumes a hierarchical relationship between a superior (settler) colonial state and subordinated peoples (e.g., refugees, indigenous peoples) that require them to seek recognition from colonialist institutions, refusal as a political stance asserts a relationship between equals.[88] Even as relationships between equals take place in a "deeply unequal scene of articulation," refusal has the potential to be an "antidote" to inequality[89] because of the ways it rejects, reconceives, and rechannels the cultural logics of colonialism.[90]

McGranahan's explication of four qualities of refusal is constructive. First, refusal is generative. More than "a stoppage, an end to something, the breaking of relations," refusal creates and produces "something new."[91] Second, refusal is social and affiliative. Its rejection of the structures of the colonial state "produces or reproduces community" through social relations and collectivity, wherein "belonging [is] a refiguring of community."[92] Third, refusal is different than resistance. Whereas resistance and recognition "[overinscribe] the state with its power to determine what matter[s],"[93] McGranahan suggested that "refusal is a critique" that denies the power of the state's institutional structures.[94] Last, refusal is hopeful and willful because it insists on the possible rather than the probable.[95] While the probable dismisses hope in privileging the calculated, "authorized anticipation" of the status quo, hope in combination with will opens opportunities for change by "moving away from the probable into the possible."[96]

Education scholars engaged the notion of refusal to foreground the importance of relationships and reject the primacy of individualism of hegemonic culture.[97] For example, Sandy Grande's theorization of "refusing the university" affirmed the need for commitments to collectivity, mutuality, and reciprocity that respectively take up a communal ethos rather than "individualized inducements," accountability to each other and communities we claim to serve, and "social relations not contingent upon the imperatives of capital."[98] Chandler documented the ways in which Native Hawaiian scholars refused the hegemonic esteem for "new" knowledge of higher education institutions.[99] Faculty and staff incorporated ancestral knowledge into the structures of the academy by bringing in elders from the community, thus situating learning within community contexts and carving out spaces for students to honor and learn from ancestral knowledge. Additionally, Yuan elucidated the refusal of Chinese Christian parents to strive for academic achievement, upward mobility, and social recognition through state schools, secular curricula, and national exams. Parents instead chose to send their children to unsanctioned religious schools that nurtured relational practices that focused on care, family, and personal development.[100]

Re-membering Culture is an intervention to the fragmentation and erasure of Hmong cultural heritage, identity, and community. I elucidate Hmong re-membering culture through practices of (re)storytelling, resurgence, and refusal in the face of white cultural hegemony. I explore the educational experiences and contestations of Hmong children and families as part of U.S. imperialism and settler colonialism's ongoing dispossession of Hmong Americans. Aligning with the scholarship of critical refugee studies, I center the experiences of the Hmong diaspora in the United States to illuminate Hmong "refugee lifeworlds as a site of social, political, and historical critiques."[101] *Re-membering Culture* asks, what are Hmong concerns, perspectives, and knowledge production regarding culture in education? This focus moves beyond a pathologizing emphasis on refugee suffering, poverty, and abjection that serves only to substantiate and perpetuate refugee rescue narratives.[102] Its analysis of Hmong Americans re-membering culture significantly elucidates school as a site of structured forgetting within U.S. imperial architectures.

THE STUDY

At the time of the study (2006–7), Harriet City was the second largest city in the state. The metropolitan area was home to the largest concentration of Hmong in the United States. The Hmong community created multiple spaces to serve the social and cultural needs of Hmong children and families, including a half-dozen Hmong nonprofit organizations and a half-dozen Hmong charter schools. The nonprofit organizations, charter schools, and programs stressed the importance of Hmong cultural heritage and the revitalization of Hmong culture. Hmong charter schools in the area sought to teach children about Hmong language, rituals, folklore, and dance as an integrated element of the academic curriculum. These Hmong-specific schools offered curricula that "integrate[d] Hmong language and culture" or curricula that were "enriched and informed by Hmong culture and language." The various Hmong mutual assistance organizations provided educational programs to families that focused on what they termed "traditional Hmong cultural practices." A variety of mission statements declared a variety of intentions: to "empower Hmong families to acculturate to life in America . . . while retaining their cultural heritage and identity," "empower the Hmong to meet the many challenges of modern American life within a context that honors and preserves their traditions, values, and heritage," or "preserve Hmong culture and language through storytelling, gardening and the arts." Adult and youth classes that aimed to preserve Hmong culture included ones that taught Hmong dance; the *qeej,* a traditional instrument used in Hmong funeral rituals; and traditional songs and rituals for Hmong marriage ceremony *(Meej Koob)* and funeral *(Kev Pam Tuag)* customs. The common theme across the organizations was the importance of retaining and preserving Hmong knowledge systems.

Harriet City Public Schools was the state's largest school district in 2006–7, with over 40,000 students and more than 6,000 staffulty (staff and teachers). The 66 schools included 48 elementary schools, 8 middle schools, 7 high schools, and 3 alternative schools. The district website underscored its diverse makeup by noting that students spoke more than 70 languages and dialects. Students of color made up 74 percent of the students in the district, with racial identification consisting of 29.8 percent African American, 29.3 percent Asian American, 25.94 percent white American, 12.9 percent Latinx American, and 1.8 percent American Indian.[103] Sixty-nine percent of the students qualified for free or reduced-price lunch, and 40 percent were designated as English language learners (ELLs). The district reported that it had the most Hmong students in 2006, and Hmong students made up 90 percent of the Asian American students in Harriet City Public Schools.[104]

Dayton High School was one of seven high schools in the Harriet City Public Schools system. During the 2006–7 academic year, its 2,107 students made it the second largest high school by enrollment (by fewer than 15 students). Fifty-one percent of the students in the school were ELLs (second highest in the district), and 77 percent received free or reduced-price lunches (third highest in the district). The student population was made up of 82 percent students of color (third in the district) including 49 percent Asian American, 21 percent African American, 21 percent white American, 10 percent Latinx American, and 2 percent American Indian. Hmong American students represented the largest Asian ethnic group at Dayton High (46.4 percent) as well as in the district (25 percent).[105] The concentration of Asian ethnic students at the school was noteworthy for the Hmong staffulty at Dayton High. For example, one staffulty shared, "I always tease them. I'm like, 'For every four kids you see out there two of them are Asians.' I mean there's some classes that it's all Asians." The staffulty described the uniqueness of the Asian American population of the school as "a world that's so different than the rest of the outside world outside of Dayton High School."

State standardized test scores for the 2006–7 year showed that across all grade levels in the district, the percentage of students who scored "meets standard" and "exceeds standard" for reading and math was lower than students statewide. Within the district, white students had the highest reading proficiency (75.9 percent) and math proficiency (63 percent). The achievement gaps between white students and students of color ranged from 33.3 percentage points for American Indian students, 33.8 percentage points for Latinx American students, 37 percentage points for Asian American students, and 39.9 percentage points for African American students. Similarly, the math achievement gaps between white students and student of color ranged from 34.3 percentage points for American Indian students,

36.3 percentage points for Asian American students, 38.1 percentage points for Latinx American students, and 41.6 percentage points for African American students. At the school level, low proficiency scores meant Dayton High School (along with five of the seven other high schools) did not achieve adequate yearly progress in reading or math as outlined by the No Child Left Behind Act of 2001.[106]

Publicity materials declared that the school's "staff and families share common goals" for high school students, particularly in the desire for "the high school experience to be academically challenging, relevant in instruction, and to ultimately prepare students to be productive citizens able to compete in a global society." Such a neoliberal approach to education embraces market principles of individualism, competition, and consumerism as foundational to educational goals and practices.[107] As a comprehensive high school, Dayton offered over six college-access programs, an International Baccalaureate program, a job-shadowing program, extended day classes, after-school tutoring, business and community partnerships, and volunteer and service-learning opportunities. The large school was divided into small learning communities structured around five distinct academies, each with its own administrator (i.e., assistant principal), counselor, and academic chairperson. School literature explained that the academy model was important for its "ability to create a sense of belonging. Teachers and students build a supportive relationship, which promotes a positive and safe learning environment." Ninth graders began in the ninth grade academy, then chose one of four academies at the end of their ninth-grade year "based on their career path of interest." The options included the academy of fine arts, human services academy, medical and environmental studies academy, or science engineering and industrial technology academy.

Re-membering Culture is animated by an interest in the social and cultural contexts of education and aligned with the commitment of educational anthropologists to better describe, understand, and reveal the salience of culture in education. My critical ethnographic research entailed "prolonged engagement" and "persistent observation"[108] where I was immersed in the everyday[109] of Hmong students and staffulty at Dayton High four to five times a week. I attended curricular and extracurricular activities such as classes, pep rallies, club meetings, dances, and athletic competitions. Outside of the school, my fieldwork sites included community organizations, meetings, and events (e.g., Hmong New Year, family gatherings). The participant observations from fieldwork were documented first in jottings or scratch notes while in the field, then written up into field notes that described the setting, activities, and participant behaviors, interactions, and conversations.[110] After each fieldwork session, I recorded my thoughts and initial interpretations in a field log, which included a synopsis of the fieldwork, analytic memos, and reflexive memos. My fieldwork also included collecting document data, such as class handouts, assignments, announcements, school information, student data, and school and community newspapers.

The Hmong American students who participated in the study either came to the United States when they were young (1.5-generation immigrants) or were born in the United States (second-generation immigrants). The Hmong adults included teachers, staff, parents, policy makers, and leaders of Hmong mutual assistance organizations. I used information that I gleaned from participant observations to construct questions for the semi-structured interviews. The individual interviews for the study included thirty Hmong students, five Hmong parents, nine Hmong community members, and seventeen Hmong and non-Hmong staffulty. The interviews with students primarily focused on information and perspectives about their daily lives and experiences in the school and community. The interviews with Hmong parents, Hmong community leaders, and schoolteachers and staff aimed to elicit their perspectives about the educational experiences of Hmong American children and families. These interviews usually lasted an hour and often took place after school in the library, in an empty classroom, or at community centers and offices.

In order to safeguard the privacy and confidentiality of study participants, I use a variety of techniques to mask their identities, such as using pseudonyms for the names of people and places in the study and withholding details for others. For example, because of the small number of Hmong American leaders[111] in Harriet City and teachers and staff in the school district, I purposely withhold details about their positions and organizations to safeguard privacy and confidentiality. Given the small number of Hmong teachers and staff at the school and their concerns about retaliation by the district, I combine teachers and staff under the larger category of staffulty. While non-Hmong students and staffulty participated in the study, because my "writing [. . .] aims to cast doubt on the validity of accepted premises or myths, especially ones held by the majority," I intentionally center and foreground the perspectives and experiences of Hmong high school students, staffulty, parents, and community leaders.[112]

As a 1.5-generation Vietnamese refugee, I share with the Hmong participants a history of displacement and dispossession from U.S. refugee-making projects.[113] My father, uncle, and great-uncle were officers in the Army of the Republic of Vietnam, the ground forces of the South Vietnamese military, which were trained by and closely affiliated with the United States. After the fall of Saigon in April 1975, my father, his brother, and his uncle spent three, ten, and eight years, respectively, in communist reeducation or forced labor camps. In Saigon, my mother faced harassment from the communist government, which included coercing the closure of her pharmacy and opening a bookstore to sell communist propaganda. After my father was released from prison camp, my family and I escaped communist persecution, along with other so-called boat people. My shared experience as a refugee was meaningful during the study, as Hmong adults and young people affirmed our bond with language use that linked our experiences as refugees and children of refugees.

OVERVIEW OF THE BOOK

Against the backdrop of a soft September breeze and blue skies, the 2006 Dayton High School homecoming court was announced, consisting of all Hmong American students in roles as king, queen, two princes, and two princesses.[114] As one of the signature aspects of American high school culture, the composition of the Dayton High homecoming court may be viewed as a testament to Hmong ascendancy and belonging within the school and American culture. As the story goes, Hmong refugees and their children have achieved the American dream. But as Moon-Ho Jung reminds us, "reckoning with empire necessitates thinking against the nation, beyond the national myths of America."[115] *Re-membering Culture* bears witness to alternate stories, with attention to Hmong Americans' recognition and rejection of the cultural logics of Western knowledge systems.

Part I examines the epistemic injustices of education. I critically examine the culture clash trope of immigrant experiences to re-present the clash as the unequal valuing of hegemonic culture and Hmong culture. Chapter 1 brings attention to the consciousness of Hmong leaders to the dismembering force of school that undermines intimacy, family, and community. I share the perception of five Hmong community leaders on school's role in excluding Hmong experiences and perspectives, making assimilationist demands, contributing to Hmong children's identity struggles, creating distance between Hmong children and parents, and being detrimental to the Hmong family. Their storytelling reveals understanding of school's function in the demand to forget that contributes to children's Hmong language loss, ignorance about the Hmong refugee experience and sacrifices of parents and elders, and disengagement from family cultural obligations. Chapter 2 explores the struggles of Hmong parents to support their children's academic achievement within Western cultural logics. I draw on insights from Hmong leaders to illustrate that school's reflection of Western ontologies and epistemologies puts Hmong parents at a disadvantage, contributing to unequal power relations that impinge on their capacity to support their children's education. I further share the perspective of one Hmong parent on navigating the structures of school to support her children's education.

Part II details (en)counters with hegemonic narratives that prioritize individualism over collectivity and denigrate Hmong culture and identity. Chapter 3 puts into context what it means for Hmong students to live between the two worlds of school and home by illuminating the ways students juggle the demands of school as well as home to contribute to the household and clan. I share facets of the home world of students to show the importance of family interdependence within Hmong households. I detail the different ways Hmong American students in an International Baccalaureate English class played central roles in their families; I describe their struggles with the pull of individualism and the push of their desire to hold on to collectivity. My focus on International Baccalaureate students significantly shifts attention from the predominant focus on Hmong and other refugee and migrant students within English as a Second Language classes. Chapter 4 elucidates the cultural racism faced by Hmong students and families, where the traditions, values, and customs of the Hmong community become proxies for race. I provide (re)storytellings of the hegemonic representations of gender that denigrate and devalue Hmong culture and identity as patriarchal, backward, and inferior to hegemonic culture. The first half of the chapter examines Hmong leaders' recognition of negative gender representations and their articulations of the role of school in perpetuating racist discourses about gender norms in the Hmong community. I spotlight their perspectives on hegemonic narratives of patriarchy and what hegemonic culture considers early marriage in the Hmong community. The second half of the chapter presents three stories of early marriage from three female students to illustrate the multiplicity of experiences and perspectives on marriage, including one story of what hegemonic culture understands to be a forced marriage and two stories of voluntary marriage. Ultimately, I extend Hmong leaders' analysis of hegemonic culture's demonization of Hmong culture, where marriage among Hmong teenagers is framed as a distinctive problem of Hmong culture rather than a problem of teenage marriage faced by all racial groups.

Part III focuses on the claiming of culture by the Hmong American community of the Harriet City Public Schools. Chapter 5 explores the engagement of Dayton High students in re-membering Hmong culture in the school's Hmong Culture Club. I first share the desire of Hmong Club students to emphasize Hmong culture due to a sense of cultural loss and marginalization, including internalized racism from Hmong American peers. I suggest that the club's Hmong New Year celebration at the school is an example of Hmong cultural resurgence that disrupted the dominant cultural repertoire of school. Last, I show the Hmong Club's construction of ethnic boundaries to differentiate themselves from other Asian American groups, which was important for affirming and safeguarding their Hmong identities and heritage. Chapter 6 illustrates an example of the refusal of the neutrality of school by the Hmong community of Dayton High and the broader Harriet City Public Schools. I document the mobilization of Hmong students, parents, and community members under a collective Hmong identity to contest school's exclusion of Hmong culture and demand Hmong representation in district and school personnel and curriculum. I detail the Hmong community's first public forum with the superintendent, where she outlined her vision for serving Hmong students and families. I then recount the community's mobilization of Hmong culture and identity to demand that the superintendent include a Hmong American staffulty on her administrative team. Finally, I explore the insights of a Hmong leader into the cultural politics of identity of the contestation.

I conclude the book with a reflection on the implications of Hmong American education as social, political, and historical critique. I identify a set of broader problems involving the Western epistemic and ontological assumptions of school. Ultimately, I suggest the coloniality of knowledge that undergirds school cannot be resolved by inclusion and recognition. Rather, it necessitates a dismembering and recomposing of school within practices of re-membering.

PART I

Recognizing the Epistemic Injustice of Education

1 The Dismembering Force of School

It hurts very much that these children don't see our past, our struggle for them to survive. Before, they rode on our shoulders, and we carried them through long and harsh mountains and jungles and rivers, and we brought them to freedom. Now we ride on their shoulders, through lands that are of gold, jungles that are of paradise—and yet I feel we're drowning, like many of our people who did not make it across the Mekong.

—Kia Vue, in Lillian Faderman, "I Begin My Life All Over: The Hmong and the American Immigrant Experience"

Kia Vue's testament about the experiences of Hmong refugee children and parents who arrived in the United States in the mid-1980s offers a glimpse of the torment of first- and 1.5-generation Hmong adults in the Harriet City Hmong American community. It is illustrative of the ongoing divestment and divisions experienced by the Hmong diaspora in the United States, where the sorrow of Hmong adults includes disappointment in children's ignorance of Hmong refugee history, mourning for Hmong family and community who died during the refugee flight through the jungles of Laos or crossing the Mekong River to Thailand, and despondency about the costs of "freedom" to their dignity, authority, and familial relationships.

School's exclusion of the views, experiences, and heritages of ethnic and racial minoritized groups has long been a concern of educational anthropologists who elucidated the implication of education that is "culturally responsive,"[1] "culturally compatible,"[2] "culturally relevant,"[3] and "culturally sustaining."[4] The deficit practices of school disregard the knowledge and belief systems of refugee and immigrant families that should be incorporated into curriculum and pedagogy. Such "subtractive schooling" advances assimilationist policies and practices that divest students of their heritage language and culture.[5]

Hmong community leaders in Harriet City understood that the lives of Hmong Americans are persistently influenced by the role and import of hegemonic culture in shaping the contours of Hmong children's education. They recognized the privileging of Western knowledge systems not only strips Hmong children of their cultural and linguistic resources but also further severs the relationships between Hmong children, families, and ethnic community. The culture consciousness[6] of Hmong leaders revealed their awareness of culture as a site of political contestation[7] and school as a dismembering force against Hmong culture and identity.

PACHEE VUE: SCHOOL EXCLUDES HMONG EXPERIENCES AND PERSPECTIVES

When school excludes Hmong knowledge production, it requires Hmong students and families to comply with and accede to Western knowledge systems that frequently do not acknowledge nor respect cultural difference,[8] classifies Hmong Americans as culturally deficient,[9] and fails to connect with them as a result of a lack of caring.[10] Hmong American leaders were critically aware of the role of exclusionary practices of school curricula that privilege hegemonic culture and perspectives. As school leader Pachee Vue insightfully noted of curricular omissions about Hmong history:

> When the curriculum encompasses all our diversity of our children, that diversity. And reading or being culturally sensitive to meeting all of our students' needs. When we have history books that is not written from just one person or one group perspective, but it's more inclusive. Saying, "You know what? This is really what happened in Vietnam, and this is how it impacted society, and this is how it impacted the world." And I think that will be the most profound, most important piece. I am sad to say, because it's very relevant—a lot of information that we're learning right now, we're learning from one group, one perspective. They write the history book. They document it. So we're learning their perspective. And I really don't know what my perspective [is]. I really don't know how the Hmong got involved. I have to do a lot of research. When can I incorporate all the information that even today we're gathering. When can this information be incorporated into a curriculum? And you don't have to give pull-out curriculum.

The school leader was conscious of the cultural exclusion of Hmong identities and experiences. She pointed out that school curricula generally are not "culturally sensitive" and thus do not meet the needs of all students.

Vue implied that school texts are written from the perspective of hegemonic culture[11] with the statement that school curricula are written from "their perspective." The repetition of "they" in "They write the history book. They document it" demarcated a boundary of difference between the contributions of Hmong and non-Hmong/white Americans.

Pachee Vue's remark about what "really" happened in Vietnam also suggests that curricular exclusions result in untruthful portrayals of history. The comment particularly alludes to the omission of the CIA's recruitment of the Hmong to assist the United States fight a secret war in northern Laos during the Vietnam War[12] that has left the Hmong neglected as "forgotten soldiers" of the United States,[13] denied of veterans' benefits and honor.[14] She suggested that structured forgetting in the Harriet City Public Schools excluded the experiences of the Hmong community and consigned children and families to pursue Hmong history on their own.

The Hmong perspective was not only unrepresented in curricula but also in teachers and staff. Vue especially noted that Hmong teachers and staff are important for Hmong parent engagement: "There's not enough teachers, there's not enough principals. There's not enough people that are Hmong that are very visible." Moreover, the Hmong leader observed that since school centers Western knowledge and belief systems and Hmong culture is constructed as "a barrier" to school engagement, Hmong staffulty are even more vital for Hmong parents:

> When their culture is a barrier, parents want to feel that sense that someone will understand me. Someone will understand where I'm coming from. And I think all of us want a sense of identity, a sense of belonging, a sense of being understood. What I've noticed is that many of our families right now, especially families that when there's a language and when there's a language and cultural barriers, they want to feel like, that they can contribute. They want to feel like they can help their children be successful.

Vue implied the alienation of Hmong parents from school exists at the psychoemotional level, marked by a sense that they do not belong. Her observation of their struggles to be understood and contribute to their children's education point to cultural exclusion that deprive Hmong parents of knowledge systems integral to their school engagement.[15]

Pachee Vue's assessment that school excludes Hmong experiences and perspectives instantiated the existence of differential power in the school curriculum. The privileging of hegemonic culture empowers Western knowledges and worldviews while disempowering those of Hmong Americans. Although school excludes Hmong perspectives, Hmong students are nonetheless required to "conform to and abide by curricula and school systems that often do not recognize nor honour difference."[16] As Apple maintained, the kind of knowledge that becomes "official knowledge" in school must be understood in consideration of educational and social inequality because "the ways in which it is organized, who is empowered to teach it, what counts as an appropriate display of having learned it" become "part and parcel of how dominance and subordination are reproduced and altered in this society."[17]

MAI XIONG: SCHOOL MAKES ASSIMILATIONIST DEMANDS

The Hmong leaders' awareness of the ways in which school privileged hegemonic U.S. culture was not categorically expressed in terms of an advocacy for the inclusion of Hmong culture in curriculum and pedagogy. Unlike Pachee Vue, Hmong leader Mai Xiong did not mourn the exclusion of Hmong experiences and perspectives even though she especially understood the pressure to assimilate. Consider her awareness of the ways in which "Americans" hold on to culture:

> So I was in Africa. They [Americans living in Africa] did not want their kids to become African. They didn't want them to learn the sentiments, to learn the language. They valued being American, they put them in American schools, through the American curriculum. I mean it's, I think when I share that example with Americans and they realize, "Oh yeah." 'Cause Americans are the ones who most hold on to culture.
>
> [. . .]
>
> Oh yeah. They are, they are the worst. 'Cause I felt really bad because again, when I was in Africa for two months—I was just volunteering with a church group over there—and what I found with the American workers, they really separated their children from the African children. I'm like, that's terrible. Some of them don't even, some of them were in junior high but they went to all-European schools or American school. And if the Africans were wealthy enough, they would send them to American school because they valued the American language or that skill for their children and then they would have American friends. So how could you live in this—Africa—but not really be engaged in your neighbors or involved in their lives. And so I'm like, "Hmm." I came away from that experience saying, "So

> what's wrong with the Hmong wanting to be Hmong? Why can't they be Hmong?"

In this observation about her travels, Xiong noted that rather than adapt to the local context, Americans in Africa infuse "American" values into local schools. While prevalent anti-immigrant discourses allege refugees and immigrants are "unassimilable" because they hold on to their cultures and refuse English acquisition and Americanization,[18] the leader suggested that in actuality, "Americans are the ones who most hold on to culture." In the second excerpt, Xiong's remark that Americans "really separated their children from the African children" underscored the ways in which Americans separate their children from African children and knowledge systems by placing them in schools for "all-European or American" children.

Despite her discernment of white cultural hegemony within schools, Mai Xiong did not espouse its incorporation into school curricula. Her explication of the role of culture in education stressed the importance of the cultural capital[19] of hegemonic society for college success and upward mobility:

> So I'm like, "Why can't the Hmong parents come here and have Hmong school, where you teach the language, Hmong history, Hmong culture, Hmong instruments?" Why's that so hard for mainstream to accept, that that's what parents want? . . . But the reality is that, when they go to college, they're going to have to interact with others from different social and cultural groups. When they work depending, they can come on and work for a Hmong employer, but the reality is that Hmong employers do not have enough jobs for Hmong employees. So they'll have to enter the job market where they will have to interact and encounter different social and cultural groups, even religious groups too. So it's hard to be separate. But again, like I said, I've done a lot of traveling. The Americans are the most strict on maintaining their American-ness.

One response to the systematic exclusion of the histories and perspectives of racial and ethnic minority groups in public schools is manifested in the creation of charter schools. These "ethnocentric," "niche," or "haven" charters[20] are purposefully created to center the specific needs of cultural, ethnic, or linguistic groups.[21] Mai Xiong recognized the desire of Hmong community members to infuse Hmong histories and experiences into their children's education, including the opening of two Hmong charter schools in Harriet City. Her question, "Why's that so hard for mainstream to accept, that that's what parents want?" simultaneously suggested the reasonableness of the desire as well as the resistance of the "mainstream" school and community. Nevertheless, the Hmong leader contended that although Hmong charter schools may provide Hmong children with an education that centers their ethnic heritage, "the reality" of U.S. school and society requires Hmong children to assimilate in order to be successful. Her recognition of white supremacy is reflected in the pointed reiteration, "Americans are the most strict on maintaining their American-ness."

Indeed, Mai Xiong was explicit about the cultural criteria that are necessary to "survive" and for "success" in the United States. She used language such as "requires" and "demands" to emphasize the dominance of "mainstream" culture. Critically, she named English language and aggressiveness as part of the "set of skills" important for survival and success:

> I just don't think that parents are getting the message that, to be a Hmong kid, you can't survive in mainstream culture. Because it requires that you know the English language. It demands that you know how to navigate with all different groups. It means that you now have to be aggressive. It means that you have to take on a whole new set of skills from the time that you are in school to when you actually get a job. People, I think people can relax once they've gotten a job. Then being a total, reverting back to the Hmongness will be OK. But in the meantime, there's still that K–12. And then even from the you know, after high school graduation to their education or employment route to become financially stable. There's all that struggle, where being totally Hmong will not lead to success in the mainstream setting.

Significantly, the Hmong leader identified assimilation as particularly important within the contexts of K–12 schools. Identification with Hmong culture and identity—"reverting back to the Hmongness"—was acceptable only after attaining education and financial security. Xiong suggested that Hmong in the U.S. diaspora consciously emphasize and deemphasize culture and identity to instrumentally acquire skills (e.g., English proficiency) and social behaviors (e.g., aggressiveness) requisite for social belonging and upward mobility.[22] From this point of view, the purpose of education is to prepare for future economic success, and success is contingent on embracing and reproducing the values of Western knowledge systems.

Significantly, the Hmong leader's construction of the Hmong community as uneducated, "traditional" antiassimilationists serves to buttress the hegemonic discourse that contributes to the stereotyping and marginalization of the Hmong diaspora in the United States. Similar to subtractive schooling, Mai Xiong failed to see the opportunity to build on the resources of ethnic and familial identities as a way to foster student engagement and academic achievement.[23] While Xiong attested to the need to embrace the hegemonic culture reflected in school, as the next three sections illustrate, other Hmong leaders disavowed school's contribution to the destruction of Hmong identity, family, and community.

KOU VANG: SCHOOL CONTRIBUTES TO HMONG CHILDREN'S IDENTITY STRUGGLES

As a prevalent discourse in academic and popular arenas, the two cultures thesis underscores the distinctive cultural differences between refugee and immigrant ethnic communities and U.S. society. According to this argument, as a result of differences in cultural values, traditions, and expectations, children of immigrants struggle to adapt because they exist "in between" the culture of their parents, who are still tied to ethnic "homelands," and the resettlement culture of the "new land."[24] As Hansen put it, "How to inhabit two worlds at the same time [is] the problem of the second generation."[25] Despite persuasive critiques,[26] analyses of refugee and immigrant experiences continue to rely on the two cultures thesis to construct the struggles of children within discourses that highlight notions of "limbo" identities that are "torn," "caught," or "stuck" in the middle, "between two cultures."

Notably, Hmong leaders also used the two cultures thesis and its related discourses to explain the experiences of Hmong children and families. Their sense making emphasized struggles of youth with cultural identities that are neither Hmong nor American. Their accounts specified Hmong youth were struggling with a limbo identity between the worlds of their family and ethnic community and that of school and mainstream society. For example, Kou Vang shared that Hmong youth are struggling with "a sense of loss of identity":

> My generation, we came here, we knew exactly where we were born, we knew exactly how we got here, and we knew that we were poor. And we weren't ashamed of being poor because we didn't know any better. And we worked hard at it, to not be poor. But we were well grounded. We knew exactly who we were. We didn't question our identity. We could speak the language, understand our parents, where they're coming from, communicate

> well with them. But with someone who was born here, I think that's harder. They don't kind of know where they're from. They hear from their parents where they were from. They hear from their parents that their parents were poor, but these kids could get almost anything they want. And so I think a sense of loss of identity goes into that.

As a 1.5-generation Hmong American, Vang maintained that he was "well grounded" and connected to his cultural heritage and thus did not question his Hmong identity. In contrast, he suggested because second-generation Hmong children "don't kind of know where they're from" they have become what wamwa Mwanga considered to be colonized peoples who are "uprooted from their ancestral heritage."[27] Children must "hear from their parents" about Hmong culture and identity because school excludes Hmong knowledge systems from curriculum and instruction. Hmong youth's lack of connection to Hmong cultural histories, language, and experiences engendered a "loss"—erasure—of culture and identity. The leader's repetition of "we knew exactly" three times underscored the deleterious change that occurred in less than a generation.

While dominant story lines of immigrant cultural conflict suggest immigrant youth are stuck in the middle between the cultures of their ethnic family and U.S. society, Vang engaged the two cultures thesis to specify the role of school in Hmong children's loss of identity:

> One of the best description I ever heard was: This kid he comes home, he tells his grandma, he says—this Hmong kid—he says, "Grandma I come home. I don't understand you. I can't communicate with you because I don't have enough Hmong. And at the same time when I go back to college, I can't understand my professor because I don't have enough English." So it's sort of like stuck in this, in the middle.

The Hmong leader observed that Hmong children struggle in school because they lack English skills while simultaneously lacking proficiency in Hmong to communicate with parents and grandparents. When refugee and immigrant children lose their heritage language, the first words to go are often the ones that convey complex thoughts and emotions, which are central to close bonds in relationships.[28] Over time, the loss of communication that fosters emotional closeness contributes to alienation between children and parents.[29]

Moreover, Kou Vang noted that the identity struggles of Hmong children are partly due to the lack of proficiency in both the Hmong and English languages because school teaches them neither the Hmong language nor adequate English proficiency necessary for college success. Hmong youth feel "lost" because they "don't belong in the mainstream community either because [they] don't look like everyone else." Consider his observation:

> With not knowing what your identity is, you're kind of lost. You don't feel like you belong with the Hmong community because maybe you don't speak Hmong anymore. Maybe your parents are doing weird stuff [shamanistic rituals] that you don't understand. But then at the same time you feel like you don't belong in the mainstream community either because you don't look like everyone else. So there's I think a sense of feeling lost for some of these young people.

The Hmong leader's articulation of Hmong youth's sense that they do not "quite fit in" or feel "quite American" critically assessed the politics of recognition of citizenship and belonging within U.S. race relations.[30] The racialization of Asian ethnics in the United States as "oriental" and an "alien body and a threat to the American national family"[31] positions Asian Americans as "perpetual foreigners,"[32] "forever foreigners,"[33] or "'foreigner-within,' even when born in the United States and the descendent of generations born here before."[34] This "assumption of foreignness" of people of Asian ancestry in the United States constructs their identities as Asian or "non-American"[35] and whites as the quintessential Americans.[36]

Kou Vang engaged the dominant discourse of Hmong children being caught "between two worlds" to assert subtractive schooling results in Hmong children forgetting Hmong language, culture, and identity. Contrary to hegemonic narratives that portray the cultures of refugee and immigrant communities as the source of their struggles in U.S. school and society, the leader's (re)storytelling makes significant the role of school in Hmong children's struggles. Hmong children are neither Hmong because of school's divestment of their ethnic language and history nor American because of U.S. practices of racial marginalization. He identified the subtractive process of language learning of school as central to the challenges faced by Hmong children and families. Hmong language loss is part of the dismemberment of children from their Hmong family, community, and heritage. As Fanon put it, "To speak means being able to use a certain syntax and possessing the morphology of such and such a language, but it means above all assuming a culture and bearing the weight of a civilization."[37]

LONG CHUE: SCHOOL CREATES DISTANCE BETWEEN HMONG CHILDREN AND PARENTS

Across ethnic groups in the United States, immigrant parents perceive processes of Americanization as the primary threat to their children and families.[38] Conflict between immigrant parents and children are often framed in terms of the push and pull of traditionalism and Americanization, where parents stress ethnic retention and children are compelled toward assimilation. The mismatch between the values and customs of immigrant communities and U.S. society is frequently described in terms of a "culture clash." For example, news headlines announce: "'People Fear What They Don't Understand': Culture Clash with Immigrants Divides Pa. Town,"[39] "*The Good Lie* Tracks Sudanese Immigrants to America and Explores a Culture Clash,"[40] "Urban Immigrants Bring a Culture Clash to Older Suburbs,"[41] and "Immigrant Parents Struggle with Cultural Clashes."[42]

In contrast to the predominant use of "culture clash" to describe the different cultural practices and worldviews between U.S. society and immigrant communities, Hmong leader Long Chue engaged the idea to emphasize the struggles between Hmong children and parents[43] that arise from different values and rates of acculturation.[44] He remarked:

> Hmong parents have a clash of cultures. There's this need to be traditional where you [children] have to follow what dad says. Whether it's right or wrong, dad is right. That's the case, and men have authority in the family, and things like that. And you [children] have to follow traditional values and all this stuff. Then you have the American culture that's seeping in. The kids are driving towards it. And there's no communication. There's no time for them to even get together. So there's even less communication. So it's even harder. So it builds even more of a barrier.

Chue's observation that part of the conflict between parents and children involved parents' demand for children to follow "traditional values" reflects the common difficulties faced by immigrant families as they navigate the demands of hegemonic culture and ethnic culture.[45] His comment, "Then you have the American culture that's seeping in" and "the kids are driving towards it" pointed to the differing influence of American culture on children and parents. Portes and Rumbaut suggested this dissonant acculturation, where "children's learning of English and American ways and simultaneously loss of the immigrant culture outstrip their parents," creates tensions in families as children move farther away from ethnic values and parental expectations.[46]

The leader's repetition of "so"—"So there's even less communication. There's no time for them to even get together. So it's even harder. So it builds even more of a barrier"—connected the tensions between parents and children to the little time they have to spend together due to the demands of work and school.[47] For the predominantly working-class Hmong families of Harriet City, parents worked long hours, often on schedules that did not coincide with their children's waking hours at home. In due course, parents and children "live parallel lives in different worlds under the same roof" but are unable to emotionally connect with each other through the sharing of daily experiences, hopes, and worries.[48]

Lisa Lowe maintained that understanding Asian American culture exclusively within hegemonic narratives of Asian American intergenerational conflict and family relations is problematic because "the reduction of the cultural politics of racialized ethnic groups, like Asian Americans, to first-generation / second-generation struggles displaces social differences into a privatized familial opposition. Such reductions contribute to the aestheticizing commodification of Asian American *cultural* differences, while denying the immigrant histories of material exclusion and differentiation."[49] Struggles between Hmong parents and children are not simply private disputes based on Hmong cultural differences that families must resolve privately. White supremacist society's privileging of English language and hegemonic culture and concomitant exclusion of Hmong language and culture substantially contribute to conflicts between parents and children. The enculturation of refugee and immigrant children by public institutions like school through exposure to American values and customs and demand for English language acquisition is a large part of the "seeping in" of American culture into the homes of families and the minds of children referenced by the Hmong leader.

Despite deploying the hegemonic narrative of culture clash, Long Chue believed the estrangement between Hmong parents and children was due to processes of subtractive schooling and acculturation that respectively excluded Hmong history and demanded assimilation:

> Growing up in this society, they don't remember the old, of how parents suffered. You ask some of these kids, they don't even know. They'll be like, "Really? That's what happened? That's what we went through?" They don't know, because they're born here. They're used to their Xbox. They're used to their cartoons. And they're used to watching the *American Idol.*

Chue stressed the influence of growing up in U.S. society on children's understanding of the history of their parents' immigration. The acquisition of American culture in combination with subtractive schooling produced an immoral knowledge that negated the suffering of parents. The phrase "How parents suffered" and questions such as "That's what happened?" and "That's what they went through?" convey the enormity of parents' hardship, which Hmong children cannot empathize with because they do not know their own family's refugee history. His examples of children's interest in and knowledge about Xbox, cartoons, and *American Idol* suggest that the topics of children's knowledge are vacuous and trivial, pointing at the futility of an education that leaves children without compassion for the pain and suffering of family members. This repudiation of Americanization brings to bear the failure of subtractive schooling to provide Hmong children with a moral education that considers and cares not only for the self but also family and community.[50]

While Stacey Lee found "Hmong adults were resisting aspects of Americanization that they viewed as either unnecessary for mainstream success or detrimental to mainstream success," such as challenging parental authority and wearing clothes associated with gangs,[51] the Hmong leaders in my study opposed the role of Americanization in stripping Hmong children of their heritage language, history, and culture. For leaders such as Long Chue, Americanization was equated with subtractive cultural assimilation[52] comprising a zero-sum game resulting in the loss of a Hmong cultural repertoire:

> They're losing a bit of what their connection was from what their parents went through. When you tell them, they're like, "Oh, really? I didn't know that." It's a new kind of concept for them to know that their parents survived the jungles of Laos just to come here. And you're pretty lucky to be born here, not experience the suffering that your brother or sister went through. They don't know that.

As Chue referred to the refugee exodus of Hmong families from Laos to Thailand after the United States pulled out of Southeast Asia, he repeatedly used "know" to bring attention to Hmong children's lack of knowledge about their family and ethnic history in comments: "Oh, really? I didn't know that," "It's a new kind of concept for them to know," and "They don't know that." For the leader, Hmong children's ignorance of the history of their family's refugee flight from the communist Pathet Lao is egregious because the history is not about the sorrow and pain of other people but of their own parents and siblings.

Chan's documentation of the personal testimony of the Chue family of Sanger's escape from Laos at the end of the Vietnam War is illustrative of the hardship and agony endured by Hmong families that are not part of Hmong children's knowledge base:

> One of the terrible things we witnessed was that people whose children would not stop crying gave them opium. If the children got an overdose, they had very little chance of survival. Some died within a few hours, these poor children looked as though the blood in their arteries and veins had become clotted. Their hearts began to beat more and more slowly until they stopped. Some of the children vomited blood within seconds, their bodies became as cold as ice. Young babies, especially, died instantaneously. Those parents with crying children who refused to give them some opium to keep them quiet were cast out of the group. People felt this had to be done to ensure everybody else's survival.[53]

Against the backdrop of the suffering of Hmong parents and family members, the Hmong leader constructed knowledge as something that is deeply cultural. Rather than being neutral, Hmong children's knowledge about Xbox and *American Idol* was viewed by the leader as part of an American cultural repertoire shaped by a nonneutral process of assimilation.[54]

As Long Chue continued to explain the conflict between Hmong children and parents, he turned to the specific role of school in Hmong children's lack of cultural competence and pointed to the need to "address the education piece":

> I wish there's more ways to address the education piece. Because every day they fall, it falls upon me to get them to learn about something or some aspect of the Hmong culture. And sometimes I have time, sometimes I don't

> have time. 'Cause I have other things I have to balance. But, certainly we can ask the other, like Mr. Thao, who's one of the older teachers that are here. He can address some of these questions. And we've been trying to outreach and go to [a Hmong community-based organization]. . . . So they have tried to go outside to get more resources sometimes.

The leader underscored the limited amount of time and resources within school to teach students about Hmong culture. His language-use of "it falls upon me" implied that Hmong culture is not only absent from the curriculum but is also missing from the capacity and willingness of non-Hmong teachers and staff to engage in Ladson-Billings's "culturally relevant pedagogy," where teachers nurture cultural competency in students and "[help] students to recognize and honor their own cultural beliefs and practices while acquiring access to the wider culture."[55] Hmong students who wish to learn about Hmong history and culture have limited means to do so within Harriet City Public Schools and must move beyond school for resources pertaining to Hmong heritage.

Long Chue's assessment that subtractive schooling created distance between Hmong children and parents held school accountable for children's ignorance—forgetting—of Hmong culture and history, and its harmful impact on family relationships. At the same time that children are quickly exposed to dominant culture in school, they are not exposed to the values and experiences of their parents and community. School leaves Hmong children with a lack of knowledge about parents' refugee history where they neither understand their hardships nor have compassion for parents in a way that could foster stronger bonds between children and parents, which are critical in the face of their dissonant acculturation. The next section extends this critique by illustrating the ways in which leaders see school as detrimental to Hmong culture and family.

TOU KHANG: SCHOOL IS DETRIMENTAL TO HMONG CULTURE AND FAMILY

Hmong social organization is based on clan and lineage systems, where the clan comprised three types of families: the subclan or lineage family, the extended family, and the nuclear family.[56] The composition of the three family tiers from largest to smallest includes the following: (1) the lineage family, consisting of all individuals of a family who descend from the same ancestral line, and who do not share the same household space; (2) the extended family, consisting of aging parents along with adult male siblings and their wives and children, who live in close geographic proximity but do not share the same household space; and (3) the nuclear family, consisting of two or more marital partners (more than two for polygamous marriages) and their children, who share the same household space.[57]

Hmong American kinship networks function as social, political, and economic support systems that contribute to the spiritual, emotional, and physical well-being of Hmong ethnics.[58] Within this worldview, "individuals find their identity within the scope of the group."[59] As Koltyk explained, the extended family takes part in (nuclear) family decisions that range from "where a family chooses to live, when they will buy a car or a home, where they will send their children to school, how they will confront an illness, all of these issues fall under the decision-making powers of families and their extended kinship network."[60] In times of need, kinship networks are mobilized to resolve crisis situations; assist with car, house, and education expenses; and find employment and housing for clan members.[61]

The Hmong leaders stressed the importance of the Hmong family structure, but they also recognized shifting values and practices. They saw patterns of relationships changing within and across generations,[62] and they mourned the deterioration of the bonds of families and kinship networks. In the Harriet City metropolitan area, Hmong families are less clustered in low-income housing; households increasingly contained only nuclear family units rather than multiple family units. With the spread of families across the city and first-ring suburbs, families became progressively less involved in each other's everyday activities. Tou Khang's explication of the decline of the Hmong family social structure is instructive:

> Well, the hardest thing for the youth is that not only are they not family oriented. . . . The Hmong family now are raising their family in isolated community. We talk about Hmong community. We talk about a physical community and a mental community. And the Hmong, we have more so a mental community than more of a physical community. So for those of us that have grown up part of our lives living in that homogeneous community where you see those physical boundaries, the function of the family, the clan together—you are able to see that, and you benefit from that so you could relate to that. But what happens now is that all these young Hmong American, they grew up in their own household, where they have never been a part of, or participated in, their family or clan activity. But their parents [are]

> still thinking that that should be a part of your life. . . . So they never really fully understood the concept of what the family activity is, or how we should support a community or a family this and that.

Koltyk observed in her work with new Hmong refugees in the early 1990s that several households of the extended family served as "multiple homes for the larger family grouping," where children "[become] familiar with many houses as home, having the liberty to eat, sleep and play in multiple places with a wide variety of caretakers."[63] Fifteen years later, Khang mourned the disappearance of such close-knit, daily interactions of the Hmong extended family as well as the overall diminishing importance of the extended and lineage families and clan, marked by the isolation of Hmong young people within the nuclear family and departure from a family orientation of mutual support and interconnectedness.

As the leader talked about the changes he saw in the Hmong community, he also noted the declining role of Hmong customs in Hmong American lives:

> Some of the things that I have observed that have changed the most: it's the physical appearance would be one, and the language and their mental capacity I would say. I mean not capacity but how—outlook—how they view themselves. Because the reason why I say that is because as a young Hmong growing up, I must say that they no longer practice, you see, a lot of the small personal or traditional etiquette that you observe. Young Hmong nowadays, they either are ignorant of it or they just don't observe that anymore. Like for example, you being appreciative of gaining knowledge from a group of family, to things like if you go past an individual or group you would lower yourself and you would say, "Excuse me for crossing your path," or things like that. Nowadays we just see young people just zoom by and have no care of the person.

Khang believed that due to Hmong youth's "outlook" or "how they view themselves," youth are no longer maintaining shared customs such as social etiquette in interactions with Hmong community members. Significantly, he saw that the way Hmong young people view themselves did not involve "being appreciative of gaining knowledge from a group of family." Since school conveys to children what knowledge is of most worth through curriculum and instruction,[64] Hmong children become partial to the hegemonic cultural knowledge of school at the expense of Hmong cultural knowledge passed down through the family.

Racial and ethnic groups distinguish themselves by creating boundaries to separate themselves from other groups.[65] For example, Filipino Americans in Espiritu's study asserted different sexual morality than American female subjects with statements such as: "I found that a lot of the Asian American friends of mine, we don't date like white girls date. We don't sleep around like white girls."[66] Hmong refugees in Koltyk's study distinguished the Hmong values of family collectivism over American values of individualism with statements such as: "Our families all help each other, just like this. Americans, they don't do this. They tell their children to 'leave home' when they turn eighteen, but we take care of our children. We help them. We work together."[67]

Similarly, as Tou Khang elaborated on the changes he saw in the Hmong community, he distinguished the Hmong and American communities by engaging binaries such as individual versus community, Hmong versus American, or Hmong versus mainstream to juxtapose cultural beliefs and practices. His observations centered on the decreasing importance of a group ethos and increasing focus on individual interests and achievements. As the leader put it: "And then the mental is thinking-wise, it's more individualized. Acclimating into the American thinking now so whereas for us [1.5 generation], we are thinking more of the community before the self or the 'I.'" Hmong leaders such as Khang saw individualism as especially apparent in the worldview of youth:

> They [youth] become more mainstream. I won't say "Americanized," because I don't know if that is a good term, but mainstream. Everybody's become more alike rather than different. So the thinking like we said earlier about more individualized. They tend to more "Me. Me." than "We. We." It's not bad. It's just how the society is functioning. They have to do that otherwise; we did what we had to do to survive, and now they are doing what they need to do to survive.

Khang understood that the shift to a focus on the individual is part of youth becoming more "mainstream." His recognition of the demands for cultural conformity and assimilation is apparent: "Everybody's become more alike rather than different." Although he acknowledged that youth are not to blame for their conformity with the remark, "It's not bad."

Similar to Mai Xiong, he also understood that assimilation is necessary to "survive" in the United States.

Hmong community leaders understood the changes in family relationships to be a part of the regular progression of life. Yet as they talked about Hmong children's relationships with their families, they also articulated a critique of the ways in which the privileging of individual achievement in schools is detrimental to the well-being of the Hmong family and community.[68] Tou Khang's explication is illustrative:

> So I see a lot of parents somewhat depressed. Because for example, a family with six or seven grown sons, but the father can't depend on them to do any of the traditional, cultural relevant activity. And then the father just found himself to be depressed and sometime even thinking about where he may have failed. Not so much what he have failed, but the kids have failed living out to be Hmong. But in the kids' mind they have not failed, they have actually become more sure of themselves. But it's the group and the family perspective thinking that they have failed. But the kids individually, they don't feel that way because they are succeeding in school and succeeding in their circle of friends. But in the eye of the Hmong, they have not.

Khang's assertion that the waning of "the group and the family perspective" has dire consequences for parents and families meaningfully implied that assimilation has brought sickness into the Hmong community.[69] His use of "depressed" to link the corrosion of a group ethos to a sickness is an indictment of hegemonic culture's focus on individual attainment. As Conquergood and Thao explained, "A sick society, according to the Hmong worldview, is one that is fragmented, alienated, highly individualistic, and ruled by competitive entrepreneurial impulses rather than communitarian drives."[70]

Crucially, Khang was cognizant of the ways in which school privileges and reproduces hegemonic culture. His repeated use of "failed" to explain children's lack of engagement with "cultural relevant" activities markedly drew on and re-presented discourses of school achievement and failure. His observation that parents believed that their "kids have failed living out to be Hmong" even though they are academically successful pointedly condemned the role of school. The leader suggested that school makes Hmong children choose either academic success or their families.[71] Put another way, because school requires students to embrace a curriculum that reflects the values and interests of hegemonic culture,[72] their academic success comes at the expense of their cultural communities and relationships.[73]

Indeed, Tou Khang intimated when school privileges Western knowledge systems, it also constructs competing versions of success. Even if Hmong children succeed in school, when they disregard family and community, parents think that they have "failed" as individuals.[74] He elaborated in this way:

> But in a lot of the family the kids have just focus on employment and academic attainment and they forget about the cultural piece. So failing the cultural piece in the family or the parents' eyes, they have failed somewhat in the life. And not able to appreciate what has been acquired because they have no experience basically. 'Cause like for example a Hmong, let's say, four-year college degree. She or he may have very good standing in terms of grade point average and a good choice of major and good degrees and would be landing a good job, but have no clue of what the Hmong life is all about. And so for the Hmong cultural piece, it would seem that the individual has failed.

The leader's emphasis on Hmong culture simultaneously denied claims of the neutral politics of school and insisted on the harmful impact of curricula that leave out the "cultural piece" that is central to Hmong kinship networks and the psychosocial well-being of the community. In light of the centrality of the family in Hmong social organization, Khang saw that even if subtractive schooling allows Hmong students to achieve college and career goals, they cannot be considered successful if they neglect family and community.

Tou Khang contended that because school requires Hmong students to embrace values of individualism and independence of hegemonic culture, their academic success comes at the cost to Hmong culture's emphasis on a group ethos and interdependence.[75] He suggests the exclusion of Hmong parents' refugee history, values, and practices serves to undermine children's cultural competency and alienate them from broader values of family and community. Ultimately, school as a dismembering project constructs competing notions of success, thus compelling Hmong students to choose either academic success or their families and Hmong community.[76]

Harriet City Hmong community leaders appropriated the hegemonic concepts of "between two worlds" and "culture clash," terms often used to describe the challenges faced by refugees and immigrants in relation to hegemonic society. In doing so, they animated the ideas in ways that exposed and condemned school as a source of the fragmentation of Hmong culture, identity, and collectivity. The (re)storytelling of the leaders is infused with social critique and a critical consciousness of school's privileging of Western knowledge systems to the detriment of Hmong culture. Their observations about the exclusion of Hmong history and experiences, the struggles of Hmong students to belong, and the role of school in the dissolution of family bonds are all part of social critique and political contestation taking place in the recognition of subtractive schooling.[77]

Illustrative remarks by Pachee Vue, Kou Vang, Tou Khang, and Long Chue underscored the various ways in which Hmong leaders perceived school requiring children and families to embrace dominant values and perspectives. Pachee Vue pointed to the ways in which school curricula reflect "their" perspective. Kou Vang remarked on the identity struggles of Hmong youth to belong in both the Hmong community and mainstream society. Long Chue incisively noted Hmong children's American cultural repertoire, to the detriment of their relationships with parents. Tou Khang astutely observed the harmful cost of school success on the interrelationships and welfare of Hmong families.

The critical consciousness of the community leaders is remarkable for its suggestive instrumentalism and politics. Mai Xiong critically understood the cultural capital of hegemonic culture is requisite for educational and economic attainment.[78] Her recognition of the pervasive, material power of hegemonic culture resulted in an advocacy of cultural assimilation as a means toward school and future success. In contrast to Mai Xiong, Tou Khang did not support the instrumental purpose of education. The Hmong leaders' divergent perspectives illustrate the ways in which school may be at the same time subjectively additive and objectively subtractive for Hmong youth.[79] That is, on the one hand, Hmong children may attain skills and knowledge useful for academic success and upward mobility; but on the other hand, they may suffer the loss of important cultural resources, such as a strong connection to family and community.[80]

Writing about African American students' "success alloyed with failure," Fordham argued that despite conformity to the expectations of hegemonic culture for school success, African Americans are still "Othered" because they still fail to achieve acceptance and inclusion.[81] Namely, school success only offers students from Black, Indigenous, or Asian (among other communities of color) a subordinated place in the U.S. racial hierarchy.[82] More than this, for Hmong American parents and adults, children's school success is alloyed—indeed tarnished—by children's failure to understand and appreciate the values, histories, and experiences of their families and community. Aspirations toward and (infrequent) attainment of school success come at the cost of Hmong language, history, and culture. As the Hmong leaders saw it, school's criteria for success not only produces family estrangement but ultimately failure in the eyes of Hmong parents and community.

2 Hmong Parents Navigating Exclusion

> Speaking in Hmong, the staffulty shared with the parents that they have time for one more question and that if they still have questions, s/he'll write them down and will forward them to the assistant principals, Mr. Sherman or Mr. Hines. Just as the Hmong staffulty finished the statement, Mr. Sherman told the staffulty that if the parents have more questions, s/he can forward their questions to him or Mr. Hines and they'll respond. The staffulty smiled and responded that s/he just did so. Mr. Sherman laughed and said, "You're way ahead of me." A Hmong female parent who was called on for the last question stood up and said, "We're parents at home, and we know that you're parents here. We want to show you our appreciation."
>
> —Dayton High Hmong Parent–Teacher Association meeting

As a type of "symbolic capital," culture is "a form of power that is not perceived as power but as legitimate demands for recognition, deference, obedience, or the services of others" in contexts such as school.[1] Cultural capital theory suggests the cultures of parents have different value in school and influence the interactions parents and children have with school, which affect children's academic achievement.[2] For parents, three types of cultural capital are relevant to school: knowledge and dispositions gained from experience with school; connections to education-related objects (e.g., books, computers, academic credentials); and connections to education-related institutions (e.g., libraries, tutoring centers, schools, universities).[3]

While all individuals have cultural capital, the various cultural capital of parents from different homes and cultures are valued differently by school and society.[4] While economic capital is the power to purchase goods, cultural capital for parents in the context of children's education is the power to support their children's academic advancement.[5] In a market context, school embodies the knowledge, dispositions, styles, language, and modes of thought and expression of hegemonic culture. It thus values the cultural capital of those from middle- and upper-class communities[6] over those of Black, Indigenous, Asian, and Latinx communities. Despite privileging Western knowledge systems of hegemonic culture in its expectations and practices, school portrays itself as universal and neutral—to the disadvantage of families from racial and ethnic minoritized groups such as the Hmong diaspora in the United States. Significantly, when parents and families do not engage with school within the parameters of its valued cultural model, they are viewed by school through a deficit lens of inadequacy and lack.[7] Often overlooked are the ways in which parents engage "navigational capital" to support their children's education by maneuvering through the institution of school—an institution that was not designed with them in mind.[8]

At Dayton High School, one example of the cultural model that guided the ways in which Hmong parents interacted with school was evident in a parent's statement at a Hmong parent–teacher organization meeting: "We're parents at home, and we know that you're parents here. We want to show you our appreciation." Such a declaration reflects a perspective that parents considered staffulty to be the authority figures in educational matters. In particular, the view that school staffulty have full authority as parents in the education of Hmong children suggests an expectation that staffulty will care for students as if they were their own children.[9] The statement also suggests a deference and gratitude to staffulty, as well as a belief in their goodwill. This assessment of the role of school staffulty and the role of parents stands in contrast to those of middle- and upper-class parents from hegemonic culture, who influence the curriculum, advocate for their children, and wield power that positions staffulty as employees who must work on the behalf of their children and families.[10] Hmong leaders such as Pachee Vue and Fue Thao recognized that Hmong parents and children are put at a disadvantage when school expects them to conform to school's Western cultural logics by possessing the knowledge, experiences, values, and dispositions—cultural capital—of parents from hegemonic culture.

PACHEE VUE: "THE EDUCATIONAL SYSTEM BACK IN LAOS AND THAILAND IS DIFFERENT THAN IN THE U.S."

In Laos, if a Hmong family was able to afford and access formal education within its village or a neighboring village, sons were typically sent to school,[11] while girls received education at home through oral histories, songs, and poems, as well as learning to take care of children and the household.[12] Similarly, the refugee camps of Thailand offered limited opportunities for formal education, up to the ninth grade at most, and were usually extended to boys from families who could afford the school fees.[13] Educational opportunities for refugee Hmong adults were extremely limited, leaving the majority of adults without formal education or literacy in any language.[14] Moreover, in Laos and Thailand, "the teacher had all the authority" and "could punish you in any way he wanted," including corporal punishment and various forms of humiliation.[15] As Lee Pao Xiong shared with Hillmer, "The teacher was sort of an extension of the parents back then, and commanded a high amount of respect."[16] The teacher held such absolute authority that Xiong remembered his "teacher taking the whole class to cut bamboo for him, to build his house. And people didn't question that."[17]

Education leader Pachee Vue reported that the frame of reference Hmong refugee parents have about their role in their children's education comes from experiences with school in Laos or the refugee camps of Thailand. From this experience, parents believed teachers are the "power of authority":

> The educational system back in Laos and Thailand is different than in the U.S. When you send a child to school, you send your child to school with an understanding that the teacher, the educator, they are the power of authority. And they will educate and for the best interests. They will do whatever it is to educate your child. And you as parents, your involvement is more limited. And so you have absolute faith almost. You send a child and you have absolute faith that this child will get a good-quality education.

Vue observed that from the standpoint of Hmong parents, teachers hold definitive knowledge about how to best educate Hmong children. This means that parents have a limited role in their children's education and must have "absolute faith" in the school system, curriculum, and wisdom of teachers. The Hmong leader concluded that the experience of Hmong parents in Laos and Thailand imparted a noninterventionist approach to education: "So the parents' involvement has always been: provide, work hard, make money, send your child to school, and education will happen."

In a similar vein, Lareau found that parents from working class communities "turned over the responsibility for education to the teacher, whom they viewed as professional" and "educated people."[18] In contrast, middle-class parents saw their role as central to their children's education, and they "described the relationship between parents and teachers as a relationship between equals" and "believed that they possessed similar or superior educational skills and prestige."[19] The cultural capital that Hmong refugee parents activate to guide their relations with school—teachers as an extension of parents—is neither recognized nor valued by school.[20]

The cultural world of school in the United States expects parents to actively support their children's education through a variety of parent involvement activities: volunteering in classrooms, assisting children with homework, attending parent–teacher conferences, attending extracurricular activities, or participating in parent–teacher associations (PTAs) or parent–teacher organizations (PTOs). Parents who are not involved in school in ways that are sanctioned by school are considered to not care about their children's education.[21] The Hmong leader noted the struggles of Hmong parents when their experience and knowledge are incongruent with those valued by school:

> It confuses parents when they come to this country and the teacher is saying, "You have to be engaging in your child's education." And parents are saying, "But you're the educator. You're supposed to be educating my child. So what do you really mean?" And so the parents are saying, "I want to help. OK. Now you want me to be engaged. How do you want me to engage?" And they say, "Well, read to your child." "Well," parents are saying, "Well, first of all, I have never—I don't know how to read myself. What other ways can I do this?"

Pachee Vue understood the bafflement of parents when teachers ask them to take part in teaching their children, partly as a result of a cultural frame of reference where teachers are "supposed to be educating my child" and partly as a result of their limited educational background. When school asks Hmong immigrant parents who had no or limited opportunity to attend school—in the United States, Laos, or the refugee camps of Thailand—to engage with their children's education by reading to them, it demands that Hmong parents have the same educational experience as parents from hegemonic culture. In other words, school requires all families to be familiar with the values and practices of hegemonic culture because "by doing away with giving explicitly to everyone what it implicitly demands of everyone, the educational system demands of everyone alike that they have what it does not give."[22]

The Hmong leader saw that although Hmong parents want to help their children, school cannot merely tell parents to "help your child with their homework." Such activities that are part of the taken-for-granted ways of hegemonic culture's view of parental involvement are not a part of Hmong parents' cultural repertoire:

> And when I say that parents want to help them, they need—They want to find out what they, what their role is. By telling a parent, "Well help your child with their homework"—Again, many parents, especially parents that lack the educational background, it makes it very difficult for them. So, I almost want to say if there was such a program that would help parents, walks them through: "How do you help a child?" And "How do you, how do you help your child with the homework?" And if the parents don't know, "What resources can you connect?"

As Vue affirmed the desire of parents to help their children and learn "their role" in relation to school, the leader also asserted the need for school to create programs that would make explicit the expectations of school.[23] She advocated for the creation of a program for Hmong parents to learn how to "do" school in the United States. Rather than focusing only on homework help programs, she called for school to take a more "holistic approach" that would help not only children but also parents in their relations with school:

> But again, it's still does not, it's not more of a holistic approach in my view. Because it helps the child, but it doesn't really quite help the parent. So there has to be an approach where the parents and the child can connect and really understand that we're working together to make sure you get a quality education. And as a parent, "What is my role and how can I support you?" Other than to say, "Your teacher said you're not doing well, so just make sure you study. And just make sure you do a good job. And that you do all your homework." I can say that, but what does that really mean? How does that really translate to how do you know success? Well, of course when the child is doing well, but in that transition to get to there, if you're not able to help your child with homework—"If I don't understand the problem, if I can't read, how can I help my child to be successful?"

From the Hmong leader's perspective, school needs to support parents in ways that allow them to move beyond simply telling their children to do their homework and do well in school. School should also address the ways in which it disadvantages refugee and immigrant parents by institutionalizing hegemonic cultural norms.

Indeed, Pachee Vue's account of school's expectations for parent involvement remarked on the "lack of cultural understanding" in its directives to Hmong parents that ignores differences in cultural standpoints, time, and finances, among other realities of refugee life:

> There are programs where they will encourage parent involvement but they are saying, "Parents, you do this. Know you drive your kids. You do all this stuff." Well, as Hmong parents, you don't have that kind of time, you don't have that kind of maybe funding, you don't have the resources. So you're saying, you're telling your parents, all parents—You're telling the mainstream parents and saying, "We want you to do this." And well, sometimes there's a lack of cultural understanding [on the part of school]. So I think there, I think there are almost—I almost want to say, there has to be programs that are specifically addressing the cultural piece of parents—Hmong parents—and helping their children.

School's directives for parents to engage in what Vue called "all this stuff" amounts to a "schoolcentric" form of parent involvement that approaches relationships with parents from the standpoint of "how can parents help the school and its teachers?"[24] while ignoring where parents are coming from in terms of time, money, and other resources. By doing so, "school defines roles for parents in the context of institutional needs and priorities" and problematically "largely ignores what families bring to school."[25] The leader understood that school's approach to parent involvement is essentially addressing "mainstream" parents while turning a blind eye to Hmong parents. She argued that in order to mitigate the inequality produced by the privileging of hegemonic culture, parent involvement programs need to address "the cultural piece" to better level the terms for Hmong parent engagement.[26] Further, Vue recognized that school's validation of hegemonic culture not only disadvantages Hmong parents but also parents from other immigrant communities. Engaging all parents requires school to address the differing cultural worlds of school and those of refugee and immigrant communities: "So it's not like just the Hmong parents. It's the

Somali parents, the Hispanic parents, the Latino parents. I don't think until there's really that [cultural] piece of that, we will have all parents engaged."

The Hmong leader also saw differences in the ways in which Hmong parents and "mainstream parents" viewed child development, which influenced Hmong children's preparedness for kindergarten. She maintained that differences in experience with education, viewpoints about what children should be doing before entering school, and socioeconomic status advantage children from middle- and upper-middle-class backgrounds and disadvantage Hmong American children from the outset of kindergarten:

> Many of the families, there's also a belief, not all, but my comment has been, when a child, before they enter school, let them be a child. And so many parents don't, they don't take the—They're not educating their children, as preparing their children for kindergarten, preparing their children for school as your mainstream parents. Where mainstream parents, a mother is home or someone's actually home. And they are reading to their child. They're teaching their child. So by the time they're entering kindergarten, they at least know their name, they know their numbers. Many of our Hmong children, when they enter kindergarten, they don't know. And so, already, when they enter elementary school, they're I don't know how many steps behind the mainstream society.

According to Vue, while Hmong parents view the time before children enter school to be a time for play, where they "let them be a child," parents from hegemonic culture consider that time to be important for kindergarten preparation. This different outlook benefits children from hegemonic culture when they enter kindergarten and leaves Hmong children "I don't know how many steps behind the mainstream society." Significantly, the Hmong leader's word choice of "mainstream" to contrast differences in perspectives and experiences between Hmong parents and parents from hegemonic culture suggests an awareness that Hmong parents have a parallel existence on the margins of U.S. society.

Pachee Vue also reported that Hmong parents' limited experience with formal education influenced knowledge about college financial aid and orientation toward college for their children. She shared, "I've encountered families where there was just so much potential, but because of the lack of resources or lack of understanding of opportunities and resources, they're not pursuing education." She particularly saw that parents' limited experience with college constrains their understanding of college financial assistance such as financial aid and scholarships and gives rise to the belief that children need a perfect 4.0 grade point average to attend college. Significantly, Vue also pointed to the role of limited financial resources on parents' college outlook:

> There's a lack of understanding that there's financial aid support, that there are scholarships, that you don't have to have 4.0 perfect score to go to college. That it is, that parents—I think both parents and students still have that lack of understanding that there is so much opportunity that you could pursue. And then meeting the immediate need—And sometime parents struggle because they are trying to meet their immediate need. And that if they have a child of that age, "Well, you just graduated so maybe it would be best for you to go and work for now. So you can help meet the basic need, paying the rent and all that stuff." Well, that turns, may be more, a temporary basis, can turn into two to three years, four to five years.

The leader's observation that Hmong parents prioritize the "immediate need" of the family over children's immediate enrollment in college after high school makes salient the financial hardship of some Hmong families who do not have enough resources to meet their everyday basic needs. Vue understood that postponing college may encroach on Hmong student's college aspirations.[27] She noted, "So then you get to the point of, 'Well, I don't know if I want to go to college anymore—maybe I should just work.'"

Moreover, the leader was concerned about the reluctance of parents to take out loans to pay for college. She suggested parents are "not understanding the investment of 'You have to invest up front because long term you're going to save.'" As Vue recounted the conversations she had with Hmong parents, she again juxtaposed a current and future view of the role education:

> I'm constantly having this conversation when I'm out in the community and talk with parents and saying, "You should go to college. It's OK to invest up front. It's OK to acquire fifty-, sixty-thousand-dollar loans. Because you will eventually—Yes, there will be a light at the end of the tunnel. And you will actually benefit more. You will get more out of this because you are getting a quality education. Because you are getting a better job. And you're not

going to work physically as hard. You may work mentally, but not physically as hard." And again, this is again some kind of lack of understanding. Lack of—It's a cultural piece too. It's a cultural piece of understanding.

The leader's comment about the "cultural piece" in understanding college as an investment underscored the different cultural perspectives that Hmong parents have about education. Her explanation to Hmong parents about taking on college debt for occupational and economic security suggests the need to make explicit the rationale for college loans.

Writing about the role of the cultural broker, Lopez and Stack maintained it is part deciphering the culture of power for community members and part affirming the community's cultural wealth, values, and rights: "[Cultural brokers are] creating a safe space in which to decode and translate the culture of power; enabling members of marginalized communities to rehearse the unfamiliar codes of the culture of power; serving as a means to deploy personal and collective social capital to gain access to networks of targeted mainstream-dominant institutions; and integrating and affirming community cultural values, resources and rights."[28] In light of the different frames of reference and cultural capital that Hmong immigrant parents bring to school, Pachee Vue saw the need for school to make explicit differing cultural standpoints. She advocated for a school "cultural specialist" or "cultural expert" to create a curriculum for parents that explicitly examines differing cultural practices and expectations:

If you have parents that are older parents, and if English is not their first language or if they have limited English, how do you communicate with them? How do you relate to them? And sometimes you have to use examples, you know, like in Laos, this is how you do things, but in the U.S., this is how it's done. How do you incorporate those two and say, "Well if you do so-and-so, well think back to when you did this. Now how did that example become a learning experience? Now if you take that and you apply it to here, how would you do that?" And so using those examples, 'cause then parents can relate to them and they go, "Oh, I understand because I did that. So, OK. I can apply something like that and use it to help my child now in the U.S. to be successful." And I don't see that happening because again, this—And I see this is the cultural piece. And you almost have to have a cultural specialist, a cultural expert to come in to help walk through this to build this kind of curriculum.

"Cultural specialists" such as parent cultural liaisons may leverage their knowledge of hegemonic cultural norms to assist parents from minoritized communities decipher school bureaucracy, understand their rights, negotiate access and resources, and advocate for cultural inclusion. Their work has the potential to contribute to the unveiling of the "subtle and not so subtle ways that formally meritocratic institutions help to recreate systems of social stratification" through pretenses of cultural neutrality.[29]

FUE THAO: "SCHOOL'S TAKING ADVANTAGE OF THE STUDENTS AND THE PARENTS AND THE COMMUNITY"

Echoing Pachee Vue, Hmong leader Fue Thao perceived Hmong parents' experience with teachers in Laos and Thailand informing their understanding of the role of school staffulty. As the leader put it, "the teacher was god" in Laos and Thailand. Although the U.S. educational system is different, parents "believe in 100 percent in what teachers do, whether it's right or wrong." He observed that Hmong parents' understanding of the authority of staffulty influenced their interactions with school, such as taking the side of staffulty during school conflicts, even to the detriment of their children:

> Or the fact that a teacher yells at them and calls them stupid or something, or degrades a student. Is that person gonna—Yeah, most teachers will blame the students or their child. Hmong parents—'Cause they're like, "You must have done something stupid." Because again, it's a culture thing because in Thailand or Laos, if you went to school, the teacher was god. And here, it's different. And they expect the same thing from the teacher. And so, they always think that it's their child [who is to blame]. . . . And so, the parents accept fully. I mean, they believe in 100 percent in what teachers do, whether it's right or wrong. And it's—That's not very healthy to have [that belief] especially if they're being taken advantage of.

Considering staffulty as a type of "god" manifests in parental support of staffulty who blame Hmong children, even if the staffulty are mistaken or malicious. Similarly, Doucet's explication of the ways in which the experiences of Haitian immigrant parents in Haiti informed their approach to U.S. school pointed to the salience of their Haitian cultural repertoire: "In Haiti, teachers are treated with utmost respect and are permitted, even expected, to reprimand their students and physically punish them if deemed necessary."[30]

While Fue Thao recognized that Hmong parents and school hold differing expectations for their roles in school, he did not see school supporting or accommodating immigrant parents' ways of knowing. In fact, he suggested that parents' esteem for staffulty, along with their quiet demeanor and willingness to accommodate staffulty, resulted in being taken advantage of by school:

> Some kids won't be as fluent in English. Or will have more of those traditional traits, like being quiet, being passive, not looking the teacher in the eye. And because of that, other students will take advantage of them. Or because of that, ignorant teachers who don't know about these customs of the Asians or whatnot or Hmong students will treat them differently or take advantage of them. . . . The school's taking advantage of the students and the parents and the community because of the cultural traits that they have. And the stereotype is that they're passive. They're quiet. They're accommodating. They're nonaggressive.

When I asked him to give an example of how he saw school taking advantage of parents and students, he reported that staffulty suspend Hmong students without notifying parents, despite district policy:

> Sometimes a kid would be caught up in some trouble. Whether they're guilty or not, it doesn't matter. They will be suspended without question sometimes. And/or without a thorough investigation. And the explanation is not offered to the parents. Sometimes the parents don't even call and the kids are sent home. I'm very, I get upset about that because it's a protocol that we have to—And it's mandated by the state that we call parents. Sometimes they skip that step because they know, "Who's gonna know about that rule?" "What Hmong parents gonna know about that rule, that administrator rule?" You know, unless it's taught to them. Unless the person is an administrator. That's a big example.

The leader's question, "What Hmong parents gonna know about that rule, that administrator rule?" alludes to staffulty abuse of parents' limited knowledge of school policies and procedures and misuse of their authority in interactions with Hmong American students, as well as the exclusion of parents in their disciplinary decision-making.

Refugee parents' limited experience with the U.S. educational system often results in a reduced understanding of various facets of school, including the curriculum and organization of school,[31] the "invisible codes of power" of school cultures,[32] and their rights as parents.[33] This in turn hinders the ways in which they may support their children's education, including the questions they ask, their assessment of school practices, and their advocacy for their children. As Fue Thao put it, "The biggest obstacle right now is that they just don't know what goes on in the schools." He emphasized the implications of Hmong parents' partial knowledge of U.S. schools in their school interactions:

> I guess they expect the best out of teachers. And they expect them to be the best, and to do what's best for the kids, and to look out for their kids. And that's not the case, not always the case. There are some that do that, but they aren't and they have to be and watch. They have to be a watchdog for their own children. They have to advocate for their own kids. And I think a lot of it is just that they're so afraid of the schools because they don't know. They just don't know. They don't know they have these rights. That's the biggest thing. They have a lack of knowledge. They don't know they can advocate for their kids. That it's OK to question authority. That it's OK to question a teacher or an administrator. "Well, what happened?" They can't just accept it.

The leader maintained that Hmong parents "have to be a watchdog for their own children" rather than believe staffulty will "do what's best for the kids." He asserted, being a "watchdog" means parents learning to monitor the actions of staffulty and learning to advocate for their children.[34]

Significantly, I suggest that Fue Thao's comment that Hmong parents "don't know they can advocate for their kids" should not be read as simply a reflection of parents' limited experience with school. It must be read as an indictment of school, where parents cannot trust staffulty to do their jobs as educators and have students' best interests in mind.[35] The necessity for parent self-advocacy rests on the problematic "assumption that parents should know that they have to fight the system to get a good education for their students."[36] The Hmong leader's assertion that school is "taking advantage" of Hmong parents and students is thus a condemnation of school's privileging of the values, dispositions, and experiences of hegemonic culture that marginalizes the standpoint of Hmong families in relationship to school. Put another way, school legitimates hegemonic culture by systematically incorporating its codes and cues into school policies and practices. It does so while simultaneously excluding and devaluing the knowledge systems of minoritized communities.[37] In order to ensure school is serving the best interests of their children, school requires parents to be involved in their children's education[38] and to know that they should scrutinize the curriculum and pedagogy of staffulty and advocate for their children.[39]

Fue Thao understood that school tacitly demands that Hmong parents and students possess the linguistic and cultural competence of hegemonic culture that it does not provide them. He declared that school needs "to make an investment to educate parents" about how school operates:

> And they're still in the transition period where they're learning to become American system parents—if there is such a phrase. And it takes time. And it takes some understanding. It takes patience. And we have to make an investment to educate the parents—the parents that are behind. The parents that are the future parents, they'll be easier because they have gone through the system. But right now, we have to have patience. We have to work with the older, traditional, conservative parents that don't know any other way or have never been touched by education.

For the leader, school should be explicit about what it demands from Hmong parents because "they're still in the transition period where they're learning to become American system parents."[40] He suggested that becoming "American system parents" involves learning about U.S. hegemonic cultural norms. Additionally, for Hmong parents who "have never been touched by education," becoming "American system parents" requires learning about school in general.

The Hmong leader advocated for staffulty to serve as resources for Hmong parents until Hmong students have acquired experience navigating school, "'Cause as the future moves on, as the students and kids move on, they will get a better sense of how to be successful because they have gone through it. Or their siblings have gone through it." In essence, the leader called on education staffulty and policymakers to be what Stanton-Salazar called "institutional agents," or "individuals who have the capacity and commitment to transmit directly, or negotiate the transmission of, institutional resources and opportunities."[41] Fue Thao insisted that educators be "proactive" with Hmong parents:

> So teachers, administrators, policymakers, whoever, you name it, we have to be resources. I think that's the biggest thing because they're not gonna come seek our help, for the most part. The conservative and the traditional, the new ones [Hmong parents], we have to kind of be a little more proactive. . . . And that holds true for every single culture. We cannot expect them to come to us. We are people who are, we are educators. We're supposed to go to them. We're supposed to educate them. We're supposed to seek them out and teach them.

Stanton-Salazar suggested, "Through relationships with institutional agents, a segment of society gains the resources, privileges, and support necessary to advance and maintain their economic and political position in society."[42] Institutional agents are imperative because institutional school structures are more influential for developing the form of social capital needed for academic success.[43] In a similar vein, the Hmong leader recognized the critical role of staffulty in Hmong parents' access to the resources and privileges required by school for the success of Hmong children. Indeed, he suggested that it is a fundamental function of staffulty to serve as a resource not only for Hmong parents but also for parents from "every single culture" to successfully navigate school.

While education leaders Pachee Vue and Fue Thao emphasized the struggles of parents who have limited experience with education, they also acknowledged the spectrum of Hmong American parents, ranging from first-generation refugee parents with limited formal education to second-generation Hmong parents who grew up in the United States and are highly educated and savvy about navigating the structures of school. In the following section, I share Xee Yang's experience with her children's education to illuminate the knowledge and resourcefulness that exist among Hmong parents. I suggest her perception of school and interactions with staffulty illustrate what Yosso called "navigational capital," which "refers to skills of maneuvering through social institutions" and "infers the ability to maneuver through institutions not created with Communities of Color in mind."[44]

XEE YANG: "I WILL SHOW UP AND SAY, 'THIS SCHOOL NO GOOD. TEACHER DO NO GOOD JOB'"

> I think they have problem, every school. It's not just only one. And I go see how the teacher teaching children. And then I can see that some teacher is very good, teaching good and then care about their job. But some of them bad. They, all they doing is just give them the material and then just sit down, do nothing, you know. Like that. So if I show up a couple of time they, I think they must be scared too. They know that somebody cares. Somebody look after the children.

These are the words of first-generation Hmong immigrant Xee Yang, a Hmong parent who was born in Laos. As a child, she fled Laos for a refugee camp in Thailand, where she married her husband when she was fourteen years old. As an orphan, she lived with an aunt in the refugee camp for six years before she and her aunt were resettled to the United States through the sponsorship of her grandparents. She was seventeen years old when she arrived in the United States with her husband and three-year-old daughter. During the time of the study, Yang worked at a medical supply manufacturing company assembling diabetes insulin pumps. As a thirty-six-year-old mother, she had eight children, two of whom were in four-year colleges, four of whom were students at Dayton High School, one who was in middle school, and one who was in elementary school.

When Xee Yang's oldest children were in elementary school, she viewed staffulty in much the same way that was described by Hmong leaders Pachee Vue and Fue Thao. She was "scared" of staffulty and believed "they have more authority to do everything." She thought parents did not have rights, even as she was upset that a teacher was keeping her daughter late after school and seeing "the principal not care at all":

> I think all the parent they kind of scared of the teacher. But I thinking that first, just tell you too that before I scared a little bit. Because I thinking that maybe the teacher they have more authority to do everything. That's how I think. Because you ask me I have to answer it true. And then like long time at school, my children in elementary school. And then one teacher is keeping my daughter late. And then the principal not care at all. And then looked like they not responsible at all. And then I'm thinking maybe—because that time I don't open my eye—I thinking that they have authority to do that or

> do this. And parents have no rights to do nothing. And I'm scared. And then after that I—The year 2003 I went to a nursing program to taking care of old people, nursing assistant. So I learn all the rule that they don't have authority to do that—the parent did.

It was only during her participation in a nursing program that Yang learned of her rights as a parent and the limited authority of school staffulty. Rather than view the staffulty as "a king" her perspective of the role of the staffulty changed: "How come I scare all those teacher? And they did not—They not a king. They not a something. They like employee. Somebody pay them to do their job. How come I am scary?"

Xee Yang's attitude toward staffulty was one of wariness. While she recognized that some staffulty are trustworthy and capable, she also observed, "Some teachers, they doesn't really care about children. They just do their job to get what they get paid." She asserted that "they don't have the right to do like that" because "they are the teacher they have to give the best material to teach the children." Despite lingering uncertainty, she pushed herself to engage more with her children's education:

> So I know that I have to make sure that they give the right material to teach. Because when I go to conference, they just—My son he not have a good reading grade. And then I ask them why. And then they say they give the material to him but he not return—Something like that. But I know that my son doing his homework and then if something's missing I force him to do, to finish. So I getting more involved with my children. I get more involved, ask the teacher more question: "How you teach my children? How you get the material? Is the principal giving to you? Or you do your own self?" Something like that. So I think, I think the teacher they kind of, they kind of want to see how much the parent care about their children. If I ask more question, if I concerned then look like they, they kind of concern. And then do their job the right way. If I don't do that then it look like they just, "Oh, parent not care." I can see it's something like that is. I don't know for sure, but that's how my vision can see like that. If I follow my children I ask him, I ask the teacher more question: "How my son doing? What's missing? How do I help my children get better? My daughter or son get better?" Then that teacher know that I care. Then he or she must say, "Oh, this and that. You make sure they return to me." So I make sure they make sure to return.

Yang believed that staffulty "want to see how much the parent care about their children" as a condition to serve her children to the best of their capabilities. She asked staffulty questions ranging from curriculum development to the progress of her children in the class. Her rationale was, "If I ask more question, if I concerned then look like they, they kind of concern. And then do their job the right way." She perceptively recognized that she needed to be an advocate for her children in order for staffulty to educate them well.[45]

Xee Yang's skepticism toward staffulty was informed by experiences that called into question staffulty's commitment to the best interests of her children. One notable experience occurred at a parent–teacher conference where a staffulty told her that her son was doing "good" in the class even though his grades were in the C and D range:

> But most of them they did good too. But just some of them they'd say, when I get there they'd say, "Oh, your children do good." But when they show me the grades not good. So I say, "How can you say it's good? Even D or C? That's not I want to see it. Even you have to say that you are concern. But you say still good." So I not happy about that. . . . They say, "Oh hi, my name's this." And then I say my name then they'd say, "Oh, your son doing good. No problem at all." But I look at his grade and then I say, "This is not good." It sound like they doing good but when I see it's not good. And then I tell him—I came back—"How do I help my son get better? You need to tell me because I'm not a good reader or educated, because I grow up in another country and this is my second language. It's hard for me. And then even I cannot help them do their homework."

In a follow-up meeting, she learned that her son's grade was reflective of some missing assignments, so she negotiated for him to redo the assignments for a better grade. Significantly, as a first-generation immigrant, Yang advocated for her son by pointing out her refugee status, limited English proficiency, and limited experience with education. In this way, she underscored what Fue Thao suggested as the role of staffulty: she needed staffulty to be her resource.

Similar to Fue Thao's suggestion that Hmong parents need to be a "watchdog" over their children's education, Yang surmised that it was her responsibility to keep an eye on the staffulty. She would go to school uninvited in order to observe staffulty in their classrooms:

> Even Dayton or when my children still in elementary school, I just sneak in. I don't know, I sneak in because my children just say, "Oh, my teacher no good. And then she just give homework. And she just reading the newspaper and then not do anything." And then she—I don't—We don't know she checking or not checking. And she just keep—I see something that I am not happy. So I say, "That's OK. Let mommy take care." (giggle) I told her let me take care. And they say, "How you do it?" I say, "Watch me." (giggle) And I said I sneak in the school and go to the principal office. I say, "I want to go to this class." They say, "What reason?" I say, "I want to see my children, how they do in school. To just say hi." But you know they, they don't know what I thinking. I just go there and sneak in and see how that teacher doing. So I kind of get an idea how that teacher doing so if I go to meeting, I will show up and say, "This school no good. Teacher do no good job." And then something like that. I care. I care and give idea like that. So, I not scared.

Under the pretense of monitoring her children's behavior, Yang entered her children's classrooms to observe the behavior of staffulty. She was motivated to do so after her children complained about staffulty neglecting to teach, instead assigning busywork so they could read the newspaper. Her pretext for entering the classroom "cultivate[d] a persona of concerned helpmate,"[46] which conveyed to the teacher that she cared about her children's education and avoided a counterproductive direct confrontation with the staffulty.[47] Yang would then report her observations at broader school contexts of PTA meetings and declare, "This school no good. Teacher do no good job" as a way to advocate for her children.

Xee Yang practiced parent involvement through "presence"[48] in her children's classrooms and schools. In fact, her engagement with her children's education not only involved surveillance of staffulty but also surveillance of her own children, to ensure that they were attending school. She wanted to be present at her children's school "no matter what":

> No matter what—I don't know, that's OK just go there. Like after school I usually pick up my children and just go a little bit early, see how they doing. Make sure they are in school. They not lie to me. (laughing) Go somewhere and then almost the time and come back to waiting for me to pick up. I know some children do like that. I know my children is not like that, but I just want to test them to see how they doing. So I go early and just go looking where they are.

Although her children told her to stop keeping tabs on them because "it's embarrassing," she stressed, "I don't care. Just want to make sure my children in school." Yang's approach to supporting her children's education demonstrates a fearlessness toward staffulty and the formalities of school. Her actions disrupt and exceed the traditional, sanctioned terms of parent involvement that manifest in parent–teacher conferences and parent–teacher associations, and lay claim to her rights as a parent to be in school outside of parent–teacher meetings.

Nevertheless, Xee Yang understood that not all Hmong parents viewed staffulty with the same confidence. She saw that other parents were afraid of staffulty, so she took it upon herself to encourage them to speak up to support their children's education:

> I don't know, the other people, the other parent they kind of scary. And then that's how I told them that, "Don't scary." I told them that "Don't scary, because we have children go to their school. They have more money and then we have right to say anything. Even we do have right to say that thing. But we have right to say not only good thing and making them better—Change." So that, that's how I do.

Yang drew on her experience navigating school to reassure other Hmong parents with limited experience with school that they should not fear staffulty. Her comment that parents should not be afraid of staffulty "because we have children go to their school" implies her recognition that staffulty are there to work on behalf of parents and their children. Her appeal to other parents to voice their concerns to improve the quality of education for their children was a call to action toward change.

Despite her navigational capital,[49] Xee Yang acknowledged that supporting her children's education was difficult as a result of her limited education and English language proficiency. Since her oldest daughter graduated from high school, her daughter has played a major role in assisting Yang with her other children:

> Before is hard for me. The only one thing that—I not good helping them to do their homework. I know that I'm not helping, I cannot help them because my English is not—I don't have education. And then I look at their homework it's harder than what I think and cannot help. . . . Before it was hard. But now, now everything's OK because I have my older daughter. She pass

> through the high school and then everything so, if my son need help, she can help him. Even she go to [college] they still talk through the phone and they're helping them.

As Fue Thao suggested, once Hmong children complete high school and understand how to navigate the system, they will serve as a resource for their siblings. Yang relied on her oldest daughter, a junior at a liberal arts college in the state, to assist her other children with their schoolwork by phone. Eventually, her daughter will also assist them with the college application process.[50]

It is worth emphasizing that school's institutionalization of hegemonic culture disregards the perspectives and community cultural wealth of racial and ethnic minoritized families and communities. When school portrays itself as meritocratic, universal, and neutral,[51] it cloaks both its privileging of hegemonic cultural norms and devaluing of minoritized cultures. Within the market context of school, where the different cultures of different racial and ethnic groups are allocated different values by school, the cultures of minoritized communities are deemed to be impoverished,[52] lacking the knowledge, skills, character, and outlook necessary for academic achievement and upward mobility.[53] This deficit view of minoritized communities not only obscures the ways in which school is designed and organized to serve the interests of hegemonic culture but also makes unintelligible the cultural wealth of Black, Indigenous, Asian, and Latinx communities.

Education leaders Pachee Vue and Fue Thao both recognized the ways in which the cultural frame of reference Hmong refugee parents have for school—particularly the role of staffulty—is not valued or recognized by school. The cultural world of school is a barrier for Hmong parents when school operates from the values of hegemonic culture but presumes Hmong parents hold the same knowledge and perspective. As Lopez and Stack put it, "Public institutions demand that communities of color acquire cultural cues and knowledge of the culture of power."[54] The leaders saw the ways in which school's privileging of hegemonic culture hindered Hmong parents' capacity to support their children's education. They advocated for school to be forthright about its values and expectations in order to mitigate the disparities faced by Hmong parents. Notably, both of the education leaders recognized that school's requirement that all parents be familiar with the codes of hegemonic culture results in adversely affecting not just Hmong parents but also parents from all minoritized cultures.

Pachee Vue and Fue Thao particularly wanted school staffulty to serve as bridges between the cultural worlds of school and Hmong families by being proactive as cultural brokers[55] or institutional agents.[56] Vue suggested that beyond offering children homework help, school needs to support parents with the "cultural piece" of doing school. Thao maintained that staffulty need to actively serve as "resources" for parents as they learn to become "American system parents." The leaders believed changing the ways in which staffulty see their role in relationships with Hmong parents is critical for supporting Hmong families, particularly in the face of school conditions where Hmong parents do not feel they belong inside school, view staffulty like a "god," and are being "taken advantage of" by staffulty. Such a view of staffulty as proactive resources—to meet refugee and immigrant parents where they are—stands in contrast to the predominant expectation for parents to engage with school only on its own terms.[57]

Significantly, Hmong parent Xee Yang's refusal of the authority of staffulty was a political stance that claimed a relationship between equals.[58] Her experiences not only echoed the observations of the Hmong leaders but also revealed the cultural wealth that Hmong immigrants leveraged to support their children's education. Although she did not embody the type of supposedly proper parent involvement accepted by school that only white middle- and upper-class mothers are able to exemplify,[59] Xee Yang used various forms of capital that are not typically recognized by school. For example, she understood she needed to be what Fue Thao called a "watchdog" in her children's education. She activated "navigational capital"[60] to gain entry into her children's classrooms on the pretense of observing her children, but instead she monitored the behavior of teachers. Her advocacy to improve her son's grades resulted in his teacher allowing him to turn in missing assignments for a better grade. Xee Yang also deployed "resistant capital"[61] to challenge the inequalities and problems she saw with school. Her oppositional behavior included fostering sociopolitical consciousness among Hmong parents about their rights in their children's education and attending Hmong PTA meetings to demand a better education for her children. Last, Xee Yang engaged "familial capital"[62] to simultaneously provide her children with homework assistance and encourage sibling ties and familial obligation. Even though her eldest daughter was away at college, Yang relied on her to help with the younger children's schoolwork over the phone.

The cultural world of school is not only a barrier for Hmong parents. As I illustrate in the next chapter, when school reflects Western knowledge systems and disregards the commitments of Hmong Americans to the Hmong family and community, it creates dissonance between Hmong students' home and school worlds.

PART II

(En)countering Hegemonic Narratives

3 Between Individualism and Collectivism

'Cause family's always gonna be there for family. Hmong, they're really about family.

—Xiong, IB English II student

The students in the group handed in their assignments and started talking and joking around with each other at their desks as they waited for others to complete their work. Suddenly, a loud gurgling sound came from somewhere within the group. When I asked the students about its origin, Alexis and Zer pointed to Teng, who laughed heartily, put his head down on his hands, and then raised it up again. Alexis explained to me that the sound Teng was making is like that of a shaman at a ceremony just before he spits out water. The group laughed at Teng, with Zer and Hli expressing agreement with Alexis about the noise being similar to that made by a shaman. Hli added that the spitting always startled her, and explained above the din of laughter from Xiong, Teng, Alexis, and Zer that she usually sits at the ceremonies in a daze, and then all of a sudden the shaman spits and jolts her out of her daydreaming. The group agreed with Hli, nodding and laughing and saying words of affirmation in Hmong and English.

The different "worlds" or spheres of students' lives comprise different cultural knowledge, values, norms, and expectations that are separated by boundaries delineated through specific sociocultural, socioeconomic, linguistic, gender, and structural characteristics.[1] When school privileges the values, norms, and expectations of hegemonic culture and disregards Hmong culture's emphasis on family interdependence, Hmong American children must traverse a disproportionately dense border compared with children from hegemonic culture. On the surface, as they laughed at a friend goofing around in class, the Hmong American students in the eleventh grade International Baccalaureate English class were like any other high school students. However, a deeper consideration reveals the incongruity in the values, norms, and expectations of the students' Hmong homes with those of the dominant culture of school that belies the group's carefree laughter.

Similar to other Asian American groups, family and kinship networks are fundamental to Hmong social, political, and economic support that provide individuals with financial, physical, and emotional care.[2] Research suggests, for example, that children are expected to submit to parental authority[3] and provide emotional, financial, and instrumental support to the family.[4] For example, Zhou and Bankston cogently maintained from their research with the Vietnamese American community that children are "constantly reminded of their duty to respect elders, to take care of siblings, to work hard, and to make decisions only with the approval of their parents."[5] The fortunes of family members are entwined because the behaviors, successes, and failures reflect not only on the individual but also have implications for parents, siblings, and extended family members.[6]

Within low-income refugee households, interdependence is essential for day-to-day survival. Coloniality's insistence on English language proficiency and low-wage labor in the United States necessitates that Hmong children assist parents as institutional brokers in roles as interpreters, translators, and advocates;[7] take care of younger siblings and the household;[8] and contribute to the household economy.[9] Problematically, the Western cultural logic of school requires students to cast off principles and practices of family interdependence and instead embrace hegemonic culture's values of independence and individualism in order to be successful. The pull of individualism and attempts to hold on to ethnic collectivity strained Hmong students' experiences with both family and school.

THE PULL OF INDIVIDUALISM

Teng: "You're in High School and You're Smarter than Your Parents"

Teng was a seventeen-year-old junior at Dayton High. He had two older sisters who were twenty and nineteen years old. He lived with his parents, fifteen-year-old brother, five-year-old sister, and three-year-old brother. As the oldest child at home, his parents depended on him for assistance as a cultural broker, including serving as an interpreter and translator for his parents in interactions with various institutional stakeholders. While some immigrant youth embrace the opportunity to assist their parents with caring work,[10] other students, such as Teng, deeply felt the strain of the responsibility:

> My dad tells me that when he came here he only passed high school. He didn't go to college. And it's every day that my mom and him ask me to read letters and everything. I get kind of mad. I always question them about why I have to read and they go, "Well, you're in high school and you're smarter than your parents. And of course you're gonna have to read it." I'm like, "Oh, OK. I guess you are right."

Even as Teng expressed that he got "mad" at his parents for requesting his assistance as a cultural broker, he also was disconcerted that his parents thought he was "smarter" than them. He understood the challenges his parents faced acculturating to the United States as adult refugees, and he pointed out the difficulty of learning English as a fourth grader to highlight their difficulties attempting to learn as a thirty-year-old newcomers:

> I wouldn't say I'm smarter than my dad. But it's just, he can't obtain that, the knowledge—But it's just—For me, like a thirty-year-old who just comes to the U.S. and just tries to learn the language. It's kind of hard compared to a kid like in fourth grade where he even have struggles trying his ABCs at first.

Significantly, Teng rejected the idea that he was smarter than his father. His explanation of his parents' struggles to navigate U.S. institutions reflected an awareness that their hardship was due to white cultural hegemony rather than intelligence.

Nevertheless, Teng was unhappy that his parents' limited English proficiency required his assistance as an interpreter and translator. Even though his parents turned to him for assistance to negotiate U.S. institutions, he was overwhelmed by his own dearth of knowledge. For the most part, he was concerned about the adequacy of his own knowledge:

> When they told me to read it, then I go, "I don't even know the purpose for what I'm doing it." Like how my mom, she told me to call this one guy. I don't even know what I'm doing. But he says, "Can you read the case number real quick," and I was like, "46744." I was like, "OK, I don't know what I'm even doing." My mom just tells me and I just interpret it.

As he talked about his duties as a cultural broker, he repeatedly fretted about not knowing what he was doing. As Teng continued, his apprehension boiled over into frustration: "It's for the fact that I'm not sure what I'm doing. That's why I get kind of pissed off, I guess you could say."

In addition to obligations to his family as an institutional broker, Teng financially supported himself and family members by working twelve to thirty hours per week at a JCPenney at a local mall. Since his freshman year in high school, Teng worked so that he could have spending money. He wanted to be self-sufficient because he felt "neglected" by his parents:

> Why do I work? Well, I've been trying to find a job ever since freshman year. Because I feel like I need to support myself because I felt like I was kind of neglected from my family. . . . Because I tell them to buy one little thing for me and they can't even buy it. So I feel kind of neglected by that. I feel like I should just support myself, instead of like relying on my family for it. So I work. That's why I get a job.

While some Hmong children are ashamed of their family's poverty,[11] Teng expressed resentment about his parents' inability to make purchases for him. His comment that his parents could not "buy one little thing" for him is imbued with hurt that his parents could not fulfill his material needs. His anger is perhaps exacerbated by the knowledge that although his parents rely on him, he could not rely on them. Since Teng believed he could not depend on his parents for financial support, he decided to earn his own money.

Notwithstanding his bitterness toward his parents, Teng shared his earnings with his younger siblings and older sisters, but also his mother and father. He did so because of his position as the oldest son in the family:

> My little brother, I give it to him because I guess I am the oldest son. But it's the fact that he needs money. So I know he doesn't want to ask money from my mom and dad. So I give him money. And sometimes, I give my little sister money and sometimes, my older sisters come ask me for money. . . . And sometimes, my dad too. At times, I would give my mom money. But since my dad and me are the only ones working right now and we can't really support ourselves too. So I would give my mom $120 every paycheck I get.

Teng's sense of obligation to his family prevailed over self-interest. Instead of saving all of his earnings for himself, he unreservedly gave money to his family. As one of two wage earners in the family, Teng tried to help his family make ends meet by giving his mother a significant sum from every paycheck. However, he saw that his contributions were not enough and declared, "We can't really support ourselves."

While Teng's contribution to his family was important to him, it also came at a personal cost to his education and general well-being. As he detailed the activities of an average day, he emphasized its lengthy duration:

> It's kind of hard because I feel like I don't have time for myself actually. 'Cause I wake up at 6:00 and go to school until 2:00. And sometimes stay after school for [a college preparatory program] too, [that] goes on until like 4:15. And after [a college preparatory program], just go straight to work until 10:00 or get home at 10:15, 10:20. It makes it seems like you don't have time for yourself. All you do—All that and let's see—You're like, seventeen hours of just going to school and going to work and all that—Makes it seems like you don't wanna do homework or touch it. Because, I guess, it's just the fact that you don't have time for yourself. That's why you don't want to do it, so.

Teng's focus on time to express the ways in which he juggled work, school, and home responsibilities reflected the stress of his obligations. He underscored the pressure of his day by repeating three times that he had no time to himself. Notably, he reported that his seventeen-hour day made schoolwork the last thing he wanted to attend to—or, as he put it, "You don't wanna do homework or touch it."

In the end, when Teng did not have enough time or energy for homework at night, he got by in his classes with the barest amount of time preparing for classes during school the next day. He tried to find "every slip of little time" during school for his homework:

> 'Cause I find, I try to find every slip of like, every slip of little time I can get. Like, if I don't have time to do something, then I'll just do it in foundations the next day and try to get it finished up. And then, if I have time in first hour, I try to get the things in second hour done. The same thing goes for third, fourth, fifth, and so on.

Whereas upper- and middle-class parents are able to assist with their children's academics by hiring tutors to assist with homework,[12] Teng worked to help himself and his family. In the face of competing obligations on his limited time, Teng chose to support his family at the expense of his homework. He used time during one class period to prepare for the next.

Hli: "I Think of College as a Way to Get Away"

Seventeen-year-old Hli was the oldest of seven children. She lived with her parents and siblings, including a sixteen-year-old sister, fifteen-year-old sister, fourteen-year-old brother, thirteen-year-old brother, twelve-year-old sister, eleven-year-old sister, and nine-year-old brother. As the oldest child, Hli was responsible for cooking for the family, assigning household chores to siblings close to her age, and making sure her siblings do their homework. Even though her mother was home, she took on minimal domestic duties as a result of an illness,[13] leaving Hli responsible for the majority of the household tasks.

In spite of "a lot of stress" that came with her home responsibilities while maintaining good grades at school, Hli found motivation in looking forward to her career and future. She especially noted that she was driven by a desire to prove her parents wrong for doubting her capabilities:

> Well, I think a lot about like my career and the future and what I want to do. And I just want to like prove to my parents that I can do a lot of things that they doubt about I can do. So. But it keeps me motivated. Keeps my—keeps me, keep my grades up high and everything.

The dissonant acculturation between immigrant parents and children results in differences in parents' cultural expectation of children as well as differences in children's cultural expectation of parents.[14] Hli thought her parents did not believe in her potential because they did not behave in ways that are typical of parents from dominant culture. In particular, she pointed out that her parents did not offer her encouragement for her achievements:

> They don't give any encouragements. So it's like when I accomplish something, I'm proud of myself and they don't really. To me, it seems like they don't really care. It's like they don't really say much about it. And then there's always problems that follow after.

One example of the "problems" that followed were arguments related to a scholarship that Hli received for a year of tuition-free French classes at a local French organization:

> I was really happy when I first got the scholarship, and my mom was happy for me too. But afterwards, after like a couple weeks into it, like, my dad doesn't, he doesn't want to take me to class. And I really wanted to continue taking class over there, 'cause the scholarship covers the whole year of classes. And so, I'm just having trouble trying to get to class and finding a ride to class. And I don't know. I just wish that he would be more into taking me to class. It's just once a week for three hours. And I don't know, it's just basic problems like that.

Although the scholarship was a significant representation of Hli's academic achievement and hopes, transportation for Hli to attend the French classes was a substantial burden for her father. He would have to drive her to another city and wait three hours until the end of the class, then drive her home. Hli thought her father should support her education more, even if the logistics of taking her to class were difficult for him.

On the whole, Hli thought her parents should be more supportive of her education. She was frustrated that they failed to acknowledge her achievements to family and friends. She shared, "They don't really say like accomplishments that I've done. They don't even say anything about it. . . . They never say any of the good accomplishments and they make it seem so negative sometimes." Echoing Hli, a Hmong American young woman in Chan's study reported:

> The kind of physical affection and words of praise that many American parents express are unknown in my family. My parents seldom converse with my sisters, brothers, and me. . . . They never tell us they love us, nor do they congratulate us when we accomplish something. They believe strongly that people should not show their feelings and emotions.[15]

Or as Kao Kalia Yang put it in her Hmong family memoir, "'I love you' are three words only Americans say,' my mother says."[16] Additionally, a Dayton High School Hmong staffulty specifically pointed to the influence of hegemonic culture and Americanization, where "Hmong kids are going to become more and more Americanized" and that "parents loving them doesn't mean providing them shelter and providing them with food anymore. They're gonna want parents to be able to verbalize and show them that they care." Whereas Hmong parents believe children should know that they love them, the staffulty stressed that Hmong children "want to be told by their parents that 'Even though you pissed me off today I still love you. And even though I'm disappointed in you I still care about you.'"[17] The staffulty continued to explain the perspective of Hmong parents:

> And I feel like there are a lot of Hmong parents who are still struggling with that, being able to verbalize how much they care about their children. And so, I always tell them it's important that you have to let your kids know you care about them, 'cause parents like to assume that they know. And they usually, they'd always say, "Why don't they know that I love them? I provide a house for them, I provide food for them. Why do I go to work every day? It's because I love them." But the kids, they don't want to hear it. They want to hear that you love them.

The widening acculturation gap between Hmong American parents and children[18] creates pain and unhappiness when parents or children are unable to fulfill expectations. Hmong American children like Hli expect the freedom, mutuality, warmth, and praise in their relationships with parents that they see in hegemonic culture,[19] which contrasts with Hmong parents' belief in parental authority, suppressing affection, and exerting greater control in the face of assimilation.[20]

Within the context of Hli's household obligations and frustration with her parents, she saw school as a reprieve from the stress of home. When she responded to my question about how she felt about school, she repeatedly remarked on the "pressure" of home in contrast to school:

> I like coming to school every day and learning. But I don't know. I think I prefer being here [at school] than being at home sometimes. 'Cause it's just more pressure at home than at school. You can be more understand—not have to worry about anything at home until you get home. And then once you get home, a whole set of new pressure dives in and then you forget about school for a minute and then you have—And then later on, you have school to think about and family life to think about. So, it's a lot of pressure at home.

In contrast to the freedom Hli felt at school that allowed her to be more of herself, home was a place that was restrictive.[21] She suggested her family responsibilities constrained not only her activities but also her self-expression:

> Well, at school I can be more free. And I can hang out with my friends. And I can just be more of myself and laugh. And just not have to worry about any problems. But at home, it's like I can't do anything fun and just go out for a few hours. I can't do that. I have to be at home all the time. And I'm expected to teach my younger siblings to cook when it's time for dinner. And teach them how to cook, and teach them just good responsibilities and manners, so that when they're older, they know what to do around the house.

Hli felt that she was unable to "do anything fun" on the one hand because of her home responsibilities, and on the other hand because her parents were among the more conservative Hmong parents who did not allow her to go out with friends, participate in school extracurricular activities, or attend school events such as dances (see also chapter 4). The restrictions placed on Hli's movement and behaviors stem from the reaction of immigrant parents to the U.S. context, particularly their fears of corruption by American culture alongside the loss of ethnic culture and identity.[22]

In addition to seeing school as a reprieve from household pressures, Hli saw college as an avenue to escape the burdens and troubles of home life. She yearned to be on her own and broaden her experiences:

> I'm still young, but I think of college as a way to get away. And just to experience things on my own. And not have to worry about all the family problems at home. So yeah. I think college is my opportunity to just get away from the house for a few years and just see the world on my own.

Unlike some of her Hmong American peers who also had household responsibilities but were able to participate in school extracurricular activities, Hli was not allowed to do so. She attended school and then went directly home. In the context of the limitations on her activities and movement, Hli aspired to studying abroad during college so that she could "explore other parts of the world," "see everything that [she] see[s] on TV," and "just have fun with life."

Hli hoped to attend a small, private liberal arts college that was about an hour away from Harriet City. She reported that although she "want[ed] to go to the best college and get the best education," her parents wanted her to attend college in the metropolitan area, close to home. She explained this was because as the oldest child, her parents depended on her to assist her family:

> Well, I don't know. They don't want me to go to a college that's far away. But I really want to go to [small liberal arts school]. And it's like an hour away and even there, they won't let me go there. They want me to go to a small community college that's close by, so they can—Because they depend on me a lot since I'm the oldest. And my younger sisters, they don't really know what to do and everything. So, they don't want me to go far away 'cause they need me. But I think that I just told them that if I go to a college like [small liberal arts school], I just want to go to the best college and get the best education, so that I can succeed in the future. And I don't know. I'm still trying to persuade them to let me go.

Low-income high school students "grapple with the micro-economics of day-to-day survival"[23] that significantly shape the kinds of college choices that are actually open for their consideration. According to Hli, her parents prioritized her role as the oldest child and contributor to the family over the best possible college education for her. They supported higher education for her, but they also expected her to care for the family.

Further, because Hli's parents received limited education in the refugee camp in Thailand and did not attend high school or college after U.S. resettlement, their frame of reference for education was significantly different than Hli's own. As she continued to explain her parents' reluctance for her to attend the college of her choice, she also shared that her mother argued against her college pursuit because her family may not have enough money to purchase books for her classes:

> I think they know about scholarships. I know that they know. And I did tell my mom that I can get scholarships and—But then she said that she's talking about buying the books and everything. And she might not have the money to buy the books for me. And she just told me to not go to college after high school and just spend a year working and then I can go the year after. But for how I see it, I think that most people who don't go to college right after high school, they never usually get to go back to college until they're like in their mid-twenties. So, I really want to just go right away and since I already have a good focus on school, I don't want to lose that focus.

As Hmong education leader Pachee Vue pointed out in chapter 3, Hmong parents such as Hli's mother had financial fears about the costs of college that at times impinged on the higher education of Hmong American students. Even though her mother knew about scholarships, she proposed that Hli take a year to work after high school graduation before going to college.[24] Conversely, Hli understood that delaying college enrollment was problematic for her educational goals because it significantly decreases the likelihood of completion of a bachelor's degree.[25] It is also noteworthy that high socioeconomic status students take a "gap year" between high school and college to volunteer, travel, or "find" themselves.[26] In contrast, low-income Hmong American students such as Hli face the probability of delaying college so that she may save money to pay for college expenses and attend to the needs of her family.[27]

HOLDING ON TO COLLECTIVITY

Zer: "I'm Like, Kind of Like a Second Parent to My Siblings"

Zer was a seventeen-year-old junior at Dayton High. Her household comprised her divorced mother, eighteen-year-old brother, fifteen-year-old sister, thirteen-year-old brother, and ten-year-old sister. Since she was twelve years old, Zer and her older brother have shared responsibility for the care of their younger siblings, due to their mother's second-shift job at a meat-packing company. Her mother's second-shift work hours meant work beginning at 1:30 PM, before Zer and her siblings came home from school, and ending at 11:00 PM, after they went to bed. Accordingly, Zer lamented that she and her siblings "barely even get to see her":

> Oh, she works during the evenings, so like, so I think that's one of the things that's really affects our family. 'Cause she's only there on the weekends and we only see her mostly on the weekends. 'Cause she's always working in the evenings. . . . Like she works from 1:30 to like 11:00, so we barely even get to see her. So by the time we get home, she's at work. And then right at the time that she comes home, we're sleeping. So, we mostly just spend, like we try to spend most of our time with her on the weekends.

For immigrant families like Zer's, her mother's second-shift job schedule allowed little overlap with that of Zer and her siblings.[28] Since her mother was less available for the daily needs of Zer and her younger siblings, she depended on Zer and her older brother (a senior at Dayton High) to take care of themselves and their siblings.

As the oldest children in the home, Zer and her brother were in charge of their younger siblings and household. She shared cooking responsibilities with her brother until the third trimester of school, when she joined the badminton team. Since then, her brother took over sole duties for cooking, providing dinner for their siblings, and overseeing homework. Once Zer got home, she would take up caretaking responsibilities:

> And I come home, usually like when I come home, and then I make sure that my younger siblings have ate and have done their homework and then I would eat and do my homework. And then I would make sure they go to bed before my mom comes home or else, she's gonna be like, "Oh, why aren't you guys in bed yet?" you know. And like, "Where's Zer?" and all this stuff.

Ultimately, Zer was answerable to her mother for the care of her younger siblings. Her comment about her mother's question if her younger siblings were still awake when she came home alludes to disciplinary repercussions if Zer did not fulfill her caretaking responsibilities. Despite difficult work hours, her mother tried to be "present" by connecting with Zer and her siblings via phone calls while at work: "And my mom would call home around every two, three hours to make sure that we're doing our homework and that we ate and stuff." During the weekday, Zer and her siblings were sometimes able to see their mother for a couple of hours before school. They relied on the weekends to spend most of their time with their mother.

Zer understood that her responsibilities were not unique to her family but rather were common among Hmong families because of parents' long work hours. Similar to other immigrant parents, her mother relied on older children to take care of younger children in the household.[29] Within the Hmong American community, she explained that "parents put more pressure on the older kids":

> Most of the parents, they're always working. And the only time you get to spend with them are like on the weekends. So the parents put more pressure on the older kids, so they have—So my brother and I, we have priorities. We have to cook and clean and make sure that my brothers and sisters are doing their homework and that they're doing their chores and all that stuff. And, it's—We're kind of like a second parent to our younger siblings, I think.

Significantly, Zer used "priorities" to explain her responsibilities as one of the two older children in the family. Managing the household and supervising the education of younger siblings was a central part of her role as an older child, taking precedence over individual needs. For example, Zer reported that on occasion, her home responsibilities left her little time or energy for schoolwork:

> Well, sometimes I would come home and my mom would call and like, "Oh, you guys have to clean this and this and this." And I'm like, "Oh, OK." So we would clean and by the time we finished cleaning—And then I would postpone my homework and then I'll be really tired and I'm like, "OK. I'll wake up in the morning and like do it." And then I have to wake up early in the morning and do my homework. And so, it's kind of hard 'cause I would be tired and I don't want to wake up like five or six in the morning to do my homework.

When her mother asked her to clean the house, she simply replied, "Oh, OK." She did not argue with her mother about how the time cleaning the house would take away from her homework. Her sense of family obligation thus took precedence over her academics.[30]

Zer's statement that she and her older brother are "kind of like a second parent" to their younger siblings reflects her recognition of the ways in which their duties are typically reserved for adults in U.S. hegemonic culture; it also demonstrates her comprehension of their substantial function in the lives of their younger siblings. She elaborated on the ways in which she was a "second parent":

> Because when my mom's not there, my sisters have to come to me for problems or situations. And I have to make sure that they're, they took a shower and that they get in bed on time and that they wake up in the morning. And we have to make them breakfast in the morning. So, I'm like, kind of like a second parent to my siblings, I guess.

Some of Zer's parenting tasks included guiding her younger siblings' personal hygiene, putting them to bed at night and waking them up in the morning, preparing breakfast, and resolving "problems or situations." Her siblings chose to go to her over her older brother to assist with problems because her brother was "a really quiet and shy person" and she was "a little more patient" with the younger siblings.

While some immigrant children become overwhelmed or frustrated with assisting parents with caring work (such as Teng above)[31] Zer understood the value and complexity of her family obligations:

> Sometimes, I wish I wasn't the oldest or if I was the only child. 'Cause things would be—To me, things would be so much easier. And I wouldn't have to have all these responsibilities and I could go and have fun with friends and stuff. But, but I love my younger siblings. And they're, I guess, they're there for me when I need them too.

On the one hand, Zer yearned to be an only child—or at least not the oldest daughter, so she could be free of responsibilities and "go and have fun with friends and stuff." On the other hand, she was devoted to her siblings and recognized the importance of their reciprocal support for her well-being. Moreover, Zer's good-natured response to her family responsibilities may be attributed to her affection for her mother. She described her mother as "like a girlfriend" to her:

> My mom, she's a very supportive and loving person. And I can talk to her about anything. Like I've—she always talk to me about like—like she's like a girlfriend, kind of. I can tell her anything I'm comfortable talking to her about, like sex and drugs and stuff that Hmong girls wouldn't normally talk to their parents.

In contrast to the distance between immigrant parents and children that arise as a result of parents' long work hours[32] and the experiences of some of her Hmong peers (like that of Teng and Hli above), Zer was able to maintain a strong relationship with her mother. Ultimately, she concluded that she did not mind because she had gotten used to her responsibilities: "I've just been doing it for a long time so I guess it just comes naturally." While Zer reported that contributing to her family is innate, I suggest that Hmong American students and families are disadvantaged when school disregards the interdependence of Hmong families and assumes all students operate from the values of hegemonic culture, which privileges individualism and independence.

Toua: "School Doesn't Matter as Long as . . . I'm with My Mom"

Seventeen-year-old Toua was a second-generation Hmong American whose family consisted of his parents, a thirty-year-old stepsister, a twenty-four-year-old sister, a nineteen-year-old sister, a sixteen-year-old sister, a fifteen-year-old sister, and a thirteen-year-old brother. Everyone lived in the same household except for his stepsister and nineteen-year-old sister. His stepsister was married and living with her husband and their family, and his nineteen-year-old sister was engaged and living with her fiancé's family.

Similar to other Hmong students, Toua's home responsibilities included serving as a cultural broker and caring for his younger siblings. Since the sixth grade, he was helping his parents pay for household bills by writing out checks. As he put it, "My mom just tells me to write it, so I just write it. And then she doesn't sign it, but she just tells me to sign it." Beginning the year before the study, Toua's responsibilities to his family significantly increased after his mother's health deteriorated from liver failure and she underwent a liver transplantation. He shared he had to "step up and grow up":

> I kind of had this step up and grow up a little bit. Me and my [nineteen-year-old] sister, we had to take care of our little brothers and sisters. We had to make food and everything since my dad was mostly in the hospital and so is my mom. So, we were the only ones at home. And the bills, we had to pay and everything. We just had a lot more responsibilities. And on top of that, you had to work also, so it was like really hard.

Because his parents spent most of their time at the hospital, Toua and his sister essentially became parents to their younger siblings. As he elaborated on his home responsibilities, he characterized them as "the stuff my mom and dad does":

> The stuff my mom and dad does. Yeah, like watch them and tell them what to do and everything. And when they do something wrong. And then, they're not telling my mom and dad anymore where they're going. They're telling us. And then we have to arrange rides for them. And then we have to buy food also for them. . . . I have to wake up and then wake up my brothers and sisters and then get them ready for school. And then I have to watch for my little brother. I have to pick him up sometimes from the bus stop and then make the food.

Toua and his nineteen-year-old sister took on the everyday duties of his parents, where his household tasks involved getting his siblings up in the morning and ready for school, picking up his younger brother from the bus stop, purchasing groceries, and cooking meals. His care for his younger siblings also included teaching them right from wrong and supervising their activities and movements.

Yet Toua was not only concerned about his siblings' physical needs. He was also deeply apprehensive about his younger sisters' social and academic lives, particularly the implications of their romantic relationships on their academic futures. For example, he worried that his fifteen-year-old sister was going to marry her boyfriend before high school graduation. He reported, "My sister always picks out guys who are bad" and noted that he disapproved of their relationship because he believed the boyfriend was a "gangster" who was "eighteen and he's still in junior year . . . So, he's flunked a couple of times."

Although Toua's sister did not share that she planned to marry her boyfriend, he surmised that she would because the two had dated for a year and a half; the boyfriend was at their house "all the time" until 9 o'clock at night, even sleeping over once; and the boyfriend even went to his grandmother's and aunt's houses with the family. He was particularly worried about his sister's future with her boyfriend because neither paid attention to their education:

> I'm worried about everything about her, but she really likes him. I'm like, "He can't provide anything for you and then you yourself not focusing on school good. You guys aren't gonna get anywhere in life 'cause you guys don't get to pass high school yet." Yeah, and "You should go to college and at least get an education and you might have a better resume or something." Yeah, but she doesn't have, she doesn't have a job yet and he doesn't really have one either 'cause I think he does something in realty, but the second one is pyramid. It's kings, you know.

According to Toua, despite daily school attendance, his sister was an "average" student. He was frustrated with her educational status and trajectory because she was particularly intelligent. He shared: "Well, I think she is gonna pass high school. It's just like barely probably. And she won't do good in her classes. Like I know she has potential cause when she was small, she was very, very smart."

The turning point for his sister's educational pathway came when she started to run away from home during middle school, and "she's just been going downhill" since then. In total, his fifteen-year-old sister ran away from home five times because of restrictions placed on her behavior and activities at home:

> What she said to us was that she was stressed out 'cause my mom was being too strict [and not letting her go out with friends]. And then she didn't want to have to deal with my mom. And so she ran away and she went to her friend's house.

His sister stopped running away from home only after a conversation with a county social worker and their mom. Toua shared that the social worker first talked to their mom and then their mom talked to his sister, and "they just kind of resolved their problems." More than the conversation with the social worker, he believed that the problems between his mom and sister were resolved because his mom was less restrictive out of fear: "And I think my mom is kind of scared also that she might run away again."

Similar to Hli's experiences, his sisters' movements were limited by their parents because they feared the corrupting influences of hegemonic culture that would damage the family's reputation (chapter 4).[33] Indeed, as Toua explained the ways in which his mom was now less exacting of his sisters' activities, he was also critical of her leniency:

> I mean, before she didn't let any guys come over and now, you can bring anyone and she won't really care. And then I tell my mom also, 'cause she lets my sisters bring their boyfriends to our grandma's house and aunt's house and they weren't even invited. And I tell my mom, and my mom's like, "That's OK 'cause it's their boyfriends." And I'm like, "But it's not your house and they don't know them. And you should ask them first before you tell them to come." But she's like, "It's OK." I think she's way too lenient now.

From Toua's perspective, his mom was "way too lenient" because she allowed his younger sisters to bring their boyfriends to his grandmother's and aunt's homes even though they were not invited. He disapproved of his sisters' presumptuousness in including their boyfriends in family gatherings. Yet his mother's forbearance was understandable within the context of her youngest daughter's recent flight from home, along with the history of her four older daughters also running away from home. For example, Toua's oldest sister "just left one day without telling anyone," and his twenty-four-year-old sister "kind of just went and bought an apartment without telling [their] mom."

In general, Toua wanted his siblings to take better care of themselves. He conveyed to his sisters his concerns about their educational progress and life prospects; he yearned for them to be more responsible, including doing more at home. Despite being only one to two years older than his younger sisters, Toua was like an adult in the ways in which he was fretful about their behaviors and the implications for their futures:

> I say that and they're like, "Yeah, I know." But I don't know if they really gonna take that, on my word and do it. But I don't know, as long as I get it out. Yeah. And then I'm like, "Well, you're gonna know when you grow old that life isn't what you think it is." Because for them, they're not, they don't have the responsibility that I do. . . . They practically do whatever they want. And then me, I have to work around the family and they don't really.

He wanted his sisters to take more responsibility for their lives, including taking care of the household. Moreover, Toua declared his brother was "lazy" for refusing to contribute by learning how to cook and helping around the house. He compared his household responsibilities from a younger age to that of his brother:

> He just doesn't want to do it. And, he's like a sixth grader and I'm like, "When I was a third grader, I did my own laundry. So you should do it too." And he's like, "Nope." He still gives it to my mom. My mom always does it.

Toua was disappointed that his younger sisters and brother do not contribute enough to the family. His remark that his brother still gave his laundry to their mother to do is particularly revealing because on the one hand, it suggests a desire for his thirteen-year-old brother to be more responsible and ask less of his parents. On the other hand, it suggests a plea to help his mother more since she was still unwell from the liver transplant.

As Toua talked about his struggles to juggle the demands of school and concerns about his family, he disclosed, "Sometimes I just want to give up, but then it's just something needy that tells me that I have to get it done." In particular, he wanted to give up on school because it was too difficult for him to manage the responsibilities of both school and home:

> I don't know. It's too hard. And I think for me, family is more, worth more than anything in the world. So like school doesn't matter, as long as my mom

> is, I'm with my mom and it's OK. Then at the same time, I'm like, "What happens if my mom passes away?" And then, "What am I gonna do if I don't have my education?" And then, my mom would probably want me to finish my education too if she was here telling me.

If he had to choose between the world of school and the world of home, Toua would choose his family, because "family is [. . .] worth more than anything in the world." He suggested that his mother was one of the primary reasons he persevered in school. Her mortality was also on his mind because during the October of my study at Dayton High and immediately after his mother's liver transplantation, his fourteen-year-old brother, who had been battling intestinal cancer for five years, died of lymphoma.[34]

Further, Toua would choose his family over school for the ways in which school did not care for him or his family.[35] Although he shared with Dayton High staffulty his mother's liver failure and brother's death, he reported that they were not supportive of him. When I asked how staffulty may better support students like him, he responded:

> I don't know. Just get more involved with their students probably. . . . Just talk to them, support them. Like if they see something that's wrong, they could just talk to them. And if they know that someone has lost a brother or mother or grandma, they can kind of like comfort them.

Toua's repetition of "just talk" brings attention to the silences regarding the home world of Hmong American students, particularly the competing priorities of the world of school and the world of home. While staffulty demanded students to care about school, students like Toua desired staffulty to authentically care for him.[36] He wanted to "be known"[37] beyond his schoolwork and grades, including the socioeconomic contexts of his family and life. Speaking about Dayton High School's staffulty, he remarked, "They try to understand, but they can't grasp."

Xiong: "Family Is Gonna Be Everything"

Xiong was a seventeen-year-old junior at Dayton High whose family consisted of his parents and eleven children, including seven sisters and three brothers. Xiong's siblings included a twenty-eight-year-old sister, twenty-six-year-old sister, twenty-two-year-old brother, twenty-year-old sister, nineteen-year-old sister, sixteen-year-old sister, fifteen-year-old sister, fourteen-year-old sister, thirteen-year-old brother, and eleven-year-old sister. His four older siblings and two younger sisters married and moved out of the family home, which made him the oldest child living at home with his parents and three youngest siblings.

Xiong reported that as a male member of the family, he was expected to attend and take part in weekend gatherings involving the *tsev neeg,* or extended family,[38] where male Hmong perform central roles in various rites during weddings, funerals, and other ceremonies.[39] His explanation of his role during the ceremonies underscored a type of apprenticeship, where sons learn from their fathers and grandfathers:

> A pretty big expectation we have is to learn how the Hmong culture, to perform special ceremonies. We have to learn that from our fathers or our grandfathers or things like that. We have to know how to do that. Whenever there's a ceremony, us guys, we just have to show up, be there and help out. So, in the future when it's our turn we need them, they'll come and help us.

Because Xiong's family continued to adhere to animism, the religious belief traditionally practiced by the Hmong in Laos (chapter 5),[40] his participation during ceremonies involving a Hmong shaman was a part of his ethnic socialization that contributed to the family's cultural maintenance.[41] Notably, and as I discuss below, Xiong saw his participation in ceremonies as important for sustaining Hmong culture and good relations within the *tsev neeg.* As a teenager, he played an active role in assisting the shaman during ceremonies, where he was able to "watch [. . .] and learn":

> I have to greet everyone who comes in. I have to greet them as a son. Greet them, show them that I know my respect and manners for the elders. So I have to greet them. And once the ceremony gets started, I have to show them, I have to listen to my parents. What my parents want me to do, I have to do it. Or if not, then while the ceremony is going on, the shaman does his ritual, I have to be there and watch in case there's something I need to do. Because while you're doing that ceremony, there's a bench where the shaman jumps on, so you have to hold sides so it doesn't—It like levels the shaman. Or there's a little drum you'll drum or play. There's these two metal plates you'll hit to each other. You'll hit to make a certain noise for a shaman to carry, help him carry him to the spirit world and back. So, you'll play or you'll just hold him or basically just watch him and learn.

During various Hmong rituals, male and female Hmong participants take up different roles. Hmong men and boys participate in chants, play musical instruments, assist the shaman, and sacrifice animals such as pigs, cows, or chickens; Hmong women and girls work behind the scenes to cook food for the feast after the ceremony.[42]

Students like Xiong attended ceremonies involving the *tsev neeg* every other weekend. Although his involvement was time-consuming, Xiong believed it was important for him to participate as a way to assist family and nurture communal relations among *tsev neeg* members:

> Around every two weeks, there's at least one ceremony that our relatives, they will have. And you go and you'll watch and you'll learn. And then, they'll sacrifice pigs, a cow or chickens or you know do all these things and you'll go help them chop up the meat, cook and when they set the table, you set the table with them and things like that. They'll pass food around, you'll eat and talk and pretty much being there, helping them. So in the future when it's your turn, they'll come help you.

Participation in *tsev neeg* events was more than an obligation for Xiong. He saw it as a way to learn about Hmong cultural practices, support family members, and invest in the collectivity of Hmong social relations, because as he put it, "Hmong, they're really about family."

As he elaborated on the importance of supporting the *tsev neeg* he underscored its meaning for reciprocity, where members of the *tsev neeg* communally support each other in ways that exceeded the support from friends:

> For example, ceremonies, weddings, funerals—Everyone's who gonna be there is your family. That's how, you get support by family. Who's gonna help you pay for things like that? Family. Who's gonna be there? Your friends and family. Your friends are always gonna be—Your friends are always gonna be there to comfort you. But family is always gonna be there. Family is gonna be everything. . . . Financial support. There can be a lot of things they can help you with. You need a place to stay? Family. They got you. You need to eat? They got you. Family's always gonna be there. . . . We need to pay off a debt, family members will help. Anything. You don't have to pay them back with family. It's OK. We'll help each other. Maybe I'll help you now and maybe in the future, you'll help me later, right? Like I scratch your back and you scratch my back. It's like that.

In a similar vein, Koltyk recounted, "The extended household provides the mechanism by which the Hmong can pool economic resources from both wage and non-wage sources" to enhance their economic welfare.[43] One example of relatives' contributing a nonwage resource includes assisting a *tsev neeg* member with bad credit purchase a car. Here, a family gives the relative with good credit the down payment to purchase the car. The relative then "holds the title with the understanding that his relatives [the family] will make the monthly payments and pay for the auto insurance."[44] Even though the relative owns the car legally, a verbal agreement exists between the relative and the family that the family actually owns the car.[45]

Participating in ceremonies and learning from shamans and elders were also important for Xiong because he was a witness to the loss of the belief in animism and Hmong cultural traditions more generally. He understood the desire to eradicate Hmong shamanism "in the name of science, progress, and Christianity."[46] Additionally, he reported that among his peers, "there's not a lot of teenagers who go . . . they think it's boring." In turn, he believed the lack of participation among Hmong adolescents in ceremonies involving shamans endangered Hmong culture:

> Why the religion is just sort of disappearing. And besides all that, all the elders who know about it, they're getting old. They're dying and I guess they don't have a chance to tell us or their kids. We are losing some memory of some information about the Hmong traditions.

For Xiong, his obligations to contribute to *tsev neeg* functions and learn Hmong cultural practices from his parents and elders is critical for maintaining Hmong culture and identity.[47] Despite the demands of school and household responsibilities, Xiong asserted:

> Because I want to keep all my religion, my cultural traditions still alive. I don't want it to disappear. 'Cause without that, why are we Hmong—What's Hmong, right? Every race has a religion, every race has a certain culture, a tradition they have. And what kind of race would it be if everyone forgets it? You don't know how to do it. So, for me, from what I think, the reason I do all that stuff is to keep all this knowledge of my traditions, of what we Hmong people do. I want to keep it. Store the memory and maybe later on, I can teach the future generations, so it continues.

Since Dayton High did not offer classes related to Hmong religion, rituals, musical instruments, or culture in general, Xiong committed to acquiring as much knowledge as possible by learning from elders at family gatherings. He also took classes at a local Hmong nonprofit organization to learn how to play the *qeej,* essential in funeral rites of passage ceremonies.[48] Although these commitments took their toll on the time available for school and its sanctioned extracurricular activities, he affirmed, "The reason I do all that stuff is to keep all this knowledge of my traditions, of what we Hmong people do."

Conquergood and Thao suggested that Hmong cosmology promotes interdependence and interconnectedness as essential for a good life. For Hmong individuals, estrangement from the clan is "a fate associated with death," and "being alone without family is considered the greatest tragedy":

> For the Hmong, standing alone, outside the village, cut off from the clan, is unthinkable as a moral alternative. Movement away from a communal center represents the loss of everything that makes one a viable person. It is a fate associated with death. Ntsuag the orphan is a compelling figure in Hmong folktales because being alone without family is considered the greatest tragedy.[49]

The Hmong worldview's emphasis on family and collectivity stands in contrast to the "sick society" of hegemonic U.S. culture's emphasis on individualism competition (chapter 1).[50] The stories of the 1.5- and second-generation Hmong American students at Dayton High School reflected the ongoing relevance of interdependent practices within the family and clan. As the oldest children (living at home), they contributed to the family by functioning as parental surrogates for younger siblings, serving as cultural brokers for their parents, and taking care of household domestic tasks.

As a project of coloniality, school's privileging of Western ontologies and epistemologies contribute to the fragmentation of relationships among Hmong children and parents as well as erasure of Hmong culture. While research on immigrant families has extensively documented family obligation as a facet of cultural values, I suggest that more than a feature of Hmong culture, the experiences of Teng, Hli, Zer, Toua, and Xiong with family obligation illustrate the dissonant values and priorities between their home and school worlds.[51] Hmong students responded in different ways to the pull of individualism and Americanization. Teng was frustrated that he needed to take on roles as a cultural broker and wage earner to contribute to the family. Hli desired the independence and freedom to travel and be on her own, unfettered by family responsibilities, that she saw in hegemonic culture. Zer saw her care for her family was mutually beneficial in its contribution to her well-being. Toua surmised that staffulty "can't grasp" his family commitments and concerns. Xiong understood the influence of subtractive schooling on his peers' lack of participation in family gatherings and the maintenance of Hmong culture.

Additionally, school leaves students to navigate complex cultural transitions with little acknowledgment inside school of the importance and urgencies of their out-of-school lives. Nell Noddings concluded from the lack of interpersonal knowledge in school social relations: "In contemporary schools, teachers and students do not know each other well enough to develop relations of care and trust."[52] Nonetheless, students face a double standard where they are required to know the world of school (i.e., Western knowledge systems) in order to succeed, even if school does not attempt to know them and their home world.[53] The exclusion of the cultural world of students from school impinges on their sense of being cared for[54] and "being known,"[55] which in turn contributes to marginalization in school (chapter 5).

Hegemonic discourses of immigrant youth living "between two cultures" or the "culture clash" between immigrant cultures and U.S. society not only mask the privileging of Western cultural logics but also reproach immigrants for being different than white, middle-class communities. Hegemonic culture is frequently portrayed as superior and normal while immigrant cultures are represented as inferior and deviant.[56] In the next chapter, I explore hegemonic narratives about the patriarchy and oppressiveness of Hmong gender relations and (re)storytelling from the perspective of Hmong American leaders and students.

4 (Re)storytelling Gender Representations

> By losing her virginity without marriage—even violently, against her will—she had violated a basic tenet of her Hmong culture. If her family found out, they would feel forever shamed. She feared her culture would require her to marry one of her attackers to save her reputation.
>
> —Pam Louwagie and Dan Browning, "Shamed into Silence"

> Hmong girls in Minnesota are regularly gang raped by Hmong men, but in the Hmong community even the girls' mothers blame the rape victims, and the attacks go unreported. These aren't cultures of strong women and criminal men. It's more like criminal men and complicit women.
>
> —Ann Coulter, "Country Overboard! Women and Children Last!"

Ann Coulter's paraphrasing of a part of a Minneapolis–Saint Paul *Star Tribune* special series, "Shamed into Silence,"[1] about the rape and prostitution of Hmong American girls by Hmong gangs, exemplifies the cultural racism faced by Hmong immigrants in the United States. Instead of focusing on biological or scientific racial differences, new racism makes significant the different cultural practices of minoritized groups to mark them as deficient and different than hegemonic culture.[2] Coulter portrayed gang rape, prostitution, revictimization, and reticence to report rape as cultural practices exclusive to Hmong Americans. By ascribing social problems that are part of all ethnic and racial groups solely to Hmong culture, cultural racism marks Hmong Americans as culturally different, monstrous, and deserving of intervention or banishment from a superior (white) U.S. culture. Here, "criminal men" and "complicit women" are represented as intrinsic to Hmong culture. As Coulter continued her anti-immigrant post, she engaged the master narrative of U.S. "rescue and liberation":[3] "Virtually every woman outside of the First World lives in an abusive society. We can't take them all in" and "How did violent, backward, misogynistic cultures become our problem?"[4] Within the new racism, the cultures of groups outside of "First World" societies such as the United States are constructed as "violent, backward, [and] misogynistic" as opposed to an implied peaceful, progressive, and prowomen culture of U.S. society.

This juxtaposition between a modern U.S. culture and archaic Hmong culture was similarly articulated in reader Lynnae Nelson's letter to the *Star Tribune,* featured as the "Letter of the Day" that ran soon after the special report:

> By and large, American Catholic families and farm families do not arrange a forced marriage after a girl is raped. Nor do they call girls sluts or say they deserved being raped. In this country, the idea that a woman or girl deserves being raped went by the wayside a very long time ago. For crimes such as these to become so widespread, a certain environment needs to be created. The victims interviewed for this article made reference time and again to the shame and blame that they would be subjected to by their families after their brutal rape. They mentioned family members attempting to force a marriage after a rape to save family honor. These are cultural factors that have helped create the current problem.[5]

Such cultural racism manufactures a cultural difference that willfully ignores the sexual abuse of children by Catholic priests;[6] a U.S. rape and misogynistic culture that was present even in the candidate selection in the 2016 presidential election;[7] the prevalence of rape myth acceptance that castigate rape survivors as "liars," "whores," and "sluts";[8] and the role of the police and medical and judicial systems in the revictimization of rape survivors.[9]

Illustrative instances reported by major popular media outlets include Pope Francis's defrocking of Theodore McCarrick, former cardinal and archbishop of Washington, D.C., for his decades-long sexual abuse of children and adults;[10] a New Jersey teen rape case where Judge James Troiano denied a request to try the teenager as an adult because he was an Eagle scout, college bound, and from a "good family";[11] another New Jersey rape case where Superior Court Judge John Russo Jr. asked the rape survivor whether she tried to close her legs;[12] and the Steubenville rape case where an intoxicated sixteen-year-old girl was repeatedly and publicly raped by two peers, and her rape shared on social media.[13] Despite an extensive record of sexual violence and misogyny that has extended into institutional structures, cultural racism claims the virtuousness and superiority of hegemonic U.S. culture.

In the arguments of the "new racism" targeting minoritized groups, race is coded as culture,[14] where culture functions in place of race in portrayals of minoritized communities as homogenous, patriarchal, ahistorical, and morally deficient in contrast to hegemonic culture.[15] Hegemonic narratives racialize the culture of Hmong immigrants through the representation of cultural practices as foreign to the dominant majority, which are marked as other and thus contemptible.[16] Thus, while gang rape, rape myth acceptance, and misogyny exist in U.S. white supremacist society, dominant discourses identify them as particular to the Hmong American community. The racialization of Hmong Americans effaces the heterogeneity of the experiences, perspectives, and practices inherent in all racial and ethnic groups.[17]

HMONG LEADERS (RE)STORYTELLING GENDER OPPRESSION

The stories of U.S. white supremacist society justify the oppression of minoritized groups by creating "a form of shared reality in which its own superior position is seen as natural."[18] Hegemonic narratives allege Hmong culture substantially contributes to the problems faced by Hmong American girls and women. According to this discourse, the norms of Hmong culture shun and stigmatize female victims of sexual violence. Hmong families allegedly value their reputation so much that they would force daughters to marry their attackers. Subsequently, cultural racism presumes that Hmong female victims of sexual assault are "shamed into silence" by Hmong culture. Hmong leaders Dia Lee and Kou Vang critically engaged in storytelling to refute, respectively, hegemonic discourses about Hmong culture's oppression of Hmong girls and women and tyrannical practices of "early" marriage and teenage pregnancy. Dia Lee suggested cultural racism blames Hmong culture for everything. Kou Vang argued hegemonic narratives incorrectly impugn Hmong culture for Hmong teenage marriage instead of recognizing it as a problem of Hmong teenage pregnancy.

Dia Lee: Hmong Culture Is Blamed for Everything

> And girls can't count on the Hmong community to take their side.
>
> Hmong have a highly patriarchal society. Girls who lose their virginity outside of marriage are devalued; the community scorns them and their families unless the girl marries the rapist. By contrast, some families and clans will rally to protect the males accused of rape or paying for child prostitutes.[19]

Popular representations such as the above excerpt from the *Star Tribune*'s "Shamed into Silence" special report are part of the hegemonic narratives of the new racism. Such stories emphasize Hmong culture as the singular source of the oppression of Hmong American women. Published thirty years after the first Hmong refugees were resettled to the United States,[20] the narrative depicted Hmong culture and its "highly patriarchal society" as frozen in time, with Hmong Americans in a perpetually premodern status. Browning and Louwagie[21] presented the social problem of the rape and prostitution experienced by Hmong girls at the hands of Hmong gangs as a cultural problem specific to the Hmong community. Such racialization of Hmong culture pathologized "tradition" and "culture" as exotic and other, thereby open to scrutiny and intervention.[22] Implied is a nonpatriarchal and modern hegemonic culture of whiteness that is the only source of assistance because Hmong "girls can't count on the Hmong community to take their side." The emphasis on the subjugation of Hmong American girls and women strips them of any agency and masks everyday acts of resistance and power.[23]

Dia Lee directly challenged the one-dimensional portrayal of a Hmong patriarchal culture that oppresses powerless Hmong women. She particularly saw the ways in which Hmong culture was blamed for all problems faced by Hmong women, using the language of a "single rationale" to underscore the ubiquitous tendency to blame Hmong culture:

> That the criticism is about Hmong culture. And Hmong culture is the reason for this. And, yes, there is a place for that analysis. But to holistically say, the patriarchy, the infrastructure is the single rational for the lack of opportunities, for all of Hmong women's problems is the culture. OK, then to undo all Hmong women's problems then just undo the culture. Which is then self-destruction. Because then you cease to be.

As Lee advocated for a more complex understanding of Hmong culture, she acknowledged that "there is a place" for criticisms of some practices within the Hmong community. However, she criticized the ways in which Hmong patriarchy is positioned "holistically" as the root of all women's problems. As the Hmong leader alluded to discourses about Hmong women's oppression that linked assimilation with liberation,[24] she rebuffed calls to reject Hmong culture as a solution to Hmong women's problems. As she saw it, to "undo the culture" would result in "self-destruction," and the Hmong would "cease to be."

Significantly, Dia Lee identified the role of school in circulating stories that tell Hmong children that their culture is oppressive and wrong, and reinforcing ideas of a patriarchal Hmong culture. She asserted schoolteachers and staff "have been too judgmental" about the Hmong community:

> I think that the schools need to be, to a larger extent, I think that a lot of people who work with and deal with the Hmong community have been too judgmental. They bought too easily into the simplistic example about the Hmong culture being oppressive.

As Lee continued to explain the complicity of school, she pointedly shared that she often heard allegations from teachers and counselors:

> I hear time and again. I hear from teachers, I hear from special ed teachers, I hear from counselors. I have people who walk into this office to lobby me to pass legislation for money for youth, particularly for girls. And they think that the way they can get to me is to tell me how oppressive Hmong culture is for these girls.

According to Lee, educators repeatedly asked her to support funding to advance educational opportunities for Hmong girls by pointing to the need due to an oppressive Hmong culture. Her comment that educators thought that they could appeal to her specifically with the rationale of a despotic Hmong culture perceptively recognized that they believed she was a victim of Hmong patriarchy.

Indeed, the Hmong leader found it presumptuous that people believed she would castigate Hmong culture because she is a Hmong woman: "And then to presume that the reason I rose to the level I have, somehow I have a secret weapon for overcoming the oppression of this culture that I've been operating under." According to the hegemonic narrative, her success was a result of overcoming Hmong culture rather than a result of its values. She elaborated:

> And so, they say, "How did you do it? What is your key to success? How did you overcome your oppression to become who you are?" What I like to think is that it's not so much a story of overcoming the oppression. But it ought to stand as a very positive vision for what a very positive upbringing or a very positive supportive mother and father can do. For any child, man or woman, boy or girl.

Lee argued that rather than "a story of overcoming the oppression" of Hmong culture, her success should be viewed as an example of "a very positive vision" of Hmong culture that includes "a very positive upbringing" that is available to everyone in the Hmong community, regardless of gender. Her repetition of "a very positive" in connection with Hmong culture counteracted its widespread negative portrayal. In fact, the leader was intentional about her refusal to "perpetuate" the story that Hmong culture is oppressive: "I'm not going to perpetuate that. Because I can't deny that I am a byproduct of a different aspect of a culture that ought to be really, that which should be celebrated."

Dia Lee's analysis of the denigration of Hmong culture included an analysis of the ways in which women's groups expected her to vilify her heritage. She shared, "When women's groups invite me to go speak to them, they expect me to harp on my culture and how bad it is. And when I don't deliver, people get confused." She again resisted the logic that equity requires the destruction of Hmong culture:

> To claim self-determination, I have to destroy Hmong culture, in order to self-determine. There's a fatal flaw to that analysis. I very much am very concerned about that because, and I've always taken that position. And I'm not, I'm not very popular among my sisters who tend to go towards that route.

Narratives of cultural racism position self-determination, freedom, and women's rights as antithetical to Hmong culture. The power and perniciousness of such stories are persuasive to even Hmong Americans. In the above, Lee suggested some of her female peers have internalized the racism and thus renounce Hmong culture.[25] Her refusal to take on an anti-Hmong stance on behalf of gender equity is unpopular among some Hmong American women.

Moreover, the leader sought to dispel notions of a static Hmong culture steeped in long-standing custom and emphasized instead the construction of culture in everyday practices. She gave an example of the ways in which she was intentional about how she constructed gender norms in her own household:

> And how we do that is that in my household, we have a very serious conversation about roles and responsibilities. And we intentionally raise our children to understand that daddy is daddy and mommy is mommy. And we have very specific roles and responsibilities, but we can cross the gender roles and responsibilities. And that my husband can have a very close, very personal, very playful relationship with my daughters; and I can have a very close, very playful relationship with my son. And that there is no difference between the boys and the girls. And then that's Hmong. I mean, that's Hmong.

The Hmong leader shared she taught her children that while "mommy" and "daddy" identities and responsibilities exist, she wanted to convey to them that they can also cross the boundaries of constructed gender roles and practices. She disrupted stereotypes of a distant Hmong father[26] and expectations of gender-aligned parenting through everyday practices, where her husband can have a close, playful relationship with their daughters and she can have a loving, playful relationship with their son. Mothers may have close parenting relationships with sons and fathers may have close parenting relationships with daughters. Significantly, her statement "And then that's Hmong" made claim to a Hmong culture that is alive, actively shaped by Hmong Americans on a daily basis.

Yet Dia Lee maintained that the ways in which her parenting practices challenged gender stereotypes is not a novel, contemporary version of Hmong culture. She continued to share that such parenting practices were part of her and her husband's childhood experiences:

> But see, I grew up in that kind of household. I grew up in that kind of household. I mean, I am closer to my father than sometimes I think to my mother. And so, again, you know, family role reversals—My husband grew up in a

> household where he was very close to his mother, very close to his mother. And we reflected on this a lot.

By pointing out that her parents' generation also disrupted cultural and gender role stereotypes, Lee again contested notions of enduring Hmong cultural traditions that are purportedly responsible for the patriarchal structures of the Hmong American community.

Further, the Hmong leader argued that some of the problems in the "gender debate" that are associated with Hmong culture are in fact problems that stem from individual, personal experiences rather than something widespread within the Hmong community:

> And some of the conversations that's kind of helping to frame the gender debate in the Hmong community tend to surface in circumstances where I think the individuals who were helping to frame the conversation are people who have had very challenging circumstances in their own personal lives. Whether they are a daughter of a product of a father with multiple spouses. And under that circumstance, there's a whole layer of other politics that come into play. We acknowledge that and we understand that, but that doesn't define the entire community. And that shouldn't define all of gender politics for the Hmong community. And that actually shouldn't define what Hmong culture is because that's a newly emerged thing of the military era of Hmong culture.

According to Lee, Hmong Americans who helped to "frame the conversation" about Hmong patriarchy are incorrectly assigning blame to the broader Hmong community on the basis of difficult experiences that should be viewed as isolated to individual families. While she acknowledged that polygyny is a problem, she insisted that it comprised "a whole layer of other politics" that emerged more recently.[27] For example, Schein suggested when more Hmong men than women were killed during the war in Laos, "polygyny became more tolerable so that widows would be able to remarry rather than remain alone."[28] The Hmong leader insisted that neither isolated experiences nor wartime practices should define Hmong culture.

All together, Dia Lee pointed to the problematic ways in which Hmong culture is viewed as uniformly and inherently detrimental to Hmong Americans. She admonished the public as well as her Hmong American "sisters" for buying into the simple story of a singularly oppressive Hmong culture.

Her counternarrative challenged normative ways of thinking about what it means to be Hmong by highlighting the multiplicity and complexity of the Hmong American experience. At the same time, the Hmong leader critiqued the insidious narratives of assimilation that demand that Hmong Americans "destroy" their ethnic heritage. Indeed, she refused to "perpetuate" narratives that condemn Hmong culture.

Kou Vang: "The Real Issue Is Teen Pregnancy"

"30 Hmongs in a house"

No room for a couch
'Cause we sleep on the floor
One big group of Vangs
Hmong family of twenty-four
Kids work in Saint Paul
Hang out at the mall
'Cause I know they dwell so well
Thirty Hmongs in a house

Hmongs get pregnant early
First baby at 16
Seven kids by 23
Over the hill by 30
Like sardines they live
Packed in a two-room house with the kids
But you know they age quite well
They be Hmongs[29]

Twin Cities KDWB radio personality "Steve-O" LaTart created the above "Hmong Parody Song," set to Eric Clapton's "Tears in Heaven," as a feature on the *Dave Ryan in the Morning* radio show. Presented as a parody, the song denigrated the unrelenting poverty of the refugee experience obscured by rescue discourses of U.S. refugee resettlement,[30] which for Hmong families often manifest in cramped housing conditions with two or more households sharing a home (i.e., "No room for a couch / 'Cause we sleep on the floor"; "Thirty Hmongs in a house"). In its response letter to KDWB owner Clear Channel, the Hmong National Development Inc. stated, "The 'parody' discounts the systemic injustices and the racial and economic inequalities Hmong Americans face daily in Minnesota and around the nation."[31]

As an exemplar of the cultural racism faced by Hmong Americans, the song pathologized large families and teenage pregnancy within the Hmong community ("Hmongs get pregnant early / First baby at 16 / Seven kids by 23"). These narratives of the new racism portray high fertility and teenage pregnancy in the Hmong American community as a cultural practice specific to the Hmong community as a whole, even though large families and teenage pregnancy are part of the experiences of all racial groups.[32] Further, the condemnation of Hmong American teenage pregnancy occurs alongside allegations that as a cultural practice, Hmong parents routinely force daughters into marriage to avoid out-of-wedlock pregnancy and save the family's reputation.[33] Such accounts persist despite long-standing and ongoing evidence of the changing form and function of Hmong teenage marriage and pregnancy in the United States, including the shifting attitudes toward postponing marriage,[34] marriage as an avenue of escape,[35] and marriage as a form of rescue[36] from unhappy home and school experiences.

Hmong leader Kou Vang sought to dispel notions of cultural difference between Hmong and mainstream U.S. cultures. He particularly framed practices of Hmong teenage pregnancy and teenage marriage as teen issues that are part of the struggles of all racial and ethnic communities. For example, to explain some of the struggles faced by Hmong American youth and parents, he argued that Hmong parents are like other parents:

> You know underage marriage. I have not met one Hmong parent who says, "Well you're twelve years old. You gotta go get married." I have not met one Hmong parent that says that. Every Hmong parent that I talk to says, "Go to college. Get a good education, then talk about marriage." That's the norm for the majority of the Hmong parents. OK, and they all hope that their daughter goes off to college, and then come back and get married. And so that's established.

Vang asserted that he has not met a single parent who tells their teenage child, "You gotta go get married." He emphasized this by repeating, "I have not met one Hmong parent that says that." Instead, he argued that "every" Hmong parent wanted their children to finish their education and then begin to talk about marriage. He underscored this with the statement that this is the "norm" among Hmong parents, and by extension within

Hmong culture. The language of the "norm" plays an important role in framing this value as widespread and customary for the Hmong community. Additionally, Vang contended that parents hope that daughters leave them and go "off to college," and then once they have completed their education, to "come back and get married." At the end of this statement, he reiterated this normative belief with the assertion, "so that's established."

In place of the hegemonic discourse about Hmong teenage marriage as a Hmong cultural practice, Kou Vang offered an alternative theory that positioned marriage as an option in the predicament of teenage pregnancy:

> What happens is this. You have two fifteen-year-olds. They go get pregnant, right? They don't understand sex. They were never taught sex ed. So they get pregnant. Now what do you do? You know, you have two fifteen-year-olds. What do you do, you know?

Vang explained the difficult position Hmong parents are put in by their children and the larger public with the statement, "What happens is this." According to the Hmong leader, Hmong teenagers get pregnant because they have not had sex education and "don't understand sex." With the question, "Now what do you do?" he positioned the dilemma as a problem of universal parenthood rather than one of Hmong culture. His question also suggested that teenage marriage becomes an option only after teenagers become pregnant.

Kou Vang extended this argument with a reference to a research study conducted by a Hmong nonprofit agency. As he shared, the study found that most Hmong parents are not against sex education in schools:

> And there was a study by [a Hmong nonprofit agency] that says the majority of the Hmong parents are not against comprehensive sex ed. They just, they don't feel comfortable talking to their kids about it. Because Hmong families just don't talk about sex. They don't talk to their kids about it, but they're willing to allow the public schools to talk to them and show them how to use a condom. And so these parents are not against, they're not talking about abstinence only. They're not against comprehensive sex ed. They just can't do it themselves, but they're willing to allow someone to do it. So there's willingness from the community to arm their kids with these tools, to say look you need to use protection.

The leader stressed that Hmong parents do not necessarily value "abstinence only" but are willing to have school "arm their kids" with knowledge about protected sexual intercourse. His assertions not only serve as a counternarrative to the hegemonic narrative that Hmong parents force children to marry and become pregnant but also points to the responsibility of school in preventing Hmong teenage pregnancy.

Moreover, the Hmong leader contended that teenage pregnancy is a part of every community. As he continued to explain teenage marriage among Hmong American youth, he argued that "many parents" do not want their teenagers getting married. His storytelling again made normative the value among parents that marriage is not the best option for their adolescents:

> OK, I have met many parents that say, "No. You're not going to get married." But OK at night, the girl keep, both, either the girl or the guy keeps sneaking out from her or his house and sneaking into the other person's house. Even against the wishes of the parents. And living as a couple.

The leader suggested that teenage marriage occurs "against the wishes of parents" because Hmong youth "sneak" out of their homes and into the homes of their girlfriend or boyfriend and live as a couple. Significantly, he positioned Hmong American youth as agents in their own right, who take specific actions to pursue desires that contradict and defy the wishes of parents.

Additionally, Kou Vang addressed the accusation that Hmong culture is patriarchal as a result of practices related to teenage marriage and pregnancy by suggesting that Hmong parents have a different frame of reference for out-of-wedlock pregnancy:

> Now what do you do? So a lot of the parents, you know they grew up in a society where if you got someone pregnant, that meant you were willing to marry her. If not, then you have to pay some fines. You have to go and admit your guilt and pay some restitution to that family. That's the other choice.

According to Vang, parents "grew up in a society where if you got someone pregnant," it "meant you were willing to marry her." The language of "grew up in a society" decreases the significance of "culture." Instead, the Hmong leader stressed the different perspectives or reference points for parents. He again suggested that marriage among teenagers in the Hmong community happens only after pregnancy. Further, and significantly, he provided another possible option for teenage pregnancy: that the boy and his family "pay some restitution" to the girl's family.[37] This second option importantly contributes to his argument that teenage marriage is a choice in response to a predicament rather than a preferred cultural obligation.

The Hmong leader asserted that Hmong American teenagers voluntarily chose to marry. In particular, "many of them choose" marriage out of a sense of "responsibility," and the teenagers may "initiate the whole process":

> So many of them choose, "OK I got her pregnant. It's my responsibility. I'm gonna get married. I'm gonna marry her." And so they initiate the whole process because a lot of these parents grew up in that tradition. What are they going to do—say no? So they're gonna start the process. And now you end up with these two fifteen-year-olds being married.

Implicitly, Kou Vang suggested that parents agree to their children's decisions because parents are familiar with the practice, since they "grew up in that tradition." In other words, the Hmong youth are co-opting the practice of teenage marriage that is familiar to their parents.[38]

The Hmong leader continued to undermine the connection between Hmong teenage marriage and Hmong culture by asserting that teenage marriage and pregnancy in the Hmong community was not an issue of Hmong cultural values but an issue of teen pregnancy:

> The real issue is not the culture. I think the real issue is teen pregnancy. You know if we could fix—if we could find ways to stop guys from [im]pregnating young girls, then I think this underage marriage will get taken care of. I think what has to do with teen marriage more than anything is teen pregnancy.

According to Vang, teen pregnancy needs to be addressed to stem teen marriage among Hmong young people. By connecting teen marriage to teen pregnancy, the problem is not specific to the Hmong community. Instead, marriage and pregnancy among Hmong teenagers are a problem of teenaged unprotected sexual intercourse that is a part of all racial and ethnic communities.

Overall, Kou Vang underscored the ways in which the practices of Hmong parents and youth are like those of parents and children from other racial and ethnic communities. In contrast to the narratives of the new racism that stress the differences between Hmong and mainstream U.S. cultures, Vang used language to point out the similarities. Significantly, his explanations anticipated and responded to discourses about Hmong teenage marriage and pregnancy.[39] According to the leader, Hmong American girls are not passive pawns who become pregnant in obedience to Hmong cultural norms that value marriage and children over education. Instead, he suggested that Hmong girls and boys are both active agents in teenage unprotected sex that results in an unplanned pregnancy. Vang proposed that marriage and pregnancy among Hmong teenagers be curbed with adequate sex education. Crucially, the Hmong leader connected the struggles of Hmong parents and youth to the struggles faced by all parents and children across racial and ethnic communities.

HMONG "EARLY" MARRIAGE: THREE STORIES

> Parents don't expect their daughters to get married until later. Education—My parents tell me that I have to get my education first before I get married. And like, way back in our culture, those—The older generation—they wanted their kids to get married and have a family and to support their husbands. Nowadays, I think my parents—More parents want their kids to have an education rather than get married for them.

Echoing Kou Vang's perspective on teenage marriage among Hmong American adolescents, Dayton High School students consistently shared that Hmong parents do not expect female children to sacrifice their education for the sake of marriage. As the above comment made by a Hmong female student illustrates, Hmong students considered the practice of daughters marrying before the completion of high school something that was part of the "older generation" and "way back in our culture," as opposed to the "nowadays" practice of Hmong Americans. As another student put it, "The parents are like, 'Get your education. Go to college, then get married and have kids' and whatever." Similarly, another student noted the recent changing views of Hmong Americans: "Most of the Hmong people lately, they are changing to be kind of more modernized people instead of more holding onto the tradition."

At the same time, the students also related that they knew school peers and friends who married before high school graduation. Despite the continuing prevalence of marriage among Hmong American adolescents, the form and nature of teenage marriage are multiple and changing.[40] For example, Lee and colleagues found that parents are supportive of children delaying marriage in order to pursue education, while Hmong teenagers still choose to marry before high school graduation.[41] Hutchison and McNall reported that "early marriage" did not have significant negative bearing on academic achievement or continued education after high school graduation.[42] Even as students acknowledged the existence of "forced" marriages, they emphasized that some of their Hmong peers marry boyfriends against the wishes of parents. According to one student, a fourteen-year-old cousin married against the wishes of her mother: "She just went with her boyfriend and they just decided to get married. And the next thing we know—Her mom didn't even want her to marry 'cause she was young. And she just got married." Another student specifically pointed out that Hmong teenagers become pregnant as a means to marry while still in high school:

> I know three of my friends who actually wanted to get married. And then I never met anyone whose parents actually forced them to get married . . . I know like four people outside of school who, their parents didn't like either their boyfriend or their girlfriend and didn't want them to be together. So, they would go and do something bad like get pregnant or something. So, that way, their parents have no choice. So they had to get married. My friend, Jenny, her mom didn't want her to be with her boyfriend. She really, really, really wanted to be with him. So, then she got pregnant. And then her mom got mad at her. So they had to get married. Because she had no choice because she was pregnant.

Comparable to Kou Vang's analysis of marriage as the agentive choice of Hmong teenagers that oppose the desires of parents, this student maintained, "I never met anyone whose parents actually forced them to get married." She instead observed that Hmong teenage marriage and pregnancy occur in instances where parents disapprove of their children's relationships and young couples opt to force the issue. In such instances, the student suggested "parents have no choice" in the relationship. While the student made this observation about teenage pregnancy, Evans-Pritchard and Renteln reported that the practice of "'marriage by elopement' in which the girl willingly goes with the boy"[43] is a mode of agency for Hmong young people because it "gives the younger generation the power to defy the authority of older generations" who disapprove of their relationships.[44] In a similar vein, Hmong teenagers become pregnant with the understanding that their parents and clan leaders would support marriage as a way to maintain social harmony between clans and preserve face or family reputations.[45] Lee and colleagues asserted that desires to maintain good standing in the Hmong community, "coupled with old and young Hmong people's acceptance of and attitudes toward early marriage, have sustained and perpetuated early marriage among the Hmong even in a modern postindustrial society."[46]

One student's explanation of the importance of the family's reputation for his father particularly pointed to its role in the social relations of the extended family:

> I think reputation kind of matters from my dad's point of view because without a [good] reputation, you won't get enough support from the relatives to come back you up or something like that when there's a big argument or dispute. So yeah. That's why I guess reputation matters for him. . . . When a person's reputation is bad, you wouldn't want to support them because you would be seen as bad too.

The reputation of the Hmong individual and family is important for garnering assistance from relatives in times of conflict. Because disagreements within and between Hmong families are often resolved within the lineage family (e.g., extended family, clan), respectability is imperative for individuals and the family as a whole.[47] As the student continued to explain why reputation matters, he gave an example of the marriage of a cousin who was pregnant before the wedding:

> Like, there's one of my cousins who got married. And I'll say just because of the fact that she got pregnant before she got married makes her reputation a little bit bad. And at the wedding, no one from our side of the family showed up at their wedding. But there was only like, I think two uncles that went to her wedding.

In addition to support in resolving disputes, a good reputation is important for the family's financial, emotional, and instrumental support from the extended family.[48] Nevertheless, in an example of the changing attitude about maintaining a good reputation, the student declared, "Personally, I don't quite care about reputation." Some parents and young people discourage teenage marriage despite social repercussions of creating "social disharmony," or *tou shia*.[49] The 1.5- and second-generation Hmong young people are not merely participants in an enduring cultural practice of teenage marriage dictated by the older generation but are actively transforming the form and function of marriage in the Hmong American community.

Although Dayton High School Hmong students reported knowing classmates, friends, or cousins who were married, they shared surprise when learning about the marriages of their school peers. For example, one Hmong female student shared: "It's like I see a lot of girls, like they tell—I don't know if they're married. But then they would tell me they're married. I be like, 'Whaaat?!' Yeah. It's just kind of surprising when I hear that they are married." Rather than a common practice, teenage marriage is unusual enough for students to be taken aback when they learn school peers are married. Another Hmong female student shared disdain for Hmong peers who yearn for marriage: "Like some girls, I think they're too desperate to go into marriage. They think that marriage life is very fun." In addition to disdain, the student's assessment that peers think marriage is "fun" suggested a naiveté on the part of Hmong adolescents. Along these lines, a different Hmong female student surmised with a chuckle that Hmong teenagers who marry "think they are in love": "Teens these days, I think they think they're in love. They just want to get married. Or they're like, 'Oh, you know, I love you, you love me. We should get married. Because I love you and you love me.'" Yet another student reported:

> I don't know why they want to get married when they've been—because this one friend, she has had a boyfriend for like two years, and she wants—they're going to get married this summer. So I'm like, "Two years and you guys want to get married?" I don't get it. They're just happy. And that's it. I don't get it.

These comments indicate that Hmong American students perceive Hmong teenage marriage to be a facet of young, foolish love rather than Hmong young people forced to follow a cultural tenet, as suggested by hegemonic narratives. Importantly, they also convey a voluntary aspect of teenage marriage that is omitted by the storytelling of white cultural hegemony.

The Hmong students at Dayton High also shared that they saw Hmong female students getting married as a way to leave unhappy home experiences:[50]

> Like, for example, if the daughter—She doesn't go to school or anything. She always goes out and play. Sometimes maybe she will come home and she won't have a good relationship with her parents. And every day they argue and stuff. Sometimes these girls think that they're tired of the family and then they might just choose to get married.

Another student similarly suggested: "Well, basically just to get out of their problems, I guess. A lot of girls are stressed. They are like, 'Yeah, my parents won't let me do anything.'" In the same vein, another student noted that for Hmong teenagers marriage was a form of rebellion:

> I think it depends on the person. Maybe their parents too, like how they are with their parents. They may get married just to rebel against their parents. And I think that's a lot of the cases. Maybe they have—The kids that aren't married have better relationships with their parents. They can guide them to don't get married early.

Dayton High Hmong staffulty also saw female adolescents using marriage to "escape" the restrictions and obligations of their families. As one staffulty put it, "So, the girls obviously, they have a yearning to escape this [household obligations], and they feel like there are only several options to do this. One way is marriage. That's why some Hmong girls get married early."[51] The above perspectives suggest Hmong daughters engage in teenage marriage because it allows them to leave or escape their parents' household to join that of their husbands.[52] For Hmong sons, teenage marriage may be a form of "rescue" that allows them to free Hmong girls from the demands of household obligations (e.g., caring for younger siblings) and restrictions on their movements by strict parents.[53]

Taken together, the observations of Hmong American students at Dayton High School point to various reasons for Hmong teenage marriage that extend beyond hegemonic discourses about the patriarchy and misogyny of Hmong culture. Below, I share the stories of Choua, Kajua, and Alexis to delve into the perspectives of Hmong American students on teenage marriage. All three students were part of the International Baccalaureate (IB) program at Dayton High School. Choua and Alexis were 1.5-generation Hmong Americans who were in the eleventh grade at Dayton High, while Kajua was a second-generation Hmong American who was in her senior year at the school. Choua's story gestures toward what hegemonic culture understands as a forced marriage, while Kajua's and Alexis's stories reflect voluntary marriage. I re-present the stories they shared with me during interviews in stanza form to highlight my retelling of them, for as Joan Scott suggests, the stories research participants tell researchers are "an interpretation and in need of an interpretation."[54] The stanzas are constructed verbatim from excerpts of their interviews with me.

Choua: "She's Gonna Bring You Guys a Bad Name"

I. I'm like, "I'm still at the mall."
"Where are the other two couple?"
I'm like, "They're home."
They're like, "We can't turn around right now because
we're way past Harriet City."
"Then what do you expect me to do? Sleep over here?
I don't have nobody over here."
They're like, "Well, why don't you call your boyfriend?"
I'm like, "OK" and I called my boyfriend.
So, I called him and he was like, "Oh, so you have no ride home?"

II. We were gonna head out of Harriet City
when my parents called.
They busted me.
They're like, "Why are you over there?
And why are you with your boyfriend?
You told me that you're with your friend.
I called your friend.
And your friend said you're not there with them."
I'm like, "I was with my friend, but they left without me."
So my mom was really mad.
'Cause my dad was so mad.
My dad told my mom to call my boyfriend's parents
and tell them that my parents don't want me back home.
So then my parents called his parents and talked to his parents.
So his parents called him and asked him where he is.
He was like, "Oh, I'm at the park."
And his parents were like, "Stop lying.

You know you're with your girlfriend.
So you better take your girlfriend home.
'Cause we don't want any issues."

III. My parents actually called the Vang leader. The actual Vang leader.
And talked to him about it. And then he was like,
"Well, if your daughter's over there already,
then just have them get married because,
we're not accepting your daughter.
Because if your daughter comes back,
she's gonna bring you guys a bad name.
So, just force her to go and marry him."
Then they just talked it over to the Xiong leader.
The Xiong leader just said, "No, we're not.
We don't want your daughter.
'Cause it's not like our son came and take your daughter.
Your daughter actually came up here."
But since my parents were being so hard on his side of the family,
they're just like, "OK, fine. We'll take your daughter then."

IV. And I'm like, "But, I don't wanna marry you. I only want to date you.
I don't wanna marry you."
He's like, "Well, I don't wanna marry you too."
I'm like, "OK."
Then somehow he came up with the stupidest idea.
He was like, "Why don't you run away? I'll run away."
And I'm like, "Hell, no. I don't know what to do.
If I run away, I don't got nowhere to go."
I was like, "Forget it. If this is where we end up,
Then this is where we're gonna end up."
Then he decided to take me home. That's why we got married.

V. [My mom] thought that probably I would not be like my sister.
And I'll be a little more smarter and think about it. (chuckles)
But she was really mad about—
Because she said that I totally make the wrong choice.
And that why didn't I come back home.
If I don't wanna marry him, why didn't I just find my way home?

I was like, "You guys were the ones who was not happy with his parents.
That he has to marry me.
So this is where I'm gonna end up."
Like I would actually kind of say that.
It's not really my parents' fault.
I would say it's kind of my fault too.
Because if I would have known and probably I wouldn't have come.

VI. All I did was I just came up here and shop and that was it.
It's not like I was with him the whole day.
It's not like I was with him or I slept over with him or anything.
All I did was I just came up here to shop and that was it.
I came clean, so if I go home, I'm gonna go home clean too.
So my dad wasn't happy.
My dad was like, "Well, when I called you, you were with your boyfriend.
So that means you guys must have did something."
I'm like, "I did nothing.
When you called me, I was just in his car. I did nothing." (chuckles)
So my dad was really accusing me of doing bad things with him.

When Choua asked her mom for permission to go to Harriet City with her friends, her mom said, "No. Don't go 'cause your dad's gonna be mad if he finds out." She convinced her mom to let her go on the day-trip by emphasizing that she "never really get to go places." When her mom relented, she told Choua, "Oh, OK. Just go. But be sure you get back home on time before your dad gets home." When Choua's dad realized she was in another state with her boyfriend, he did not allow her to come back home. She shared, "All he said to me was, 'If you come back home, for sure, you're not coming back into my house. So if you wanna have a house to live, you better marry your husband, 'cause I'm not accepting you back.'" From her father's perspective, because Choua's honor was put into question, if she did not marry her boyfriend and simply went back to her parents' house, her tainted reputation would reflect poorly on the family and clan.[55] To move forward, her father gave Choua two choices. She could strike out on her own—"run away," as her boyfriend suggested to her—or she could marry her boyfriend, after which she would become part of his parents' household.[56] In other words, Choua was "forced" to choose between being on her own or becoming a part of her boyfriend's family.

Consequently, Choua married her boyfriend of one month and two weeks during her sophomore year of high school. She then moved to Harriet City to live with her new husband and his parents.

According to Choua, teenage marriage happens in the Hmong American community when parents—like her father—are "really cultured" and strictly monitor the actions of daughters. She implied that not all parents are "really cultured" or as strict as her father. Choua explained the mindset of strict parents:

> They don't really let their daughter have friends. And then once their daughter go off with a person that they don't know, they'll be accusing their daughter like, "Oh, yeah, I know you. You went and did this and this with your friend. You must have did bad things with your friend."

Billson suggested that as "keepers of culture," immigrant daughters are expected to "conform to the image of an 'ideal' ethnic subject" because they carry the weight of protecting and preserving the family name.[57] Across ethnic groups, the exacting control of immigrant daughters is part of broader efforts to maintain the ethnic group in the face of acculturation and demands for assimilation.[58] According to Yen Le Espiritu, "Women's moral and sexual loyalties were deemed central to the maintenance of group status, changes in female behavior, especially that of growing daughters, were interpreted as signs of moral decay and ethnic suicide."[59]

At Dayton High School, Choua was initially embarrassed about being married, but she gradually told more people:

> When I first married, I was kind of like embarrassed to tell people that I'm married, but after a while, I don't feel embarrassed about it anymore. Because I'm like, "It's a natural thing. Girls get married. If they don't leave now, they leave later." So, either ways, they're gonna end up telling it to people that, "Yeah, I'm married."

At the same time, she was selective about who she talked to about her status as a married teenager. She had no problems telling Hmong male students who would "smack" on her: "They'll be like, 'Dude, what's your name? Can I get your number or stuff?' I would be like, 'I'm sorry, but I'm married. Don't ask me.'" However, Choua was more reluctant to tell non-Hmong students because they were "shocked," audibly gasped, and asked her questions such as, "Why did you get married? Why didn't you just go back and live with your parents?" and "Why marry at such a young age?" To these questions, Choua told non-Hmong classmates, "I don't know. That's the way our culture is." Choua's reticence to tell non-Hmong students was a response to their reactions of astonishment and her concerns about their judgment.[60] Her response to non-Hmong peers that she married her boyfriend because "that's the way our culture is" simplifies Hmong culture to an easily understood narrative by echoing the rationale of the hegemonic discourse. In actuality, and as illustrated below, Choua understood the complexity of Hmong teenage marriage.

Significantly, Choua was not only concerned about the criticisms from non-Hmong students but also wary about telling Hmong American female peers that she was married:

> But [Hmong] girls—Like when they ask me, I don't really tell them, because they kind of like have a bad point of view. . . . They just think, "Oh, is it because you're pregnant? Is that why you got married?" Like, they kind of have a bad point of view. Yeah, that's why I don't really tell Asian girls a lot. So whenever they ask me about it, I would just be, "Yeah." And sometimes if they heard me saying like, "Oh, yeah, my husband," they'll be like, "You're married?" And I'm like, "Yeah." They'll be like, "Oh, OK. That's surprising. I never knew about that."

Her emphasis on the "bad point of view" of Hmong female peers implies, first, that her Hmong peers disapprove of teenage marriage; and second, that Hmong girls who marry often do so because they become pregnant. Marriage among Hmong American teenagers was not a cultural norm in terms of being broadly embraced or practiced. Additionally, like other Hmong students, Choua reported that Hmong peers were surprised when they learn of her marriage. Belying hegemonic narratives about the pervasiveness of Hmong teenage marriage as a cultural practice, Hmong students are taken aback when they learn of the marriages of their school peers.

Even though Choua was upset with her parents for refusing to allow her back into their household after her father found out she was with her boyfriend, she understood that her story of Hmong teenage marriage was not the only story for all Hmong American adolescents. She observed Hmong teenagers marrying out of different motivations. For example, she reported some of her peers marry because "they either get pregnant, they either like—Somehow like their in-laws caught them somewhere, or like in the bed together." For other teenagers, she underscored the ways in which male and female adolescents make the intentional choice to marry:

> The guy just wanted to marry her and that's probably why the guy bring her home. . . . "Oh yeah, my husband just wanted to get married. That's why he took me home." Or some girls, they'll just be like, "Oh yeah. I really wanted to marry him. So that's why we just got married."

In exerting their choice to marry, a Hmong American couple may "elope" by going to the boy's home to declare their desire to marry and instigate the negotiation process between the boy's family and the girl's family.[61]

Moreover, and significantly, Choua echoed other Hmong students who mocked peers who chose teenage marriage. She especially thought some of her peers got married for "dumb" reasons:

> I think some girls wanted to get married—Well, for me, I would say that it's kind of dumb why they think that, "Yeah, he's my first guy. He's gonna be my last. I'm gonna marry him." Some girls, they think like that. And then once they're married to that guy and it didn't turn out what they expected, they ended up running back to their parents.

From Choua's perspective, some Hmong girls marry their boyfriends out of the nonsensical desire to make their "first guy" their "last" one. Notably, she related that when the marriages do not work out, girls went "running back to their parents." This suggests that Hmong parents are not all like Choua's father, who refused to allow her to return home. Despite the context of her own marriage, she ultimately asserted, "Like, there's many reasons of why people get married."

Kajua: "'Cause He Wouldn't Like Let You Do Things"

I. Mom, I would have to say she's more modern than my dad.
My dad, he's much more traditionalized.
He follows the Hmong religion and everything.
Like he expect what the Hmong people would expect in you.
But my mom, she's more understanding.
'Cause I guess she's a woman.
So it's kind of like a mother–daughter thing and she adapts.

I guess she adapted more here to the environment.
And how the social community and everything is.
So it's just my dad that sometimes, we get conflicts with.
'Cause he wouldn't like let you do things.

II. So, like if you want to go have fun sometimes,
like just go hang out with your friends or whatever,
he wouldn't let you.
I don't know why, but he would let my younger brothers,
just 'cause they're guys.
I don't know why. Maybe it's just 'cause we're girls and we're vulnerable.
We can get pregnant and stuff like that.
They just think that like people—well, like strangers—
They're afraid of what can happen to us.
'Cause we're daughters, and
we can get raped and stuff like that.
But it's not like we're going we're bad.
Just to the mall and stuff.

III. I have to work harder now [since marriage].
Sometimes when my mother-in-law, they want money,
then they come ask us.
So you can't say no, 'cause if you do that,
they'll bad-mouth you and say,
"Oh, my daughter-in-law's so greedy."
So I guess I have to work hard
just to get money, and it's hard.
Yeah, I have to kind of give it to them.
When I was still with my parents,
I could save money and I can use it on my own stuff.
And when they really, really need it, they just ask, and that's it.
But if my in-laws and them—I work and I have money.
And then they ask us to go buy groceries,
then we have to use our own money
to go buy groceries and stuff like that.

IV. Well, I get more freedom [since marriage].
If you wanted to like just go out for a while, have a little bit fun,

like all you had to do is just ask them.
And tell them where you're going,
who you're going with,
and tell them like what time you'll be home by.
And they're like, "OK, you can go.
But just don't do anything bad. Or just don't get into any trouble,"
'Cause they know how it is, I guess,
since they grew up here.
I mean, like it doesn't really matter to them,
as long you're still going to school
and you're still working hard,
then it's good.

V. I can just talk to her [mother-in-law] like she's a friend.
Well, my mom's like that too.
But my mom, I talk to her like she's an older person, not like a friend.
And then, she's not that Americanized like my husband's mom.
It's just like, sort of like she's [mother-in-law] a teenager to me. (chuckles)
So she understands a lot.
And she got married when she was also very young too.

VI. She [mother-in-law] says just wake up whenever you can.
But if we were to go live with my husband's real father and his stepmom,
she would expect us to wake up like at six or seven
just to cook and have breakfast ready when they wake up.
And then clean and then cook lunch again.
And then clean and cook dinner again at certain time and stuff.
If you're married into a family that's more traditional,
they would expect you to do more, so it would be harder for you,
'cause you have to put what they want first and what you want second.
But for me, like my mother-in-law and my father-in-law—my
 step-father-law—
they want us to put what we want first.
So if you wanted to like get a good job and education,
they want us to do all of that first.
And then come back and take care of them later.

In the spring of Kajua's senior year at Dayton High, she married her boyfriend of almost four years, who was also a senior at the school. When she told me about the upcoming nuptials outside of her guidance counselor's office, she tearfully mentioned she was going through a hard time. She later shared in our interview at the end of the school year that at the time, she was partly upset "'cause a lot of people didn't think that I would [marry]. Well, *I* didn't think that I was gonna get married. But I did." Kajua explained that people did not see her marrying before high school completion because "stereotypically, whenever a Hmong girl gets married, it's either 'cause she's pregnant or her parents walked in on her having sex with her boyfriend." As she continued, she told me, "But that didn't happen to me," distancing herself from the stereotype:

> So if they, like the people, if they found out that you were married—Like Hmong people, if they found out that you were married, they'll go, "Oh, is she pregnant?" And I'm like, "No, I'm not pregnant. I just got married 'cause I wanted to." I don't know. That's probably why. And I didn't want people to say that like, "Oh, she got married because she's pregnant."

In the face of hegemonic narratives such as the KDWB "Hmong Parody Song" that ridiculed Hmong Americans for marrying at young ages and having numerous children, students like Kajua sought to dissociate herself from the negative typecast that her marriage was an outcome of an unplanned pregnancy. When she shared the news with me before her marriage, she asked me not to tell anyone, and afterward, she only told a few close friends and teachers.

For students such as Kajua, marriage was a means to achieve independence[62] from a "traditionalized" father who was "a little too protective"—to the extent of not allowing her to go to the mall or even hang out with girlfriends. She recounted that when her older sister was considering colleges and wanted to sleep over "to get to know the college campus," her father did not allow her to do so, "just because she's a girl." During Kajua's own college exploration, her father barred her from applying to a state college that was an hour away. Kajua explained, "But my dad wouldn't let me go over there 'cause I would have to live on campus. But my mom was OK with it, 'cause she understands." Her father did not want her reputation and that of the family exposed to the perceived debauchery of campus life. Although she had a close relationship with her mother, who was "more modern" and "more understanding," she could no longer tolerate her father's strict control of her movements. Marriage was an avenue for Kajua to gain more freedom from restrictive home conditions. Put another way, the "traditional" practice of teenage marriage was appropriated and re-expressed by Kajua in her negotiation of gender, power, and identity within the institution of the family.[63]

The struggles of Hmong American students like Kajua (and Choua) with restrictive home conditions is well documented in the immigrant research literature. Studies across ethnic groups in the United States showed that immigrant female children are monitored and limited to the home outside of school hours, in contrast to the freedom male children have to enjoy public spaces, extracurricular activities, and employment.[64] Lee and colleagues point to Hmong parents' concerns about the corruption of dominant culture:

> A primary duty of parents, according to Hmong tradition and custom, is to protect the reputation and purity of daughters until they are married. Many Hmong American parents worry about young girls becoming corrupted by bad influences from the mainstream American society and consequently ruining their own and their family's reputation. This worry leads some parents to monitor their daughters more closely than their sons, who are given more leniency and latitude.[65]

Whereas Coulter's narrative[66] and other racist discourses blame Hmong parents for the rape of Hmong daughters, Lee and colleagues suggest it is the "primary duty" of Hmong parents to safeguard the reputation of daughters and protect them from the "bad influences from the mainstream American society."[67] From the perspective of daughters, Hmong parents' lower levels of concern and restrictions over their sons[68] make the limitations on girls' movements and behaviors seem overly strict and controlling.[69] To this point, Kajua relayed that her father perceived that she and her sister were "vulnerable" because they were female: "They're afraid of what can happen to us. 'Cause we're daughters and we can get raped and stuff like that."[70]

Subsequently, the double standards for male and female immigrant children create experiences in immigrant households where "boys and girls lived in two very different worlds and by different rules at home and school."[71] In Kajua's experiences, the unequal treatment between her and her younger brothers contributed to her conflict with her father as well as a sense of gender oppression in his household.[72] The desire of immigrant parents to maintain their ethnic culture, coupled with observations of the negative impact of Americanization on children,[73] can result in Hmong parents' becoming more stringent with children's behavior in the United States than they would in their ethnic homeland.[74]

When Hmong female teenagers leverage marriage as a tactic to gain freedom from parents, they replace the authority of their parents with that of their parents-in-law, since Hmong women join their husband's household upon marriage.[75] Kajua explained what it would have meant if she had married into a "traditional" family: "If you're married into a family that's more traditional, they would expect you to do more, so it would be harder for you, 'cause you have to put what they want first and what you want second." She recognized that because her mother-in-law was "Americanized," she afforded Kajua more freedom, which would not have been the case with a more "traditional"[76] stepmother-in-law, who would expect her to "wake up and cook for them first and then go to school later like at twelve in the afternoon or like one or two." Her parents-in-law understood the importance of college:

> They know about college and how important it is. 'Cause my husband's parents, they didn't go to college, they just finished high school. So they want us to go to college and help them out. They want us to be successful and have a good job, and not have to worry about money and not have to worry about not having enough to eat and stuff like that. So yeah. And then they want us to go live on our own someday too. Yeah, 'cause the oldest son will have to move out eventually.

Kajua saw that parents-in-law may be equally or even more strict than the parents of Hmong American female children and require daughters-in-law to contribute to household labor (e.g., cooking, cleaning, caring for young children) and household economic resources through employment, which may impinge on their education.[77] Importantly, unlike hegemonic discourses that portray all Hmong families as the same, Kajua recognized that not all Hmong parents are as strict as her father.

Alexis: "There's Actually Somebody Telling Me What to Do"

> I. I just decided that maybe, it's like about time.
> 'Cause his parents really, really wanted us to get married anyways.
> 'Cause his parents really, really loved me like their own child.
> 'Cause she, Johnny's mom, she knows the way how I feel.
> 'Cause she was an orphan when she was little too.

Yeah, she was an orphan when she was like five.
And she had to live with her uncle and aunt.
And she was like, "They didn't love me.
I had to walk five miles to school every day."
They didn't even care like to pick her up and take her to school or stuff.
She's like—She feels me.
So it's OK. If I ever feel I need them,
then they'll take me in as their own daughter.

II. My brother, it's not like I'm getting married to get away from him.
It's like I'm getting—I think that I made my choice because
I want them [younger siblings] to realize their place in the family more.
Because when I'm not there,
it's like they're so disorganized and stuff.
There's nobody telling them what to do.
They're just do whatever. They would go out on the streets,
playing around on the streets and I'm like,
"No, there's a car coming. Get out of the street."
They're still playing on the street.
I was like, "If I'm gone, what difference would it make to them?"
But then, I want them to realize the difference.
'Cause it's really hard for them to realize anything still.

III. I think they have to take care of themselves more.
They're not independent or anything.
They rather be with their friends or something
instead of just doing family dinner and sit at the table and eating.
They would go eat in their room and stuff like that.
I'm like, "Bring the dishes back up," and it's still there the next day.
And I'm like, "Oh, my god."
I don't know, it's really hard to—
They got to realize what's happening and me as an older sister,
I'm not gonna live with them forever.
I'm not gonna be like, "You do this, you do that."
They gotta learn how to do it themselves.

IV. No. We don't get along [older brother], we don't get along.
We don't tell each other we hate each other up front or anything.

It's just that some part of me just doesn't,
it's that I really don't love him as my brother.
It's that sometimes I can't accept the fact that he's my brother.
Sometimes he doesn't treat us equally to his wife.
He looks at his wife like she's god or something.
We would ask for money, he'll be like,
"No, I don't have any money."
The next thing you know he gives her like $300 to go shopping.
And we're like, "You just said you didn't have any money."
He's all like, "Well, that's my wife. What you gonna say about that?"
I was like, "I'm your sister, I'm your blood.
You're not gonna even treat me like your wife. Oh, my god."
I always tell Zer and them, and Zer and them are like,
"Gosh, I hate your brother."
Zer and them, they're really there for me though.
They really stand by my side.

V. Yeah, Zer and Mai and Hli and Christina and them. Yeah.
They all help me, yeah.
I always tell them about what happened during the weekend.
And I would be like, "Yeah, my sister-in-law was like this and like that,"
and my brother and my sister-in-law argue constantly
about weird, stupid things that are like, I don't know,
if she doesn't get money to go shopping,
she would throw a big fuss about it, like a baby.

VI. I think it will be different [being married].
But yeah, basically what I do at my house
is probably gonna be like the same thing
I'll do when I get married.
Because it's like, if I go get married, then
there's actually somebody telling me what to do
instead of me being independent and
tell others what to do.

Alexis married her boyfriend of two and a half years during the spring of her eleventh grade year. Similar to Kajua, her boyfriend was a student in the same grade whom she met at Dayton High and chose to marry before high school graduation. She shared with me that she decided it was "about time" and emphasized that her boyfriend's parents "really, really wanted [them] to get married" and "really, really, loved [her] like their own child." His parents especially appreciated that she's "the only person that can tell him to do things." Before their marriage, her boyfriend's parents talked to her about using her influence to urge him to quit smoking. Additionally, because Alexis and her eight siblings were orphaned when her parents died in a car accident when she was in the eighth grade, she felt an affinity with her mother-in-law, who was also orphaned when she was young.

After the death of her parents, Alexis and her siblings lived with their uncle until her older siblings were old enough to take care of her and her younger siblings. As one of the older siblings during the time of the study, this meant she had to take on parenting responsibilities for younger siblings that are typically the role of adults. Alexis conveyed the burden of the task, disclosing that one of her motivations for marrying and moving in with her husband's parents was because she wanted her younger siblings "to realize their place in the family more" and understand that she would not be around indefinitely: "I'm not gonna live with them forever. I'm not gonna be like, 'You do this, you do that.' They gotta learn how to do it themselves." In addition to frustration with her younger siblings, Alexis also did not get along with her older brother, the eldest of the siblings and the head of the household. Her dislike for her brother centered around his preferential treatment of his wife with spending money while rebuffing requests from Alexis and their other siblings. On top of her conflicts with her brother over money, she also hated that her "brother and [. . .] sister-in-law argue constantly about weird, stupid things."

Despite Alexis's denial that she was marrying to get away from her older brother, marriage allowed her to leave a difficult home situation, one shaped by the weight of her relationships with her older brother and younger siblings. Indeed, as a form of escape avoidance, marriage for Hmong female teenagers is a "type of individual coping strategy [that] is characterized by the effort to escape from having to deal with a stressor like a negative home environment."[78] The relief from responsibilities of caring for her siblings that Alexis would achieve once she joins her husband's family is evident in her statement about not having to "tell others what to do": "Because it's like, if I go get married, then there's actually somebody telling me what to do instead of me being independent and tell others what to do." In the context of her adolescence as an orphan who was obliged to care for herself and her younger siblings, marriage offered Alexis a way to leave behind the stress of sibling conflict and gain a form of independence. By joining the household of her husband's parents, she could let go of some of her worries and depend more on her husband and parents-in-law.

In contrast to Choua and Kajua, Alexis announced to school classmates and friends her intentions to marry before the ceremony. When I asked her to describe the reactions of peers, she reported that some were surprised but happy: "'Oh, my god, really?' I was like, 'Yeah.' Some were like, 'Oh, congratulations. Oh, my god, I'm so happy for you.'" Others responded less favorably: "'Oh, you gotta be kidding me? Oh, my gosh!' stuff like that. Like Zer. Zer's like, 'No way!' And I was like, 'Yeah.' She overreacted a little bit." While Alexis thought her good friend "overreacted," Zer was deeply concerned about the possibility that her friend's marriage would interfere in her schoolwork and attendance:

> Alexis is a really good friend to me. And she's like a sister. So when she told me she was getting married, I'm like, "Oh, my gosh!" You know, "What about all this stuff that you have to do for your family?" And then, "You have to come to school. And who's gonna take you to school?" and all this stuff. And I just think it's like a really big step.

In addition to household responsibilities (the cooking and cleaning mentioned by Kajua above), Zer was worried about how Alexis would get to school because her husband's family lived closer to a different school, and he transferred from Dayton High in order to be closer to home.

Students like Zer and Mai feared that the marriages of Alexis and another girlfriend from the same IB English 11 class (who married shortly before Alexis) would create barriers to their education because they would have to juggle school responsibilities with those of married life. Zer explained:

> I guess I'm just scared they might drop out or give up on school. And they might regret it one day about getting married. Or if they get pregnant and then they miss school and then they're really far behind and they're gonna get stressed out. And I think it's a really big step into getting married. Like a lot of people, I think a lot of people when they get married, they don't think about the consequences of getting married.

Zer was particularly concerned that her friends might miss too many days and drop out of school. Notably, she talked about marriage as a choice of school peers where "they don't think about the consequences of getting married." In a separate interview, Mai similarly lamented about the decisions of Alexis and her friend from the same IB class to marry before high school graduation:

> I think that they could have made wiser choices, waited a little bit longer to get married. I mean it would have been all the same later on. But then, it's their decision, I guess. And if they're gonna still do well, then I guess it's OK. But if they're gonna start slacking off and not coming to school and stuff, then it's a bad decision that they made. Like they could've just waited longer. Because really, they could have graduated from high school and then gotten married. It would have still been the same, I think.

Mai's reflection on the marriages of her friends notably included assertions such as: "they could have made wiser choices," "it's their decision," "it's a bad decision that they made," and "they could've just waited longer"—all of which underscore the voluntary nature of the marriages. Whereas hegemonic narratives emphasize Hmong American teenage marriage as a compulsory cultural practice, Alexis's story elucidates the complexity of the practice, which includes her experiences as an orphan and navigating relationships with her siblings.

Hegemonic narratives portray Hmong culture as premodern, patriarchal, and misogynistic.[79] The racialization of the cultural practices of Hmong Americans categorizes them as emblems of difference and demeans them.[80] As a focus of censure, teenage marriage among Hmong American adolescents is racialized as a practice specific to Hmong Americans although it actually occurs across all racial groups and is dependent on factors such as group demographics, family background, and religion, among others.[81] For example, individuals whose parents have higher educational attainment and financial resources are less likely to marry young,[82] and individuals whose parents married early are more likely to marry at young ages.[83] While racist discourses about Hmong teenage marriage vaunt the superiority of Western knowledge systems, white Americans are second most likely to marry, followed by Latinx Americans, and with Asian Americans and African Americans more distantly following as the third and fourth groups, respectively.[84]

As this chapter showed, Hmong leaders Dia Lee and Kou Vang were keenly aware of the prevailing negative narratives of an oppressive, deviant Hmong culture. Dia Lee contested the vilification of Hmong culture that framed it as the singular source of oppression of Hmong girls and women. While she acknowledged the need to address problems in Hmong American social relations, she rejected the destruction of Hmong culture in the struggle for gender equity. Her recognition that educators entreat her for educational funding for Hmong girls by pointing to the oppressiveness of Hmong culture illustrates a discernment of the anti-Hmong discourses prevalent in education. As she pointed to practices that nurture strong, educated women, Lee advocated for a more complex understanding of Hmong culture that accounts for the multiplicity and transformation in Hmong social relations.

Likewise, by attributing teenage marriage to teenage sexuality, Kou Vang disputed the widespread perception that Hmong parents do not support the education of daughters and force them into marriages during their teenage years. He suggested the blame for Hmong teenage marriage lies in the lack of sex education rather than in Hmong culture. The Hmong leader especially called attention to the existence of out-of-wedlock pregnancies across racial and ethnic groups.[85] Yet hegemonic narratives mark nonmarital pregnancies as a problem of Hmong culture. Vang countered the negative portrayal of "traditional" Hmong parents averse to assimilating to U.S. cultural norms with an empathetic interpretation of teenage marriage that arises from finding their children in the predicament of teenage pregnancy.

The stories of Hmong American students at Dayton High School similarly reflect the complexity of teenage marriage conveyed by Hmong leaders. Choua, Kajua, and Alexis's experiences with marriage are examples of just a few of the reasons Hmong young people marry during high school. While some teenage marriages occur as families attempt to maintain the good name of the family and social harmony between clans,[86] the Hmong community should not be defined by them. While Choua's marriage may be reflective of her family's concern for maintaining the family's reputation, her father's stringent control over her movement is also reflective of the concerns about the harmful impact of Americanization on the behaviors and morals of Hmong daughters.[87] Kajua's and Alexis's marriages are examples of the ways in which Hmong female students have taken up the practice as a means to respond to undesirable home conditions.[88] Their Hmong American peers echo similar sentiments about the multiple motivations as well as surprise and disdain for teenage marriage. The homogenizing effect of hegemonic narratives of an oppressive Hmong culture makes unintelligible the ways in which Hmong young people marry as an attempt to exert control over their lives.

In the face of hegemonic culture's racist vilification of Hmong culture, some Hmong American young people respond by rejecting Hmong culture and identity, while others seek a "return" to their ethnic roots. In the next chapter, I elucidate the perspectives of Dayton High School's Hmong Culture Club students, who sought a culturally relevant education that increased the presence and esteem of Hmong culture within the spaces of the school.

PART III

Claiming Culture

5 Re-membering Culture in Hmong Club

Hmong students don't know how to speak the Hmong language, and they're like, "Yeah, Hmong people are so ghetto and blah blah blah." But I'm like, "Nah, you can change your thought and you can always change your way, but you can never change the color of your hair."

—Pakou, vice president, Hmong Culture Club

Mr. Moua asked the officers to introduce themselves to the two newcomer Hmong students by sharing their names and a little about their positions as leaders in the Hmong Culture Club. This started fifteen minutes of much laughter and amusement for the group, as the students struggled to speak Hmong. Tom Lor went first, but he did not explain his position very well, which drew much laughter from the other club members. Twice during his introduction, he lightheartedly remarked "We're Hmonglish here" to explain his struggles. Blia then introduced herself with, "Hi, my name is Blia." Ms. Lor interrupted her to ask her to speak in Hmong and explain her role in the club. As Blia switched languges and attempted to describe her position in Hmong, Tom Lor interjected, "That's what I said!" and received more laughter from the rest of the club members. At this point, Mr. Moua stepped in to explain the officers' positions to the two newcomer girls. Kajua and Mai both said, "Yeah, what he said" and commented to me that the explanations in Hmong would take their peers forever to accomplish without assistance. After the officers introduced themselves, Mr. Moua asked the rest of the club members to go around the room and share their names and grade level. Like the officers, the first member struggled to use the correct Hmong words. Instead of saying "I'm in the eleventh grade," she said, "I'm eleven years old." Once more, the students erupted into laughter.

Similar to the more common term "Spanglish," the "Hmonglish" of the Hmong Culture Club members was a practice of code-switching or code-mixing[1] between Hmong and English that involved switching from one language to the other within and between sentences. The majority of second-generation Hmong American students spoke a mixture of Hmong and English—what they termed Hmonglish—with each other as well as their parents. Students like Chris Vang explained: "Because we're the generation known as the mixed generation. Where when we were born our parents didn't know English so they also teach us just Hmong." Tom Lor particularly noted that "older people" speak only Hmong:

> At the same time we're learning English so both things, both things jamming together. So sometimes when we speak Hmong we mix it with English. We can't just speak Hmong always like the other, the older people. Like we have to mix some English in there. Or else we can't, we don't know what we're saying. But when we talk in English we could be mainly talking English, but just can't talk in Hmong only.

The language practices of the second-generation Hmong American students at Dayton High School reflected the phenomenon of language shift from heritage or minority language to that of the dominant majority. Language shift occurs when minority language groups such as Hmong refugees encounter dominant cultural groups that have the social, political, and economic power to shape language policies—such as the language of instruction in school.[2]

The "hegemony of English"[3] that demands children of immigrants speak only English is a central component of immigrant children's language loss.[4] This process typically occurs over three generations. The first generation continues to speak the heritage language at home while learning the majority language. The second generation continues to speak the heritage language on a limited basis at home while learning advanced levels of English, and speaks English without an accent. The third generation speaks English exclusively, with limited or no working knowledge of the heritage language.[5] Without intervention, immigrant groups completely shift to majority language use within three generations,[6] with research suggesting that an increasing number of language minority groups undergo a complete shift within two generations.[7]

Although Hmong Club members laughed at one another's struggles to speak Hmong, they were keenly aware of the negative impact of white cultural hegemony on the Hmong community. Their struggles with Hmong language provide a glimpse of the intergenerational rifts described by the Hmong community leaders (chapter 1) as well as the divisions among Hmong students. As Pakou, the Hmong Club's vice president, suggested (in the epigraph above), the hegemony of English has resulted in not only Hmong language loss but also in the belief that "Hmong people are so ghetto." Like the leaders, Hmong Club members were aware of the negative impact of the erasure of Hmong heritage. They sought to infuse Hmong culture and identity into their education at Dayton High School.

"I'M NOT ASHAMED TO ADMIT THAT I'M HMONG": REVIVAL OF HMONG ETHNICITY

Paul Vue looked a little like the hip-hop artist Nelly, a piece of thin black athletic tape under his left eye evoking the use of eye black by football players to reduce glare. The secretary of the Hmong Culture Club wore jeans, an orange T-shirt, and a gray zip hoodie. In the absence of Blia, the club's president, he started the meeting by casually saying, "Hey, everybody!" and jumping to sit on the teacher's desk at the front of the room as members ended their conversations. The other officers, Tom Lor and Pakou, smiled at him from their seats at desks in the room. He asked, "So, who has a joke?" Several of the club members laughed. In Hmonglish, one student offered a joke about his mom using oil in cooking, which ended with the punch line of his mom exclaiming, "Oy, oy, oy, oy!"[8]

As the members erupted into laughter, Blia walked briskly into the room and passed out the meeting's typed agenda. She positioned herself at the podium at the front of the room and called the meeting to order again with a curt, "OK, listen up!" She told the members the meeting would cover the items on the agenda and added that they could "skip" item number 3, "review of last meeting," because she had already received an update. Blia then pointedly noted, "I heard it was very loud and chaotic." All the officers were convened at the front of the room, leaning against the whiteboard, faces downcast and somber.

Mr. Moua raised his hand and suggested, "You should ask students if there are other items that they want to add." A Hmong female student new to the club asked, "What's the purpose of the Hmong Club?" In a serious voice, Blia responded, "The purpose of the Hmong Club is to establish a Hmong community at the school, to bring together Hmong and other students. Americans and Somalians can also join."[9] Blia added that the club was also intended for students to "learn about your history." Mr. Moua stood up and told the students that the club is a "support group" where students can learn about Hmong culture and Hmong language. He continued, "Every few weeks, I'll give a Hmong language lesson."

In this meeting, which occurred a few weeks into the school year, figureheads Blia and Mr. Moua asserted the aims of the Hmong Club as nurturing cultural competency and cultural resurgence,[10] a space where students could learn about their history, culture, and language. This desire to underscore Hmong culture and identity echoed concerns of the larger Hmong American community about the importance of retaining Hmong culture, language, and identity. Stuart Hall theorized that such attempts to keep culture unified and intact as the "revival of ethnicity," where ethnic minority groups emphasize ethnicity as a "strategy" for cultural survival in the face of cultural domination.[11] Similar to charter schools and organizations serving the Hmong American community in Harriet City, in the face of the assimilationist demand to forget, the Hmong Club at Dayton High sought "to hold fast to cultural traditions, to reaffirm those elements of the culture which maintain the links to one's past."[12]

"Hmong Is Not Really Known"

In the mid-1980s, the Southeast Asian Club, also known as the SEA Club, was established at Dayton High School for newcomer ELL Hmong refugee students who wanted to be a part of the school's extracurricular activities. Members of the SEA Club were primarily Hmong students, who for the most part conducted the meetings in Hmong or Hmonglish. Over time, the membership of the Southeast Asian Club consisted of only a few ELL students and an increasing majority of what staffulty termed "mainstream" Asian American students, who were primarily second-generation Hmong American students in the IB program. In the early 2000s, Hmong ELL students who did not feel comfortable speaking English and who did not feel welcomed in the SEA Club established the Hmong Culture Club as a way to reconnect with and center their Hmong identity. At the time of the study, the leaders and members of the Hmong Club included students from various academic tracks, including the vice president of the club, who was an ELL student, as well as a few newcomer Hmong refugee students who were resettled to the United States after the closure of Wat Tham Krabok, the last Hmong refugee camp in Thailand.[13]

On the surface, the members of the Hmong Club and the SEA Club at Dayton High were the same: second-generation mainstream Hmong American students. As a longtime staffulty who was involved in the establishment of the SEA Club put it,

> SEA Club originally started as [focused on ELL students], and that evolved into a mainstream dominance. And then the Hmong Club was started because of that mainstream dominance and now the Hmong Club is evolved. So now we've got two Asian groups that are pretty much dominated by mainstream kids.

While staffulty viewed the Hmong student members of the two clubs as the same "mainstream" students, the students saw distinct differences between themselves, as well as between the purposes of the two Southeast Asian ethnic clubs at the school. For Hmong Club members, the evolution of the Hmong Club from primarily ELL students to primarily mainstream students was less important than the original impetus of the Hmong Culture Club to focus on Hmong culture and identity.

Students viewed the Hmong Culture Club as an avenue for the recognition of the Hmong as a distinct Southeast Asian ethnic group. Vice president Pakou shared that the Hmong Club was important for "explaining to people when they ask, 'What is Hmong?' 'cause a lot of people, they tend to not know Hmong." Blia, the president of the club, elaborated:

> Hmong Club is important because it opens up doors to the Hmong kids to know each other. I wish that more people would come. I wish that it wasn't just Hmong people. I wish that it was Americans [white students] or African Americans who would come. And the Mexican kids and even the new refugee kids . . . but I just wish that more, a lot more people—minorities or majorities from different ethnic groups would come. Because we need to educate people on what Hmong people are. I mean, having a path like having a history of our people's history. It's not everything, but it does give you a sense of identity.

In a school where almost half of the students were Asian American, and the vast majority Hmong, members of the Hmong Club expressed the desire for others to know about their ethnic culture and heritage. Blia's assertion that knowing her Hmong history would offer "a sense of identity" mirrored the concerns of the Hmong leaders in the local community (chapter 1) that Hmong students did not learn about their own history at school. The exclusion of Hmong history and culture from the school curriculum left students like Blia and other Hmong Club members longing for legibility. Chris Vang particularly saw the need for Hmong Americans to be "acknowledged" and distinguished from other Asian American groups:

> I just wanted to expand, expand the fame of Hmong. 'Cause you look around the United States. Hmong is not really known. Only [this state] know Hmong people. In other places in the [United] States they don't know about Hmong people. They know Japanese. They call you like, "Are you Chinese? Are you Japanese?" . . . But then, it's kinda like a stereotype. I just really want to make Hmong people act more, be acknowledged.

Student members viewed the Hmong Culture Club as a means to garner attention for Hmong culture and identity. As the students pointed out, although dominant culture knows about Asian American groups such as Chinese and Japanese ethnics, there is a lack of recognition of Hmong ethnics in the United States.

Critical theorists of the "politics of recognition" suggest that groups that engage in identity politics seek recognition because they desire to be recognized for (1) different markers of identity (e.g., ethnicity, gender, sexuality); (2) inclusion (as a result of being excluded or silenced); and (3) distinctiveness (as a result of being overlooked or unvalued).[14] Taylor claimed that "recognition is not a courtesy we owe people. It is a vital human need,"[15] while Fraser argued that recognition is a matter of justice because of the ways in which "institutionalized patterns" treat some social "actors as peers, capable of participating on a par with one another in social life" while treating "some actors as inferior, excluded, wholly other, or simply invisible, hence less than full partners in social interaction."[16] Significantly, misrecognition viewed as "status subordination"[17] rather than identity politics is better able to highlight the injustices of being denied the status of a full community member.[18]

The Hmong Culture Club at Dayton High School sought to overcome the ethnic and cultural subordinated status of Hmong American students inside and outside the spaces of the school. Hmong Club members wanted their Hmong ethnicity affirmed, to be included in the curriculum of school, and to be distinguished from other Asian American groups. I turn next to their perspectives on the denigration of Hmong Americans, which prevented them from "participating as a peer"[19] in the social life of school.

"Some People Call Us Jingle Bells"

The processes of subtractive cultural assimilation not only stripped students of their heritage Hmong language but also supplanted a sense of ethnic self-worth with deficit views of Hmong culture and identity. Hmong Club members understood the ongoing dispossession of Hmong heritage and expressed a desire to revalue and affirm Hmong culture and identity. As Kajua saw it, Hmong students disliked their own people: "Some Hmong students, they ignore their culture. They say they don't like Hmong people and stuff like that. . . . Some Hmong people, they're like, 'I don't like Hmong people.' Like, why don't you like your own race and your own culture? It's just weird." When I asked her to explain further, Kajua shared her male cousin "hates our culture and traditions":

> My cousin, he's a perfect example. He's very—he lives in his own house. He doesn't get along with his dad, and he hates, he hates our culture and our traditions. I don't know why. He says that we're too strict on everything, and that we don't live in Thailand anymore. We're here in America, so we have our equal share in everything. We have freedom, we have our rights, you know. And his dad, he's traditional; he's very traditional too. . . . I don't know, he just don't like, he just don't like our race and culture. I never understood why, though. He would always say, "I don't like it. I hate how they [get] around this—all these rules. I hate all these rules."

While Lee found divisions between "traditional" 1.5-generation and "Americanized" second-generation Hmong American students, where "Americanized youth ridiculed traditional students for being too traditional, conservative, and old-fashioned,"[20] second-generation students at Dayton High like Kajua claimed that some Hmong students generally disliked Hmong people and Hmong culture as a whole based on a similar rationale of restricting freedom through conservative traditionalism. This intraethnic othering or internalized racism among Hmong Americans that is marked by contempt for their own ethnic and racial group[21] occurred within a context where Hmong students were taught implicitly and explicitly that their culture is other and loathsome (chapter 4).

The internalization of racism produces what W. E. B. Du Bois called "double-consciousness," or the "sense of always looking at one's self through the eyes of others, of measuring one's soul by the tape of a world that looks on in amused contempt and pity,"[22] and what Franz Fanon considered an existence with "Black skin, white masks."[23] Internalized racism imbues individuals with self-contempt and motivation to dissociate from members of their own ethnic and racial groups in efforts to become "more white."[24] In the case of Asian Americans, the "hidden injuries of race"[25] manifest as deflecting the stigma associated with Asian ethnics (e.g., racist stereotypes) where Asian Americans demonstrate assimilated status by denigrating coethnics for being traditional, speaking with an accent, wearing unfashionable clothes, and being "fresh off the boat" (a.k.a. FOB), among other negative stereotypes.[26]

In Harriet City, the Hmong American community termed the intraethnic conflict "Hmong versus Hmoob"[27] to describe the schism between "Americanized" and "traditional" Hmong Americans, respectively. Traditional Hmong Americans particularly faced ridicule from Americanized peers for maintaining Hmong religious practices of animism rather than converting to Christianity. Pakou poignantly recounted the derision from Hmong students:

> I guess 'cause I was born into a really traditional family. My parents, they, they're still like the old-fashion way, you know. They don't tend to take the American way yet. . . . We're shaman. . . . It doesn't really affect me, like I feel nothing—Like other people, like the [Hmong] Christian people, they kind of make fun of us for doing jingle bells. But I don't really—it doesn't really bother me 'cause—Jingle bells, they call us shaman people jingle bell. . . . Yes, some people call us jingle bells, 'cause you know we have the ceremony where the shaman dude came in, and then like do a little tradition and stuff. We have like a bell, so they call that jingle bells.

Before refugee flight, the Hmong in Laos practiced animism, a religion grounded in a belief in the spirit world, where all animate and inanimate objects have one or more souls.[28] Separation of one or more souls from an individual's body (e.g., a soul may be frightened from the body) or the presence of a foreign spirit in the body may cause illness and death.[29] As the "master of spirits,"[30] the *txiv neeb,* or shaman, oversees the spiritual, mental, and physical health of Hmong clans. The *txiv neeb* plays a central role as a healer able to travel between the spirit and corporeal worlds to communicate with spirits and conduct curing rituals through trance and animal sacrifice (e.g., soul calling rituals).[31] The pejorative "jingle bells" used by Pakou's Hmong peers refers to the shaman's left index finger bell rings, one of several accessories used by the shaman during rituals.[32]

It is important to underscore that the contempt some Hmong students have for their ethnic culture is a manifestation of internalized racism. As an adaptive response to racism, the combination of the disrespect for Hmong ethnicity and abandonment of Hmong customs as an acquiescence to the demand to assimilate results in a form of acceptance of hegemonic culture's racist views and values that are part of efforts to belong.[33] In other words, the scorn for Hmong religious beliefs did not exist in isolation among the Hmong students at Dayton High; rather, it was part of the context of the anti-Hmong, anti-immigrant discourses of the hegemonic culture of the school, local community, and U.S. society. One white staffulty's explanation of the "relevant" education offered by Dayton High hints at the disdain for the traditional animist beliefs of Hmong families that some Hmong students internalized:

> It matters. It's up to date. It's current. It's accurate. It's, it may challenge—like everything with our Hmong students, it may challenge tradition, it may rock the boat at home, but damn that's relevant. Ya know. We talk about an infectious disease, and there's a little activity that I have my students do about remedies, how the family heals you, or cures you. And kids won't share those remedies unless they feel safe. So we've got, in our different pockets of ethnicities, and the practices are absolutely inconsistent with Western medicine, ya know. This is very superstitious. This is not based on any kind of science. The coining thing. A number of our Hmong families boil eggs, and they'll rub the egg over parts of their body. They'll have to drink tea, ya know, and just do certain kind of rituals. But they won't share that stuff. And then to, to rock the boat and say, "Well, here's your immune system, and this is how science works. These are your T cells, your B cells, antibodies, pathogen enters. You get a fever 'cause of this. It's not 'cause a spirit has entered you. It's 'cause you have pyroxenes that your cells actually manufacture, and

> sends it to your hypothalamus, it generates this temperature increase. (clap) That's what's happening." "Ya mean, ya mean, what my mom tells me isn't right?" "No, I'm not sayin' that. I'm just sayin', think about this!" (clap) Ya know? Kids, they hear stuff at home, which just cracks me up, you know, regardless of culture.

From the perspective of the staffulty, Hmong animist views about the role of spirits in illness and health are "superstitious" and "not based on any kind of science." This implied that the science of Western knowledge systems is "accurate" and "up to date" while traditional Hmong beliefs are wrong and dated, even backward. As the staffulty privileged Western medicine, s/he derided the coining technique used to treat illnesses. This technique is still widely practiced by various groups in China and Southeast Asia. Hmong cultural narratives of illness were disregarded, but the general wisdom of parents and the very underpinnings of Hmong culture were also called into question. Indeed, the staffulty acknowledged that "everything" the school taught Hmong students had the potential to "challenge tradition" or "rock the boat at home." As Phenice and colleagues put it, within the contexts of school, "Typically, minority children have been placed in contra-culture learning experiences that exuded with such messages as 'your parents' ways of behaving are not good, and if you want to achieve success you must become like the dominant group.'"[34]

In physician Yeng Yang's review of Anne Fadiman's *The Spirit Catches You and You Fall Down: A Hmong Child, Her American Doctors, and the Collision of Two Cultures,*[35] he noted the double standard of the ways practitioners of Western medicine have accepted the role of prayer in the care of Christian patients but have rejected the role of soul calling ceremonies in the care of the book's young Hmong patient, Lia Lee:

> Western-trained doctors claim to practice scientific-based medicine and therefore cite religious and cultural differences as the main impediments of effective healing for patients of different ethnicity. Yet we have no conflict with the faith of our Christian patients. All other cultural and religious practices seem to compromise the practice of medicine except for prayer. Prayer is not grounded in science but in faith much like that of the Hmong's *ua neeb* and *hu plig* (soul calling ceremonies), yet it is an interwoven part of medicine and healing in the western culture. Should not the Hmong culture and religion enjoy similar treatment?[36]

Yang's juxtaposition of the attitudes toward Christian and Hmong religious beliefs within Western medical practice calls attention to a colonial epistemology where the values of Western knowledge systems are viewed as normal (e.g., Christian prayer), while those of minoritized communities are judged as deviant (e.g., Hmong animist soul calling). To this point, Conquergood observed that various groups have sought to eradicate Hmong shamanism—the animist practice of spiritual healing—"in the name of science, progress, and Christianity."[37] He understood that "the resistance to shamanism that the Hmong resettled in the United States now experience, recapitulates a history of oppression that traditional people everywhere have been subjected to when confronted with Western powers."[38]

Goodwin suggested that in the context of U.S. schools, Asian American education occurs within practices of "curriculum as colonizer."[39] At Dayton High, the regard for scientific evidence and Christianity alongside the disdain for Hmong religious beliefs are arguably a part of an ongoing colonial project of assimilation that has succeeded in colonizing the minds[40] of some Hmong students who subsequently disavow Hmong cultural practices and beliefs. As Pakou reported, her Hmong American school peers even functioned as a coercive force of assimilation:

> I think that a lot of Christian people, Hmong Christian people, they do make fun of old traditional shaman people. . . . Like one of my friends, she's Christian and she be asking me like, "Are you Christian?" And I'm like, "No, I'm still a shaman." And they're like, "Why don't your family go into Christian?" I'm like, "'Cause we just like the old way of how we're in right now." And they're like, "That's a little bit older. You know, you guys should like change to Christian instead of shaman, 'cause sooner or later, everybody gonna turn to Christian." So I take that really personally, but I didn't say anything to her.

As Pakou spoke about the pressure from Hmong peers to convert from traditional Hmong religious practice to Christianity, she repeatedly used the language of "old" or "older" to explain her family's desire to practice shamanism. Such a characterization reiterates hegemonic narratives about immigrant culture that construct binary oppositions of old world/new world or traditional/modern, where the divestment of ethnic culture is associated with the newness of a future orientation that is superior than an old or traditional past orientation of cultural maintenance.[41] Pakou's recount of her friend's rationale for converting to Christianity—"'cause sooner or later, everybody gonna turn to Christian"—suggests the demand for assimilation is incessant and eventually requires surrender. Yet such capitulation would have tragic consequences for Hmong culture, for as one Hmong shaman put it, "If all Hmong were to become Christians, we would lose Hmong culture forever" (see also Xiong in chapter 3).[42]

Within the milieu of the cultural imperialism of U.S. school and society that assaults and erases the core components of Hmong knowledge systems, the Hmong Culture Club at Dayton High became a means for Hmong American students to affirm their heritage and culture. It was evident to Hmong Club members that the internalization of the anti-immigrant, racist views of hegemonic culture produced among their peers ethnic shame and embarrassment. Hmong Club was important to students like Chris Vang "because at school you're not with culture." Although he saw that some of his Hmong peers disliked Hmong culture, he deemed their school experience to be a sort of exile: "And you're Hmong, and you don't have a culture, you feel like really an outcast. You know, you're not down with your culture." In light of the intraethnic othering among Hmong American students, members like Paul Vue wanted the club to function to "help unite Hmong people." In a similar vein, Tom Lor saw the need to "bring Hmong people out there to Hmong Club because we should have pride in being Hmong. So we established a Hmong Club." Resounding Tom Lor's focus on ethnic pride, Pakou wanted a way "to show that I'm Hmong and that I'm not ashamed to admit that I'm Hmong."

HMONG NEW YEAR AS CULTURAL RESURGENCE

As the group walked around the school, we stopped every few minutes to talk about whether or not a wall space was a good site for a Hmong Club recruitment poster. At one of the stops, the group wanted Paul Vue to hang a poster higher, but he had difficulty getting it high enough. Long, who at five foot six was the tallest, stepped in to help get it higher. Mai See remarked, "Hmong people are short." During this poster-hanging activity, we came across several staffulty who acknowledged the students with a simple "Hello" and then walked on their way. Midway through the activity, a white American male staffulty tried to engage the students in conversation by remarking, "I'll join the club if you have food. Do you have food? Egg rolls?" None of the Hmong students responded to this staffulty, but instead merely smiled and continued to walk down the hall. Mai See and Pakou glanced at each other uncomfortably.

In U.S. schools, liberal multiculturalism frequently manifests as a "month" or a "day," with posters, display case exhibits, and cocurricular student groups that aim to "celebrate," "respect," "recognize," and "include" various ethnic and racial groups.[43] Dayton High School included all of the above "contributions approach" to multicultural education,[44] including an "Asian Culture Show" showcasing dance, music, and other talents and a signature "Multicultural Festival" that featured a fashion show with ethnic music, dance, and clothing as well as themed student booths that sold "ethnic food."[45] Although these practices of liberal multiculturalism acknowledge the existence of various groups, its neglect of power and inequality essentially operates as a form of appeasement that offers minoritized groups "representation" while maintaining the authority of hegemonic culture.[46] Problematically, such an approach to ethnic and racial difference constructs culture as exotic and other, thus endorsing and reinforcing racial or cultural stereotypes.[47] In the context of multiculturalism's trivialization of cultural difference through a focus on food, festival, folklore, and fashion[48] and the school's Multicultural Festival, the staffulty's above comment to Hmong Club members effectively reduced Hmong culture and identity to egg rolls.

Nevertheless, liberal multiculturalism's offer of representation is often alluring and taken up by marginalized groups. At Dayton High, even as the Hmong Club embraced Hmong culture and identity in a politics of recognition, it also took up liberal multiculturalism's ideology of ethnic representation. For example, early in November of the school year, as the Hmong Club was considering ways to incorporate more aspects of Hmong culture into the school, Ms. Lor told students, "If you want to do something about Hmong culture, you could try to 'represent' for Hmong New Year." She explained that the members could potentially recruit more students to Hmong Club and that the club would be "more respected" at the school. She specifically suggested they put on a dance to celebrate Hmong New Year, where they play Hmong music the whole night, and students could have their "own celebration." She warned that they would have to move fast, since they did not have much time left in November (when Hmong New Year is typically celebrated), and suggested that the club leaders speak with the principal the next day. When Ms. Lor asked, "Would you like to do something like that?" the students responded with an emphatic "Yes!"

Over the next two and a half weeks, the students worked to secure permission for the Hmong New Year event and funding for food from the principal; order catered food for an estimated three hundred students; and plan for the event within specific groups for food, security (ROTC students), activities, miscellaneous gifts and artifacts, decorations, and marketing and communications. The event flyer provided details against a *paj ntaub* watermark that invited "everyone"—Hmong and non-Hmong students—to "learn our cultural celebration." The New Year celebration that took place in the school cafeteria included a buffet meal catered from a Hmong food vendor, invited song and dance performances, and an open dance at the end. The Hmong Club members staffed a table at the entrance of the cafeteria with a number of Hmong cultural artifacts, including a *qeej*, two flutes, Hmong coins, bracelets, and a good luck charm; served food to students; patrolled the cafeteria and adjacent hallways as security; served as the masters of ceremony for the invited performances; and kicked off the open dance during the second half of the night.

By and large, the Hmong New Year event was a resounding success for the Hmong Culture Club. On one level, the celebration was an achievement because an hour and a half into the event, the cafeteria space reached capacity with five hundred students—two hundred more than the members had anticipated would attend. Consequently, Mr. Moua took to the microphone to apologize for the shortage of food and announce that the doors to the school would be locked to bar new admission or reentry. On another level, the event was an accomplishment for the club for the ways in which it allowed members to assert their ethnic identity and relevance into the cultural context of Dayton High School. As the host for the well-received celebration, the Hmong Club brought attention to Hmong heritage. Since the larger Hmong New Year in Harriet City was popular with Hmong youth (and the broader Hmong community), the success of the school celebration arguably increased the student group's visibility and reputation.

As described by Yang Dao, the Hmong New Year celebration in Laos traditionally was (and remains)

> the most exciting and colorful tradition. It is an annual reminder of Hmong cultural identity. With people gathering from all over, it serves to strengthen

> social ties, allows new ones to be forged, and provides widespread sharing of information about how best to survive and prosper in the mainstream. It also serves as a bridge between the past and the future.[49]

The festivities included household feasts and *lwm sub,* a ceremony to transition to the new year, as well as a public village celebration that included singing contests, sport competitions (e.g., top playing, kicking, bullfighting), *qeej* performances, and a *pov pob,* or ball-tossing activity.[50] The ball toss was a courtship practice that only occurred during the New Year celebration:

> These young people leave their family homes and make their way toward the common area of the village. The girls line up facing a row of boys, and begin to throw cloth balls back and forth, along with verses of complex extemporaneous courtship songs. Many visitors from other villages have come to join the *pov pob* ritual, and the possibility of meeting one's future husband or wife heightens the excitement.[51]

Since Hmong girls and boys were prohibited from speaking in public, the *pov pob* was the only occasion where they were allowed to interact and communicate with a potential spouse.[52]

In the United States, the Hmong New Year brings together Hmong individuals from across the United States and world. Organizers in major U.S. cities with large Hmong populations intentionally schedule their local community's New Year celebrations to avoid conflicting with those of others as a way to promote national and international attendance and increase opportunities for Hmong Americans to connect at the events. For Hmong American adolescents, participation in cultural events such as the annual New Year celebration is the most common form of ethnic socialization.[53] As a cultural event, the Hmong New Year is part of what Gary Yia Lee considered a "cultural re-creation"[54] in the Hmong diaspora, and what Lynch, Detzner, and Eicher described as

> a juxtaposition of ancient ritual and American popular culture. The auditorium floor is dominated by young people engaged in a ball toss courtship ritual by day and a rock and roll dance by night. Middle-aged and elderly Hmong Americans watch from the balcony and the sidelines on the main floor. The stage features spectacles ranging from shamanistic rituals performed by elders to heavy metal rock and roll performed by punk Hmong teenagers.[55]

During the time of the study, Harriet City's Hmong New Year took place over a three-day period, with programming from eight o'clock in the morning to eleven o'clock at night, including the following: "Hmong Music (Instrument)," "National Anthem," "Welcoming the New Year," "Honorable Guest Speakers," "Dance Performance," "Pageant Contest" (to crown the state's Miss Hmong), "Dance Contest," "Modern Song Singer Contest," "Traditional Folk Song Singer Contest," "New Year Songs," "General Shows" open to volunteer talent, and evening "Entertainment" with music and dancing for the younger generation. In addition to these stage activities, one exhibit hall was dedicated to vendors who sold merchandise including videos, medicinal herbs, clothes, embroidery, jewelry, and artwork, among numerous other items; and another exhibit hall dedicated to food vendors, within which was a large open space allocated to ball tossing, with both Hmong teenagers and elders participating in the activity. The annual Hmong New Year celebration is a gathering of the Hmong ethnic community and a representation of cultural re-creation and affirmation.[56]

Similar to the Hmong New Year in Harriet City and elsewhere in the United States, the Hmong New Year at Dayton High School was a display of cultural contrast and fusion. The Hmong Club's program for the Hmong New Year celebration consisted of seven components: (1) a welcome by the president of the Hmong Culture Club (Blia) and the Dayton High principal, (2) a "history of Hmong New Year," (3) a dinner, (4) a "traditional show," which included a "Hmong rap" and singing by male and female groups, (5) a "Hmong American show," which included rap and song performances by solo and group artists, and a Hmong group break-dancing performance, (6) games (e.g., ball toss) in the atrium of the school, and (7) an open dance to DJ music. With the exception of one rap performed in English, all of the songs were performed in Hmong.

As "an annual reminder of Hmong cultural identity,"[57] I suggest the club's Hmong New Year celebration amplified the presence and significance of Hmong ethnicity at Dayton High. Although Hmong Club students were categorized and denigrated as "traditional" and other by hegemonic culture, and even by their Hmong peers at school, the Hmong New Year celebration disrupted essentialist notions of what it means to value Hmong culture and identity within the school context. The hybridity of the Hmong Club members was reflected in the clothes, performances, Hmong language use, and overall tenor of the celebration. For example, the male master of ceremony styled his black hair spiked with gel and wore a crisp white dress shirt with black dress pants and a traditional Hmong sash; and the female master of ceremony wore a Hmong dress over black leggings and stiletto heels, long hair swept from her face in dramatic waves. The combination of dress shirt, slacks, leggings, and carefully coiffed hair contributed to a contemporary, stylish presentation.[58] One of the performers was a young man who looked like a beatnik Bob Dylan, who wore a cap with a small rim placed slightly cocked to the side atop his chin-length hair. He dressed in dark jeans, a button-down shirt, and a worn suede jacket. He performed an original song in Hmong on an acoustic guitar and finished to resounding applause from students in attendance. Another song was performed by three young men dressed in white shirts, dark pants, and tan Timberland boots, who harmonized and crooned a song in Hmong to the adoring screams of female students in the crowd. The response from the audience was comparable to those at popular music concerts.

Although the event was motivated by liberal multiculturalism's ideal of "representation" and club members' pedagogic desire for their peers to "learn our cultural celebration," the outcome was more than "education about the other" where non-Hmong students were taught about Hmong culture.[59] Student attendees were 97 percent Hmong American, 2 percent African American, and 1 percent white; the Hmong New Year thus ended up being a curricular intervention that affirmed Hmong culture and disrupted the erasure of Hmong dignity and pride among Hmong students. As Hmong Club members saw it, "most schools, they don't really do a New Year." The "first ever" school Hmong New Year in the district "brought in some newer things that the Hmong kids do into [school]." In other words, the club brought into school a culturally relevant activity that was of interest and importance in the lives and heritage of Hmong Americans.[60] By making Hmong New Year a school event, the Hmong Club infused a significant Hmong custom into Dayton High. Significantly, the event was a version of the broader community's Hmong New Year in miniature, rather than a typical school diversity event or ethnic festival.[61] Although the school already offered an Asian Culture Show (as well as hegemonic culture's ubiquitous dances, such as homecoming, Sadie Hawkins, and prom), the Hmong New Year celebration was a uniquely Hmong-specific custom that instantiated a Hmong cultural repertoire into the practices of school. As a curricular intervention, it was an everyday act of cultural resurgence that reconnected Hmong adolescents with their heritage and fostered community.[62]

CONSTRUCTING BOUNDARIES: THE IMPORTANCE OF HMONG ETHNICITY

> The immigrant signifies a person in a specific relation to the nation and contains within it a sense of movement—the immigrant has moved or is moving, crossing a border to get from "there" to "here." What negotiations must the immigrant make in traversing the border to gain entry into the United States? Once "inside," what other borders remain? The immigrant may learn after crossing the border that she has not left it behind, that the border is not just a peripheral phenomenon. . . . Indeed, to be an immigrant is to be marked by the border. This is not to say that all immigrants are marked in the same way. Some immigrants are able to "pass" while others (and sometimes even their U.S.-born descendants) remain perpetual foreigners.[63]

In the above excerpt, Asian American legal scholars Robert Chang and Keith Aoki mused that "to be an immigrant is to be marked by the border," where gaining entry is one of many socially constructed borders that structure (and constrain) immigrant pathways within the United States. For immigrants of Asian descent such as the Dayton High School Hmong students and families, their racialization as "perpetual foreigners"[64] leaves them in a precarious position of "unsettled" belonging.[65] They are expected to assimilate as a condition for incorporation into U.S. society but are nevertheless refused inclusion because of enduring nativist racism (i.e., racial nationalism) that constructs them as a racial other to whites as well as a foreign other to (white) Americans, thus precluding them from "real" American identities and belonging.[66]

Although hegemonic discourses construct the Hmong American community as homogenous, the students at Dayton High are marked (differently) by the border, exemplifying the heterogeneity that exists within Hmong and other minoritized communities. Differences in Hmong students included those who were born in the United States (second generation), resettled as refugees at an early age (1.5 generation), and resettled more recently as teenagers (first generation). Further, the Hmong students were marked differently by self-constructed as well as imposed borders to differentiate themselves from one another. In addition to the "Americanized" and "traditional" student categories noted earlier in the chapter, students and staffulty separated Hmong students by academic tracks (i.e., IB students, traditional track students, and ELL students) and Hmong language proficiency. For example, Ms. Lor discerned between

> Hmong kids who can speak Hmong fluently, and then you have kids who are just kind of like, "OK, I know my basics." And then you have Hmong kids who are just like, "Sorry, I'm clueless. I understand, but I can't say it, any of it." And then you have the ones that can write, can write and read Hmong, and then the ones that are totally like lost.

More than Hmong American heterogeneity, the differences reflected the subtractive cultural assimilation that contributed to the formation of social boundaries between various groups of Hmong students. In addition to the intraethnic othering shared by Hmong Club members earlier in the chapter, Ms. Lor particularly noted that socially, 1.5- and second-generation Hmong students "don't associate much with new arrival Hmong kids 'cause they're way too Americanized" and "both of them are afraid of each other, basically." Newcomer students are "scared" of being teased by "Americanized" students, and both groups feel a sense of "uncomfortableness around each other."

For Hmong Club members, boundary making through the production and maintenance of culture and ethnicity was a means to combat the structured forgetting of school.[67] As students created a sense of belonging within the club, they also delineated in-group and out-group boundaries.[68] Pakou asserted that Hmong students in the club are more fond of Hmong heritage: "Well, Hmong Club would be more like, we like our traditional more. We like our culture." In a school with the largest number of Hmong students in the district, where nearly half of the students were Hmong, Pakou constructed a border between Hmong Club members and other Hmong students by claiming that the students in the club are the ones who "like" Hmong culture. The boundaries constructed by Hmong students who pursued cultural renewal[69] or a "revival of ethnicity"[70] through the Hmong Culture Club to differentiate themselves from other Hmong students became most obvious during an early November meeting of the Hmong Club.

Once Blia reviewed the agenda for the meeting, she asked the members for other items they would like to add to it. As Mr. Moua leaned against the classroom's doorframe, he raised his hand and announced that he would like to add to the agenda a discussion of the "merger" of the Hmong Club and Southeast Asian Club at the school. Students immediately started whispering. Mr. Moua briefly explained that Ms. Tanner, the advisor of the SEA Club, wanted to combine the two clubs because "the students are the same" for both clubs: they are all Hmong students. This explanation caused commotion in the room as students expressed their opinions more loudly to each other. From the front center of the room, Tom Lor put his right fist in the air and cried out, "United Asians!" To my left, Pakou informed Mai that the Southeast Asian Club was "not welcoming." Mr. Moua interrupted the impromptu discussion by telling the students, "For now, the item should just be put on the agenda. We can hold the discussion later."

During the second half of the meeting, the group turned to the agenda item about the clubs' merger. Mr. Moua reiterated that Ms. Tanner asked if students from the Hmong Club would like to combine with the SEA Club, since Hmong students made up the membership of both clubs. He explained that the clubs had slightly different functions: the Hmong Club was "more focused on culture" and the Southeast Asian Club more focused on students and experiences of the larger Southeast Asian region. Mr. Moua then asked students for their input. Pakou was the first student to make a comment, sharing with the group that she did not want the clubs to combine out of a concern that if they merged, the students in the Hmong Club may not be able to follow their own rules, and instead have to follow the rules of the Southeast Asian Club. Tom Lor, always the comic relief, announced, "We'll make them follow our rules!" Pakou continued to say that the Hmong Club's focus on Hmong culture was good, and that it was important to have that freedom. She added that it was good to work collaboratively with the SEA Club on projects, but it's also good to be independent. When Mr. Moua asked for other comments and none of the students voiced an opinion, Ms. Lor raised her hand. As she pointed to the two new female students sitting in the first row in seats just in front of her, Ms. Lor said, "There are two ELL students in the club now." She added that the students were able to understand the conversation in the club because student members speak in Hmong. She told the members that she would like to have even more ELL students in the club because the ELL students could help Hmong Club members "reconnect with your Hmong culture."

When I asked Mr. Moua for more details about Ms. Tanner's rationale for suggesting the merger of the two clubs, he simply restated that she thought it made sense because "the students are the same." All of the students in the SEA Club were Hmong students, with no other Southeast Asian groups represented. Kong then asked the group, "Who else is in SEA Club?" Paul Vue and Tom Lor, secretary and treasurer, respectively, of the Hmong Club, quickly raised their hands and held them up for a while. Teng announced twice that he was planning to join. Mr. Moua stated that even before they go to meet with the SEA Club officers, they should see if there is "any interest at all" to merge with the Southeast Asian Club. He pointed out that it was election week and that in order to remain true to the Hmong Club's belief in the democratic voting process, as reflected by votes for game planners and special events planners, the student members should vote on the merger. Mr. Moua proceeded to announce, "Raise your hand if you want to merge with the Southeast Asian Club." No member raised a hand. He then stated, "Raise your hand if you want to stay separate as a Hmong Culture Club." All of the members raised their hands. It was a unanimous vote to center their Hmong ethnicity and maintain their distinctiveness as the Hmong Culture Club.

Although members of the Hmong Club and Southeast Asian Club were all Hmong American students, with some of the same students participating in both, Hmong Club students rejected Southeast Asian "panethnicity"[71] in favor of maintaining the boundary between Hmong ethnicity and other Southeast Asian ethnicities. Their cultural politics constructed and required a place specifically with "Hmong" in its name. The Hmong Club gave students a cultural location where they were able to claim belonging to a particular place exclusive to their ethnic group where students could amplify their sense of cultural identity.[72] Mr. Moua particularly saw the Hmong Culture Club functioning in a protective role for the Hmong American students at Dayton High School:

> It's a group and a social group and a gathering of people who want to do things that are positive and have the Hmong name to it. We can support this thing and it's the Hmong Club. That's helping. So then, it's keeping the image of the Hmong students here in a good name, I suppose. And it's also, I think an avenue for them to feel positive about their culture and where they come from.

In the face of internalized racism and the status subordination of Hmong culture and identity, Mr. Moua suggested the Hmong Club protected students in at least two ways. First, it provided an avenue for fostering a positive image of Hmong American identity, to combat prevailing deficit discourses in the school and community about Hmong youth (involved in violence and delinquent behaviors). Second, given the denigration of Hmong culture from inside and outside of the ethnic group, the Hmong Club served as an alternative source for students to nurture self-esteem and maintain ethnic pride. In other words, the construction of ethnic boundaries offered Hmong Club members an option to consider their self-worth without relying on the standards of hegemonic culture.

In a different way, Ms. Lor also observed the Hmong Club served as a protective role for the Hmong American students, emphasizing the importance of the word "Hmong" for the construction of their ethnic identity:

> It's the identity. It's the feeling of using the word "Hmong." It's the purpose of saying, "We're Hmong. We're not this other Southeast Asian." 'Cause the other Southeast Asian group, they have, they can point to themselves on a map or globe or something . . . And the funny thing too is that most of the SEA [Club] kids are Hmong. . . . The Hmong Club, the kids who want to be in Hmong Club, want to identify who they are. And the word "Hmong Club," it's a security-ness.

According to Ms. Lor, the Hmong Culture Club was an ethnic location with geopolitical significance because while other Southeast Asian groups have identifiable political geography, Hmong students do not have a country of their own. She suggested that students wanted a student group with "Hmong" in its name because it provided them with a sense of identity—"We're Hmong. We're not this other Southeast Asian"—and afforded them with the "security-ness" of a place in the world.

Along the same lines, members like Long saw Hmong Club operating to safeguard Hmong language and culture. As a response to the unremitting weight of coloniality and fears of cultural loss, he sought a sort of refuge for his Hmong language and culture within the boundaries of Hmong Club:

> I went to Hmong Club because like I thought I was losing my culture. Because my sister says that the fastest way to lose your own culture is through language. So I was thinking about it, and it seemed kind of true, right? So I thought that Hmong Club was going to be surrounded with Hmong. And they do. So I don't feel bad about losing my culture. So, they do kind of keep me in touch with my culture. And that's what I like about it. . . . It just seems like, it just keeps my culture. I just know that it keeps my culture kind of safe.

Long's comment about being "surrounded" by other Hmong students suggests a function of Hmong Club as a place for cultural immersion or as a stronghold to keep his culture and identity "safe." The implied comfort of being among other Hmong Americans echoes Stuart Hall's suggestion that people often consider their culture to be a home:

> We think of our culture as a *home*—a place where we naturally belong, where we originally came from which first stamped us with our identity, to which we are powerfully bonded, as we are to our families, by ties that are inherited, obligatory and unquestioning. To be among those who share the same cultural identity makes us feel, culturally, *at home*. Culture gives us a powerful sense of belongingness, of security and familiarity.[73]

Notions of "home" and "homeland" have been important sites of freedom and resistance for oppressed groups.[74] Thus, the Hmong Culture Club was a space that afforded Hmong American students sanctuary and belonging at Dayton High School.

For minoritized groups, the emphasis on the "loss" of culture or the need to "'return' to one's cultural roots, [as a way] to hold fast to one's founding identity," and thus "close up the community around its foundational cultural beliefs and values,"[75] must be viewed as a response to power relations rather than a nostalgic cultural revival or a simple attachment to originary ideals about culture.[76] In the context of U.S. cultural imperialism, the yearning of immigrants for tradition needs to be situated within the nation's extensive history of imperialism, militarism, and nativism[77] and school as a project of coloniality, which excludes the cultures, histories, and knowledges of immigrant families, and divests students of their language and culture.[78]

The privileging of Western knowledge systems at Dayton High School relegated Hmong ethnicity to a subordinated status[79] where Hmong culture was deemed inferior and other even by Hmong American students at the school. As the Hmong Club members shared, their peers were ashamed to be Hmong, disliked Hmong culture, and viewed Hmong people as "ghetto." This internalized racism is what Stuart Hall considered to be "the 'subjection' of the victims of racism to the mystifications of the very racist ideology which imprison and define them."[80] Significantly, the racist ideology faced by Hmong American students pivots on culture, where the shedding of culture—language, religion, values—to become more like cultureless whites is the benchmark for normal Americanness; maintaining Hmong ethnic culture is grounds for contempt and maltreatment. In the case of Hmong Americans in Harriet City and at Dayton High School, the demand to forget enunciated within school by subtractive schooling pitted Hmong Americans against one another—Hmoob versus Hmong—which left Hmong Club members perceiving the need to foster Hmong unity and pride as well as a broader recognition of Hmong ethnicity.

The Hmong Culture Club provided students with a context to carve out belonging and create a sense of security and affirmation for their ethnicity and heritage. Its discursive emphasis on a collective Hmong culture offered students a means to construct self-recognition and a positive self-image in the school. Writing about the "homeplace" of African American families as sites of humanization and resistance, bell hooks stressed the importance of such places of racial and ethnic belonging:

> The task of making homeplace . . . was about the construction of a safe place where black people could affirm one another and by so doing heal many of the wounds inflicted by racist domination. We could not learn to love or respect ourselves in the culture of white supremacy, on the outside; it was there on the inside, in that "homeplace" that we had the opportunity to grow and develop, to nurture our spirits.[81]

As hooks elaborated, the healing of wounds and nurturing of spirits took place at kitchen tables, constructed out of conversations and laughter. Similarly, the Hmong Club students played games like 7-Up, Mafia / Werewolf, and Motorcycle; watched Korean and Thai movies with English subtitles or dubbed in Hmong; and organized events like a Halloween party and a Secret Santa gift exchange. The jokes, laughter, and time simply being in the same room together allowed the members to interact in social relations as peers, engaging in reciprocal acts of recognition that are requisite for the affirmation of humanity.[82]

Beyond student members, the Hmong Club made claim to the importance of Hmong culture in the broader space of school. As this chapter showed, the Hmong New Year event infused Dayton High with meaningful Hmong cultural practices. The celebration was an act of cultural resurgence that disrupted the dominant cultural repertoire of the school. In Trask's analysis of the practice of hula dance in Hawaii, she contended, "The cultural revitalization that Hawaiians are now experiencing and transmitting to their children is as much a repudiation of colonization by so-called

Western civilization in its American form as it is a reclamation of our own past and our own ways of life . . . its political effect is decolonization of the mind."[83] Similarly, I suggest the Hmong New Year celebration was an act of cultural politics toward the "decolonization of the mind" of Hmong American students. While the cultural production was celebratory and playful, it engaged in what Ngũgĩ wa Thiong'o calls the "politics of knowing."[84] Indeed, the insertion of a Hmong cultural repertoire into the school district via subsequent Hmong New Year celebrations in other schools received backlash from white parents, who petitioned the district to ban Hmong New Year from school events on the grounds that Hmong New Year is a religious event, and its inclusion in school unfairly excludes other groups. This response from white parents sought to portray and reaffirm school as culturally universal and neutral despite its privileging of Western knowledge systems, particularly white, middle-class culture (see chapters 1 and 2).

As a cultural production, the Hmong Club's New Year event revitalized ethnic boundaries and made explicit the importance of Hmong ethnicity. I illustrate in the next chapter that such cultural politics was not confined to the activities of Dayton High School's Hmong Culture Club. The revitalization of ethnic boundaries and emphasis on Hmong culture and identity occurred more broadly in the district and community as Hmong Americans struggled against the structured forgetting of school toward culturally relevant education for Hmong students and families.

6 Refusing the Neutrality of School

> As the first Hmong speaker moved toward the podium to address the Board of Education of the Harriet City Public Schools, Hmong community members in the audience stood up and raised handmade poster board signs to address Superintendent Finch and other members of the school board. The signs emphasized the basis of the community's request for Hmong representation in the district: "Equal voices for all in school decisions," "Institutional racism," "We demand respect," "More staff = better grades," "We need inclusive leadership," "Got cultural competence?" "School staff needs to reflect community," "I have a dream too," "I need my voice heard," "Charter schools for my kids."
>
> —Board of Education meeting, Harriet City Public Schools

The Board of Education of the Harriet City Public Schools hired a new superintendent with a unanimous 7–0 decision five months before the beginning of the 2006–7 academic year.[1] Superintendent Deborah Finch was an African American educator who received her master's and doctoral degrees from Harvard University and was formerly the chief accountability officer of a large school district in an Eastern metropolitan area. The youngest of five finalists for the position, Finch was considered "aggressive" by previous colleagues and a "rising star," "fast-rising phenom," and "rock star" by Harriet City school board members and city leaders. In contrast, Hmong American community leaders and staffulty were wary of the superintendent. They especially remarked on her snobby East Coast attitude and negative stance toward English Language Learner (ELL) programs. Hmong community members reported that the superintendent did not believe in ELL classes and instead wanted all students in mainstream classes.

Less than a year after the new superintendent's hiring, the Hmong American community demanded that Superintendent Finch and the Board of

Education attend to the cultural education of Hmong students. The community underscored the importance of Hmong culture and identity for the academic success of Hmong American students by drawing attention to the district's institutional racism, lack of cultural competency, and marginalization of Hmong perspectives. The emphasis on Hmong ethnicity refused the neutrality of school and demanded a place in the structures of Harriet City Public Schools. Despite the superintendent's membership in the African American community, the emphasis on her East Coast arrogance, Harvard education, and disdain for ELL served to minimize her minority status, accentuating her difference from the marginalized experiences of Hmong immigrant students and families.

Highlighting the importance of "ethnicity" over "culture" for understanding the sociocultural contexts of ethnic group identity, Barth suggested:

> Ethnic categories provide an organizational vessel that may be given varying amounts and forms of content in different socio-cultural systems. . . . The critical focus of investigation from this point of view becomes the ethnic boundary that defines the group, not the cultural stuff that it encloses.[2]

According to this view, focusing on the cultural traits of groups confounds the responses of racial and ethnic groups to their social contexts, whereas attention to ethnic boundaries affords insight into changes in beliefs and behavior as products of the social milieu and interactions between groups. The construction of ethnic boundaries may thus be understood as a means for groups to achieve personal or collective advantage when confronted with white supremacy.[3] For example, in the United States, various groups have emphasized ethnic identity in struggles for political access, such as using higher education affirmative action admissions to increase postsecondary opportunities for underrepresented groups;[4] including ethnic studies curricula to incorporate the histories, experiences, and perspectives of racial and ethnic communities;[5] redistricting U.S. congressional districts to reflect racial and ethnic communities in federal government representation;[6] and revising racial classification of Asian groups in the U.S. census to better disaggregate the diversity of Asian ethnics for increasing and improving equal opportunity to programs and services.[7]

Similarly, in the struggle against cultural hegemony, the ethnic mobilization of Harriet City's Hmong American community organized around Hmong culture and identity to attain a critical speaking position.[8] Hmong community members activated ethnic boundaries to demand that Superintendent Finch and Harriet City Public Schools attend to the cultural aspects of Hmong students' education through the inclusion of a Hmong staffulty on the superintendent's senior leadership team and more broadly increase the number and presence of Hmong staffulty across the district.

THE HMONG COMMUNITY FORUM WITH THE NEW SUPERINTENDENT

Ms. Lor spoke to Hmong Club members for fifteen minutes about the Hmong community meeting with Superintendent Finch, emphasizing to students that "This is a very important meeting" and that they should know the superintendent's name because she is in charge of all the schools in the district, so she is the "face" of the Harriet City Public Schools. She shared with the group that she was appointed to organize the food and decorations for the meeting and that she would like "Dayton High School's Hmong Club" to come at 3:00 to Marion High School to help school district leader Shoua Her and community leader Dia Lee with the event. Their work would involve decorating, moving tables, setting out food, and ushering. As Ms. Lor explained the need for students to usher at the forum, she noted, "You know how Hmong parents are," and students responded with laughter. She stated that there are three types of Hmong parents: parents who have been in the United States for a long time and still don't know English, parents who have been in the United States for a long time and are fluent in English and are very Americanized, and parents who were just resettled to the United States and do not know English or U.S. culture. Ms. Lor pointed out that the last category of parents would need help at the meeting. The Hmong Club, Ms. Lor announced, will be her "right and left arms" at the meeting.

At the end of October, members of the Hmong community were invited to a community forum with Superintendent Finch, which was part of the district's efforts to reach out to various constituent groups.[9] The forum was the school district's approach to providing community members with an opportunity to meet the superintendent, hear about her plans for the district, ask questions, and share their concerns about the education of Hmong students. For the Hmong American community, one primary aim of the community meeting was to demonstrate to the superintendent through a show of numbers that she needed to respond to the needs of Harriet City's Hmong community. The Hmong American community—

including both well-established, second-generation families, and recently resettled refugee families—came together under a collective Hmong identity. Since Hmong students represented 25 percent of the district's student population and Hmong American adults comprised a significant voter base in the city, Hmong leaders hoped the superintendent would be more responsive to the concerns of the community.

The Hmong community forum with Superintendent Finch took place over a two-hour evening in the great hall of the district's Marion Senior High School. The flyer inviting the community to the "very special community conversation" indicated that "Dr. Finch is eager to listen to your concerns and ideas. She will also share her goals for the district." Two hundred Hmong Americans participated in the forum, including Hmong community leaders, district staffulty, and parents. Middle-aged Hmong husbands and wives as well as young Hmong couples with four to five children in hand attended the meeting. Reflecting varying immigrant generations and degrees of acculturation, some of the women dressed in simple, dark-colored pants and basic crew-neck sweaters with their hair pulled back in a low-set ponytail or bun and no makeup; others wore heels, shorter skirts, figure-fitting sweaters, nylon stockings, and a considerable amount of makeup. Shoua Her, the charter school liaison and special projects coordinator for the district, coordinated the Hmong community forum in partnership with Hmong leader Dia Lee, six Hmong community organizations, and three local businesses, which made in-kind contributions for the event. She actively participated in the management of the logistics and decoration of the great hall for the meeting, and she personally picked up the entreés at a local Asian grocery store that catered the dinner for the community members. A dozen members of the Dayton High School Hmong Culture Club assisted Ms. Her with the event, taking part in various tasks, including creating signs to direct guests from the school's main entrance to the great hall, decorating the cafeteria tables, working at the sign-in table, and assisting with the food service and cleanup.

The meeting opened with a performance by a Hmong female dance troupe of eight elementary-school-age girls while the attendees were getting their food and sitting down to eat. After the dance recital, the associate director of a large Hmong community organization presented Superintendent Finch with a welcome gift from the community—a *paj ntaub,* a traditional Hmong embroidery textile. When the Hmong leader stepped off the stage, Superintendent Finch commenced remarks about her vision for the district. She pointedly announced that she did not intend to answer questions from the podium but planned to answer questions at the table groups or on a one-to-one basis.[10] She added that community members may write their questions on the index cards being distributed, which Shoua Her would pass on to her for consideration.[11] The superintendent then thanked the various Hmong organizations for making the event possible.

Superintendent Finch's brief remarks focused on her vision for improving the education of students who were ELLs in the Harriet City Public Schools. Her threefold plan involved goals consisting of (1) more early childhood family education, including all-day kindergarten; (2) all Hmong students graduating from Harriet City Public Schools receiving at least one acceptance letter to college; and (3) a Hmong dual-language immersion program or magnet school where Hmong children may experience Hmong language and culture in a comprehensive program. The superintendent especially observed that for the Hmong immersion schools, three current elementary schools already have components of an immersion program, making the schools ideal candidates for her plan. Moreover, she shared that because the district currently did not have enough Hmong staff and leadership to comprehensively grow a Hmong immersion program, she planned to focus the school year on developing additional Hmong leaders in the district. This comment received enthusiastic applause from the Hmong community members.

Significantly, the superintendent made a point to address issues that were of particular concern to Harriet City's Hmong American community. For example, she repeated her intention to increase Hmong leaders in the district, reporting that she met with Hmong community leaders in June to talk about the community's concerns. She planned to return to the Hmong community in the future to work toward increasing Hmong leadership in the Harriet City Public Schools. This reiteration of developing Hmong education leaders again received applause from the audience. Additionally, the superintendent attempted to allay concerns about her stance on the ELL program by lauding the "impressive" work of the ELL program to increase students' English language skills in the district, noting that the program served 41 percent of the students in the district who were ELLs. She expressly praised the Hmong community for investing in the ELL program and noted that their efforts produced "great momentum" in the district.

After closing her remarks with an acknowledgment to the community leaders for their work on the forum, Superintendent Finch announced she was going to walk to various tables to take group or individual questions. When she stepped down from the stage to begin her rounds, she was joined by district staff member Shoua Her and Tong Yang, the ELL department's program manager for Hmong enrichment programs. The associate director of the Hmong community organization again took the stage to introduce another dance group, which consisted of twenty elementary-school-age Hmong boys and girls. He explained in Hmong and English that the group's dance represented rice planting in Laos. As the music came on and the Hmong children started to dance, Superintendent Finch stopped fielding questions and sat down to watch the four-minute performance. At the end of the applause, the superintendent continued her visits to the tables to answer questions.

In the limited time allocated to the question-and-answer interaction with the superintendent, Hmong American staffulty focused questions on the ELL programs and Hmong representation in the district. Staffulty asked questions such as: Do you plan to reduce or eliminate funding for ELL programs? What do you mean when you say you want to fund ELL equitably throughout the district? The superintendent pointed to the budget shortfall that she did not know about before her hire, which would involve cuts to programs; if the city did not pass the referendum, the district would need a more drastic cut of $10 million to its budget. Reports earlier that spring noted that the budget shortfall would necessitate a $10 million cut from the general fund, with a proposed 30 percent coming from schools and 70 percent from central administration. The largest cuts would impact special education ($3 million savings), operations and maintenance ($1.02 million savings), and the ELL program ($688,479 savings). Pointedly, the superintendent emphasized to Hmong staffulty that a smaller group of middle-class residents was "driving" the ELL agenda in the district. She remarked that "white people" who own homes with a value of $400,000 and above, 80 percent of whom do not have children in the Harriet City Public Schools, were not interested in the issues facing ELL students in education. She asserted the referendum had implications for which programs would be cut due to the budget shortfall, and she emphasized the need for the Hmong community to vote for the referendum.

Another Hmong staffulty emphasized to the superintendent the need for "more Hmong representation" within the teaching staff and administrators because most of the current staffulty were white. This was important for the staffulty because s/he was "tired" of non-Hmong staffulty bringing Hmong students to Hmong staffulty to resolve issues because non-Hmong staffulty "can't handle it." S/he remarked that despite a heavy workload, s/he did not turn away parents or students who white staffulty bring to him/her because of cultural or language barriers. Moreover, s/he observed that when white students need assistance, s/he did not similarly send the white students to a white staffulty. The Hmong staffulty pointedly asserted that s/he was expected to be "culturally sensitive" and support all students, so white staffulty should be able and expected to serve all students as well. S/he underscored the need for Hmong representation at the administrative level to support practices where all staffulty serve all students, regardless of race or ethnicity.

In different ways, the conversation between Deborah Finch and the Hmong staffulty acknowledged the racism underpinning the education of Hmong American students in the Harriet City Public Schools. The superintendent put considerable stress on the influence of white middle-class residents on the funding of ELL services for Hmong children, making salient the role of white supremacy in education policy. As a non-Hmong district staff of color put it to the Hmong staffulty after the superintendent left the group, if the superintendent needed to cut ELL programs, it would be a difficult decision because "there are issues of racism involved in all of this." S/he noted the superintendent was aware of it because she's African American, suggestively aligning her minoritized identity with the marginalized experiences of Hmong Americans.

The Hmong staffulty's claim for increased Hmong representation in the district stemmed from experiences where s/he observed non-Hmong staffulty unwilling to serve Hmong students on the premise of cultural mismatch. Echoing research on culturally responsive leadership, the staffulty wanted district leaders to enact what Johnson called "practices [. . .] that help to empower diverse groups of parents and make the school curriculum more multicultural."[12] S/he believed educational administrators should perform a central role in ensuring race, ethnicity, class, and gender, among other dimensions of difference, do not impinge on the academic success of students.[13]

The concerns of Hmong community members for district representation were exacerbated by their advance knowledge (before the community forum) that Shoua Her, the only Hmong senior staff member in the district who reported directly to the superintendent, was leaving the district within a few months. Notably, the Hmong district leader planned to open a Hmong charter school focusing on Hmong language and culture as a way to "[try] to meet the needs of the community." At the time of the study, 7 percent of the district's 6,700 staff self-identified as Asian American. The number of Hmong administrators within the 67 schools in the district were exceptionally limited, with only two Hmong principals, one Hmong assistant principal, and one Hmong administrative intern. The majority of Asian Americans were in positions as paraprofessionals or educational assistants who provided instructional support in the schools.

Less than two months after the Hmong community forum, Superintendent Finch announced her newly restructured leadership team, which was unanimously approved by the Board of Education. The team reflected a reduction of the superintendent's direct reports from seventeen district administrators down to seven.[14] For the Hmong community, noticeably absent from the senior administrative team was a Hmong American to make up for Shoua Her's departure from the Harriet City Public Schools. The absence of a Hmong staff on the leadership team was particularly glaring because the Black, Latinx, and white American communities were duly represented among the senior administrators. Against the backdrop of the Hmong community forum and meetings with Hmong leaders, the Hmong community felt "betrayed" by the superintendent because she had convincingly portrayed herself as someone who genuinely cared for Hmong children. Hmong community members vowed to organize to ensure that the Hmong American community was represented in district leadership to attend to their concerns and desires at the senior administrative level.

MOBILIZING UNDER HMONG ETHNICITY

> We, the undersigned, urge the Harriet City Board of Education to increase the diversity of educators at all levels of the Harriet City Public Schools—first and foremost in top administrative positions—to reflect the student population. Studies show that increasing teachers of color is directly connected to closing the achievement gap. Students of color tend to have higher academic, personal, and social performance when taught and led by educators from their own ethnic groups or by culturally competent educators. Increasing the diversity of staff at top administrative positions is the main ingredient to this solution. It is the first achievable step in the short term to attaining the long-term goals of increasing teachers of color and bridging the achievement gap.

> The history of the district has proved that without top administrators of color advocating on behalf of each group of students of color, there will be no increase of teachers of color and culturally competent educators. As parents, students, and community members, we are greatly concerned that our school district does not reflect the people and community it serves. It is therefore not serving us. It is the role of the Board of Education to correct this glaring oversight. IDEAS (Increase Diversity for Excellence and Achievement in School) is committed to working with the Board of Education and all concerned groups to increase the diversity of our educators in order to create a school culture of respect, excellence, and achievement.[15]

Long relegated to the margins of school curriculum and policy, the announcement of the district's new senior leadership team without a Hmong administrator became a call to arms for the Hmong American community. Hmong community leaders met individually and in groups with Superintendent Finch to advocate for Hmong representation on her team. The superintendent justified the composition of her leadership team by asserting that no Hmong American staff qualified for the senior staff appointment, despite receiving a list of potential candidates from Hmong education leaders. Community leaders rejected the superintendent's rationale, suggested her outreach efforts were empty, and mobilized parents and students in a petition drive to address the community's concerns. The community petition demanded an appointment of a Hmong staff to the leadership team as well as an increase in Hmong staffulty at all levels of the district to provide Hmong students and families with culturally competent educators. The Hmong community contended that without a Hmong staff who directly reported to Superintendent Finch, the district could not adequately serve the academic needs of Hmong students.

High school students across the district participated in the petition campaign, soliciting signatures from peers, family members, and community members. At Dayton High School, the Hmong Culture Club invited the Japanese Club and Southeast Asian Club—the only two other Asian American student clubs at the school—to join them in collecting signatures for the petition. Notably, while the Japanese Club joined the Hmong Club in the petition drive, the Southeast Asian Club declined to participate in the effort. In addition, Hmong students on the student council collected signatures throughout the school for the petition. Hmong representatives on the student council like Zoua believed that additional Hmong teachers and administrators would enable students like her to "see that someone like us can succeed, so we would want to succeed." KaBao, another Hmong student on the student council, wanted "someone up there [at the district office] who could speak the [Hmong] language and understand the culture" because "then maybe the Hmong people could have someone who can help them out in school, and be the advocate for them." She also thought that "the superintendent [. . .] should do something more to help out the Hmong community" because "Hmong people are not getting enough help." These student leaders considered Hmong educators at the school and district levels to be critical for increasing the cross-cultural understanding, educational support, and social mobility of Hmong Americans.

In mid-March of the academic year, central figures of the planning committee for the petition drive met at a Hmong community organization to plan for the presentation of the petition outlining the community's demands during the public comment portion of the upcoming week's Board of Education meeting. The group of approximately twenty-five Hmong American students, parents, and other community members prepared for the meeting by discussing various logistics such as the deadline for the collection of petition signatures; the expected number of parents, students and petition supporters who planned to attend the school board meeting; designation of individuals to create support signs for the meeting to articulate the various reasons the district should hire more Hmong staffulty; and the coordination of volunteers to drive parents and other stakeholders who needed transportation.

In contrast to hegemonic narratives portraying Hmong immigrants as stuck in an antiquated world,[16] the Hmong community's response to the exclusion of a Hmong leader from the district's leadership team reflected sophisticated social and political insight and organization. A good portion of the planning meeting focused on the committee's strategy for the public comment at the Board of Education meeting. The group finalized the order of the speakers, determining student speakers would open the comments, followed by parents, then community members at large. The speakers would share their personal stories navigating the Harriet City Public Schools, particularly difficulties involving cultural barriers, language barriers, and racism, among other issues. The chair of the committee emphasized the need to demand broad representation among the schools in the district and the need to exclude current Hmong staffulty in order to protect them from district retaliation, which may result in the loss of jobs.

S/he also detailed the etiquette of addressing the city's Board of Education in the three minutes allocated to each speaker, including introducing themselves, thanking the board members for their time and for listening to their comments, and reiterating thanks at the end of their statements. More than once, the chair stressed the importance of preparing a written statement and practicing before the meeting. S/he also emphasized coordinating the content of the statements to avoid repetition and provide board members with a multifaceted perspective on the need for more Hmong staffulty in the district.

Approximately ninety Hmong American adults, high school students, and children attended the packed Board of Education meeting of the Harriet City Public Schools. Several people were still in line to sign the attendance log when the chair of the board announced it was time to listen to community comments on topics of concern. The chair advised community members to provide the board with a written copy of their statements or concerns if possible. Then s/he explained the protocol: (1) the community member speaks and the board listens without comment; (2) the comments made by speakers about staff should be made in writing and exclude names in the public commentary; (3) each speaker is allotted three minutes, and unused time cannot be rolled over to the next speaker; and (4) speakers will be called to address the board in the order in which the speakers signed in to request public commentary time.

Student leader KaBao, a senior at Dayton High School, commenced the public comment by introducing the name of the Hmong community's group, IDEAS (Increase Diversity for Excellence and Achievement in School). She explained the group comprised "concerned parents and friends" who came together to create a petition to increase the diversity of staffulty in the district, which garnered more than a thousand signatures from community members. KaBao then read the petition out loud to the school board. The statement specified the need for the top administrative positions in the district to "reflect the student population" of Hmong Americans. In addition, it noted research evidence that teachers of color directly influence the increase in the "academic, personal, and social performance" of students of color. The petition further pointed to staff of color in top administrative positions as essential for an increase in teachers of color as well as culturally competent educators. Notably, the petition maintained that "the history of the district has proved that without top administrators of color advocating on behalf of each group of students of color, there will be no increase of teachers of color and culturally competent educators." Drawing attention to the sizable Hmong student population in the district and the lack of Hmong staffulty, the petition maintained, "As parents, students, and community members, we are greatly concerned that our school district does not reflect the people and community it serves. It is therefore not serving us." Importantly, the petition expressed a desire of the group to "[work] with the Board of Education and all concerned groups to increase the diversity of our educators in order to create a school culture of respect, excellence, and achievement." KaBao concluded by reiterating, "We need FULL representation!"

Next to speak was student leader Zoua, another senior at Dayton High, who remarked on the Asian American student and staffulty composition of the district and spoke at length about the need for staffulty who understood Hmong culture:

> Thank you for giving us your time. The population of Hmong and students of color in HCPS are growing; 73.5 percent are students of color, with 29.8 percent Asian American. Less than 7 percent of the staff are Asian American; 0 percent of the top staff are Asian American. The school district has not done all it can to meet our academic and social needs.
>
> As a Hmong American student, I, along with other Hmong American students, have to cope with and live in two very different cultures. My parents, along with many other Hmong parents, do not fully understand the American culture. Their help with things involving the American culture is very limited. Our non-Hmong teachers at school are unable to give us all the help we need without the understanding of our Hmong culture. We struggle living in two different cultures. This struggle that we face affects our education. It brings us down. It makes us not want to strive for the best.
>
> With Hmong staff in the administrative team, our struggles will be understood. They understand our struggles because they've lived through it. They understand us when we explain our issues dealing with the Hmong culture at home. They understand us when we have our issues in school. It takes one who has lived the culture to truly understand this struggle. They will be able to better provide us with the help we need.
>
> Having a Hmong person in the senior administrative level also gives us Hmong the determination to succeed because we see that there is a successful person who looks like us. It shows us that, just like that person in the administrative team, we can succeed.

> My parents do not know how to speak English fluently. If my parents have issues concerning my education, their voice will more likely be heard when there is a Hmong-speaking person in the administrative team.
>
> The education of us Hmong American students will grow richer, better, if we have Hmong representation. This Hmong representation needs to be in the top senior administrative team.

Zoua's statement emphasized that despite having one of the largest student populations in the district, Hmong Americans were not well represented among staffulty—and were conspicuously absent from the new leadership team. She asserted that the Harriet City Public Schools was not culturally responsive to the needs of Hmong American students. Reiterating the experiences of the students featured in chapter 3, she underscored the ways in which Hmong American students must "cope with and live in two very different cultures" because parents have limited understanding of the cultural norms and expectations of U.S institutions. According to Zoua, the majority of non-Hmong staffulty in the district's schools exacerbated Hmong students' "struggle living in two different cultures" because the staffulty's lack of knowledge about Hmong culture precludes them from assisting students to navigate between cultures. Echoing research on the importance of teachers of color,[17] she contended that a Hmong staff on the superintendent's administrative team would be able to provide Hmong students with the educational assistance they need because "it takes one who has lived the culture to truly understand [the] struggle" of Hmong students.

Nine other Hmong parents and community members participated in the public comment, speaking in both Hmong and English, to reiterate the need for a Hmong senior staff and additional Hmong staffulty. Their statements underscored the importance of district staffulty with deep knowledge about Hmong culture who could represent and advocate for Hmong Americans at individual schools and the broader district. One Hmong community leader, a father of children who attended schools in the district, urged the Board of Education to diversify staffulty and appoint a Hmong representative on the senior leadership team by specifically making connections to the civil rights movement, reminding Superintendent Finch of her personal history and racial heritage. Accompanied by four of his children, the parent pointed out that the majority of Hmong staffulty are in entry-level positions in the district. He asserted that the Hmong community has moved beyond "the need for liaisons, teachers' assistants and interpreters." Instead, the Hmong father declared the community "need[s] real staff with decision-making abilities." Summoning the legacy of the Reverend Martin Luther King Jr., he entreated, "We are now asking you for a seat at the table." This appeal was not only a request for self-representation on the leadership team but also a reminder to the superintendent of her African American heritage and the community's struggles for civil rights.

Moreover, a Hmong mother shared her sentiment that without Hmong representation on the leadership team, she and other Hmong families do not have a mechanism to solve the problems and challenges they face within the district. She requested that the board increase the numbers of teachers, administrators, and other school personnel within six months. Additional Hmong staffulty would decrease the problems related to language barriers and communication difficulties that currently existed between Hmong families and the school district. Hmong staffulty would "help the majority of parents who don't speak English and have difficulties" with school interactions. Further, the Hmong mother specified that she had eight children in the Harriet City Public Schools and warned that if the board did not place a Hmong staffulty on the leadership team by June, she intended to remove them from the district because Hmong "charter schools [would be] better" for her children. This threat was considerable: district leaders were worried about the district's increasing loss of student enrollment to charter schools and neighboring school districts.

The last speaker, a male community member, maintained that the district leadership should reflect the community that it serves. He asserted that everyone deserves a voice and an advocate in decision-making processes that affect him / her / them, but there was currently no "voice" for the Hmong community on the superintendent's administrative team. He stated that it is the Board of Education's responsibility to "do what is best for the students and community. Look around you, [high school 1, high school 2, high school 3], what do you see? Teachers, administrators—not representative. Not an issue of race—it is an issue of representation. We want someone who has real authority, [a Hmong representative] who reports directly to the superintendent." The community member urged the board to commit to making "real changes" and taking "immediate steps" so that within six months, the top administrative staff may reflect the Hmong student population.

Moreover, he requested that the Board of Education put into operation a comprehensive plan to increase the diversity of staffulty throughout the district and partner with the Hmong community to make the necessary changes: reform hiring practices, mitigate obstacles to hiring educators of color, establish Parent Teacher Organizations (PTOs) for parents of color at schools with high populations of students of color, involve the PTOs in school site councils, improve the recruitment of teachers of color, prepare teachers of color for leadership positions, and expand support pathways for prospective teachers of color. The community member closed his public comment by emphasizing the IDEAS group's eagerness to work with the district to achieve the group's goals and shape the Harriet City Public Schools into a district that better serves all students and communities.

As Hmong American adults, parents, community leaders, and youth pursued representation on the leadership team, they mobilized under a Hmong ethnic identity and emphasized Hmong collectivity. The public comments from Hmong community members underscored the importance of cultural representation on the district leadership team. Resounding the literature on culturally relevant leadership and culturally relevant pedagogy,[18] the statements highlighted the importance of ethnic representation and knowledge of Hmong history, worldviews, and experiences for the academic achievement of Hmong American students. The Hmong community members underscored lived experience in advocating for a Hmong staff on the leadership team. This point of view put emphasis on the need for an administrator to intimately and authentically know and understand Hmong culture and identity as requisite toward meeting the educational needs of Hmong families. The group wanted school staffulty to be a cultural insider and share the ethnicity of students and parents.

Even as Hmong Americans engaged in a cultural politics that highlighted the importance of ethnic representation for the academic achievement of Hmong students in Harriet City Public Schools, representation on the superintendent's leadership team was one means toward culturally relevant education. In the next section, I turn to Hmong leader Dia Lee's insights into the cultural politics of the controversy.

DEMANDING SELF-REPRESENTATION

I. And that's my test to the superintendent,
is to say to her, "Tell me and show me
that even if there were no Hmong people who operated at the senior level,
even if there were no Hmong teachers,
even if there were no Hmong principals,

but your school district is filled with Hmong children,
do you own these children as your children of [the]
Harriet City Public Schools system, and
how willing are you to really make them learners in your school district?"

II. And what I find so ironic about Harriet City Public Schools system
is that there are these silos that have been set up.
And then we have an expectation that the community should be satisfied with that.
Hey, Hmong community, you have your Shoua Her,
who is connected to the superintendent,
although her job description doesn't say that. . . .
So then the Hmong children are getting a lot of resources.
They have access to the superintendent.
Their needs are being taken care of, right?
No, they're not.
We have a system that is so siloed
that we don't have any quality control
because I think that we have become satisfied
with the first level of the facial representation.
And now, it's time to move on to the second level
of demanding results.
Now, I think facial representation is very important,
but I think it's unfair to those individuals sitting in those positions.
I think it's been tremendously unfair to Shoua Her
to make her the only access to the school district for the Hmong community.

III. Now, that being said, I see that there is a value
to creating role models
and making what we do reflective.
I guess I have often said to boards and organizations
that recruit me to sit on their board. . . .
"Well, do you want me as a workhorse
or do you just want me as a show horse?
Because if you just want me as a show horse,
I don't have time.
If you want me as a workhorse

and you have a specific task
that you need me and my unique identities to help you achieve,
I'll sign up for that for the time period that
you need me for to achieve that.
And then I'm out of there because I have other things to do.
But if you just need me to be a show horse—
I don't have time to be somebody's show horse."
And so, that's the question I place when we talk about role models and reflection.
If we really truly want our children to have good role models,
they better be workhorse role models.
And not only that, but they better be workhorse role models
that can really make a difference in the children's lives.

IV. And so it shouldn't matter if the teacher is Hmong, or white, or Black,
or if the principal is Hmong, white, or Hispanic.
Because at the end of the day,
that principal is going to make sure that the culture is there and is responsive.
But because I'm confident that because
Hmong students are such a large population,
that if you were to assess a certain culture, right, or a certain school building,
that your logical conclusion is gonna be,
"I'm gonna need a Hmong American person to help shape that.
And I got to seek out who that is."

Hmong American leader Dia Lee was one of the Hmong community leaders who met individually with Superintendent Deborah Finch, played a role in the organization of the Hmong community forum with the superintendent, and participated in community meetings to discuss Hmong representation on her district leadership team. In our interview, the leader shared with me her perspective on the identity politics of the leadership team controversy and her conversation with the superintendent about race, culture, and representation. Lee believed individuals in leadership positions needed to "own every community and every child," regardless of their ethnic or racial background. As she spoke of her own leadership position, she underscored her general goal of representing all communities and not just the Hmong community:

> I hope that I can use this position to speak to and to represent and do good work to a broader group of people than just the Hmong community. Because it would be too much of a shame if I didn't strive to do that.

From this standpoint, she conveyed her expectation for Superintendent Finch to also "own [Hmong] children as [her] children of [the] Harriet City Public Schools," even without senior Hmong administrators at the district office or Hmong staffulty in the schools.

Dia Lee's insight into how the protest was "read" by Superintendent Finch reveals not only her perceptivity of the politics of the community's demands but also the superintendent's politics:

> She said, "I have been too often in your shoes. That's why I know what you're talking about." She said, "My fight here is not to symbolically put somebody in a symbolic senior leadership position because that is just an empty promise. My fight here is about systemic change that will really respond to the needs of students. Not to create silos so that I can temporarily satisfy the political needs of certain communities." She said, "Don't you think that the Black community comes to me and say, 'Well, now we have a Black superintendent, so what are you gonna do about our Black kids?' Don't you think they say that to me? And you know what my response to them?" What she said is that, "Yeah, I may be Black, but I'm the superintendent for all the children in this school district. And so, just 'cause you're Black and I'm Black—yeah, we may identify—but that doesn't mean that Black kids are any more deserving of any more services than any other children."

The Hmong leader shared that the superintendent saw the demands of the Hmong community as a political request for "symbolic" representation that undermined her goals for "systemic change." These remarks criticize the identity politics of "representation" for impeding broader goals of social change. They also indicate the problematic ways in which identity politics promotes separatism or "silos" that requires individuals to work only within racial groups (i.e., "Black superintendent" working only for "Black kids") and undercuts educational equity initiatives that serve all students.

As Lee saw it, the controversy was in part a manifestation of parents' frustration with their access to high-level administrators and in part due to the lack of response to the concerns about the education of Hmong children. Consider, for example, what she said about language, communication, and the "siloed" school district:

> Because this school district has been so siloed for so long they have somehow become trained into the thinking that the only people who could competently address the needs of the Hmong community is gonna have to be somebody who speaks Hmong. But at the end of the day, the Hmong community has access only to a low-level administrator, never access to the person who has the ability to make the decisions. . . . When nothing happens, the parents get frustrated and they feel like nobody hears what they have to say.

The leader understood that the desire of the Hmong community for a Hmong representative was a result of frustration about the lack of access to decision makers with the capacity to actively and effectively respond to their concerns. The use of the word "siloed" reflects her assessment of racial and ethnic clustering and marginalization in Harriet City Public Schools. Within the context of Dia Lee's attempt to make sense of the community outcry, "siloed" particularly alludes to the separation and exclusion of the concerns and perspectives of Hmong students and families. The protest and focus of the Hmong community on ethnic representation is a result of experience—"being trained" to understand—that teachers and staff will support the educational needs of students and parents only if they come from the same ethnic and racial group.[19]

The Hmong leader contended that as the district's charter school liaison, Shoua Her's position on the district leadership team was not intended to focus on the educational needs of Hmong American students, noting, "Her job description doesn't say that." Remarking on the unreasonableness of making Shoua Her the singular entry point to Harriet City Public Schools for the Hmong community, Lee said, "The community placed tremendous burden on her by creating it into this position where she became the community's mouthpiece to the superintendent. And while she was trying to do that though, she didn't have the power to do anything about it." Moreover, the leader observed the culpability of the district for propagating the misconception of Shoua Her's clout: "I think it was grossly unfair of the school district to continually perpetuate that when she was in power, [she had] any real power to do anything, other than to just be a messenger back and forth to the community." Her criticism of the district thus alluded to the token gestures of including minoritized individuals in apparent positions of influence that are empty of actual authority.

Even as Dia Lee acknowledged the importance of "the first level of facial representation" of having a Hmong administrator on the district leadership team, she also insisted, "It's time to move on to the second level of demanding results." For the Hmong leader, the second level involves holding non-Hmong staffulty answerable for the academic achievement of Hmong students:

> What if now that Shoua Her is gone? There's no Hmong person in the administration and there's no Hmong person sitting there? The reason why the community is up in arms is because we never went the next step. Once we lose the facial representation, we've lost all hope—that our views are no longer gonna be represented. Why can't we go the opposite to say, "We want facial representation, but god damn it, whoever else you have over there better have our interests at heart! And, by the way, even if you're not Hmong looking, I'm holding you accountable for the performance of Hmong kids." Why don't we do that? Because the facial representation is fleeting and it is not permanent.

As the leader saw it, Harriet City's Hmong American community was upset—"up in arms"—because the community did not move beyond ethnic representation to require all district administrators and school staffulty to serve the best interests of Hmong children. Since representation is temporary and "fleeting," she suggested it was critical to demand systemic accountability that included all district personnel. Notably, Lee's call for systemic accountability echoes those of Hmong staffulty at the Hmong community forum with the superintendent, who expressed frustration about non-Hmong staffulty who choose to refer Hmong students and families to Hmong staffulty rather than serve them.

Although Dia Lee recognized the ways in which the protest politicized Hmong ethnicity and advocated for the community to move beyond ethnic representation, she also saw "a value to creating role models and making what we do reflective [of the community]." She suggested that the mobilization of the Hmong community under a collective identity may be an avenue for institutional change that would benefit the community. This is possible because as a representative of a particular group, you may be a "show horse" or a "workhorse." When organizations recruit Lee for their advisory boards, she shared that she often asks, "Well, do you want me as a workhorse or do you just want me as a show horse? Because if you just want me as a show horse, I don't have time." According to the leader, the distinction between show horse and workhorse makes all the difference in calls for representation, because "if we really truly want our children to have good role models, they better be workhorse role models." Lee's analysis of "show horse" and "workhorse" acts of representation revealed her recognition of the pitfalls of representation that may result in the token addition of minoritized individuals in superficial displays of the inclusion of diverse perspectives.[20] Beyond tokenism, the Hmong leader saw the possibility of ethnic representation serving as a platform for workhorse social change.

For example, Superintendent Finch justified the absence of a Hmong administrator on her senior leadership team with the assertion that there were no Hmong staff who were qualified for the position. Following her advocacy to move beyond representation, Dia Lee responded by asking, "What are you gonna do for Hmong students?" She encouraged the demand for "physical, visual representation" as one component of advocating for Hmong children:

> So I say to the superintendent, "I'm perfectly OK if you don't have any Hmong senior staff person, if you don't have any Hmong principals or any Hmong teachers. What are you gonna do for Hmong students? You make that commitment to me." . . . And this is where I think it's very, very important, for the Hmong American community, for the communities of color, but in particular for community leaders—for community leaders to demand for the physical, visual representation. But also then to not be satisfied with that access. But to also then demand for representation for Hmong from all of the people who are supposed to be working for our kids.

Lee suggested that once Hmong Americans are in positions of power—have "access"—the community must also "demand for representation *for* Hmong" from staffulty from all ethnic and racial backgrounds (my emphasis). Thus, while self-representation is important, systemic support for Hmong culture and identity requires institutional change.

The Hmong leader concurred with the desire of Hmong parents for a Hmong principal to reflect the large Hmong student population in Dayton High's search for a new principal.[21] This was because within the site-council-driven district structure, where principals, teachers, and parents at individual schools wield substantial power, she recognized the culture of a school—its values, beliefs, and traditions—is largely shaped and sustained by its principal.[22] Dia Lee shared her conversation with the superintendent about the need for a principal who is responsive to the concerns of parents:

> So, of course, the parents are absolutely right. They need a principal who can manage the building and shape the culture that's reflective of their needs and their concerns. So, that's why I said to the superintendent, "You know that. I know that. What are you gonna do about that?" She said, "You're right. That's why if I was gonna make any changes that is going to affect the culture of my school buildings, I need to assess my demographics. I need to assess the students' needs and then I need to find a school principal who will fit that culture and will help to shape the needs of that school, and be responsive to the needs of the parents."

According to the Hmong leader, Superintendent Finch recognized that the hire of a school's principal required the assessment of the demographics of the school because the principal is responsible for establishing the goals and culture of a school. Lee was thus "confident" that if an assessment revealed the school had a large Hmong student population, the superintendent would reach the "logical conclusion" that she would "need a Hmong American person" in the role as principal.

Dia Lee believed a school with a significant Hmong American student population should have leadership representative of Hmong ethnicity. She considered it worthwhile to strive for ethnic representation and culturally responsive educators, which were important for increasing the value and maintenance of Hmong culture and identity. As the leader put it, "The community has to take pride and think about us as a community because that is worthy of preserving." Beyond ethnic preservation, the leader also recommended that Hmong Americans keep in mind how the community may be a part of a more extensive effort toward social transformation. In particular, she advocated: "We have to be willing when it comes to access to resources and systematic changes—we have to be willing to then think broader than us as a siloed community. Because I think that there is more than one way to skin a cat." Put another way, moving past what she called the "first level" of ethnic representation meant the community must "think broader" than the Hmong community as a separate, "siloed community" focused only on its own interests. Dia Lee recognized that the construction of ethnic boundaries may be helpful for a racial or ethnic group to attain the group's goals toward equity. Yet she also understood that another way to "skin" the "cat" of racial disparities would involve working more broadly across racial and ethnic (among other) boundaries to construct coalitions toward dismantling structural inequities.[23]

Nearly three months after the Hmong community advocated for Hmong representation on the district leadership team at the Board of Education meeting, Tong Yang, the ELL department's program manager for Hmong enrichment programs and a member of the school district since the mid-1990s, was promoted to a position as the special projects officer for the Harriet City Public Schools. This was one of two positions on the superintendent's leadership team that still needed to be filled at the time of the Hmong community protest. His new responsibilities included part of Shoua Her's community engagement as well as work with various departments in the district to develop and launch strategic planning projects. Superintendent Finch acknowledged that it was important for Hmong parents to have someone at the district administration who understood their worldview. She stressed that Tong Yang reported directly to her as the Hmong community liaison and is part of direct reports who meet with her twice a month on community-related issues. Moreover, she noted that her open-door policy meant that Tong Yang and other staff members may come into her office at any time to talk to her.

Hmong community members affirmed that Tong Yang's presence enhanced the leadership of the Harriet City Public Schools by providing the superintendent with culturally relevant insights for education policy and practice. They recognized differences in the knowledge systems within Hmong culture and those of hegemonic school and society, and subsequently yearned for a member of the district leadership team who could authentically represent the community. In the cultural contestation with the superintendent, the Hmong community affirmed the worthiness of Hmong identity, language, and cultural values. The demand for self-representation on her leadership team was an assertion of the community's right to advance their ethnic values and interests in the face of cultural hegemony.[24] Instead of considering Tong Yang as simply a special projects officer in the district, they considered him to be a voice for the community who would provide Superintendent Finch a Hmong point of view for school leadership.

Audra Simpson's analysis of the Haudenosaunee people's refusal of Canada's governance, where Chief Deskaheh appealed to the League of Nations for the recognition of the Six Nations Confederacy as a sovereign nation-state, contended that the attempt "demonstrates the possibility of history and of so-called failure as incitements to not only mobilise but also maintain structures away from domination."[25] She suggested the consciousness of dispossession and a "deep cognisance of differing social and historical facts [. . .] make for the posture of refusal."[26] For the Harriet City Hmong community, keeping structures from subjugation necessitated staking claim to Hmong culture and identity and structuring the fact of school's privileging of Western knowledge systems as a political stance. Hmong students and families were critically aware of the status subordination[27] of Hmong ethnicity and the unequal representation of Hmong worldviews in district curriculum, policy, and personnel.

Indeed, the Hmong American community's ontoepistemology was evident in the Hmong community forum with Superintendent Finch, where education intertwined with culture, family, and community.[28] The superintendent was welcomed into the Hmong community as a guest, even though the space of the forum was a district high school under the superintendent's purview. A Hmong community leader hosted the event and made a point to honor the superintendent with a gift of a Hmong *paj ntaub*. The programming for the forum included a communal dinner as well as the sharing of culturally relevant arts in the form of Hmong dance performances. Hmong American parents who attended the forum did not come to the forum alone but came with their partners and children. Rather than the typical town hall–style forums of politics and policymaking, which are marked more by formality and lackluster oration, the Hmong community forum transformed the institutional space of the school into what Khalifa and colleagues referred to as "overlapping school–community spaces" that are part of culturally responsive schools.[29] The inflection of Hmong culture and commitments to family and community at the forum refused the pretense of school's cultural neutrality with Hmong cultural presentation and the presence of laughing, playing children.

Conclusion

> The March 23, 2007, Amnesty International Report on the Hmong hiding in the jungle of Laos condemns the action of the Communist Government for their continuing murder, rape and detention of the Hmong who supported the U.S. And yet, the U.S., in denial, is still deaf to their cries.
>
> —Chong Jones, *Hmong Today*

On June 4, 2007, with just over a week left in the Dayton High School academic year, the continuing dispossession of Hmong peoples reached a crescendo when General Vang Pao was arrested in California and charged with conspiring with nine others to overthrow the communist government of Laos.[1] The Hmong diaspora in the United States and across the world, as well as Hmong in Laos, were stunned by the U.S. government's actions.[2] National news accounts and commentaries reaffirmed the Harriet City Hmong community's sentiments of U.S. hypocrisy and betrayal, highlighting General Vang Pao's "open and ongoing activities" since he first came to the United States in exile more than thirty-two years ago:

> But for the U.S., this arrest is shameful. The CIA could have discreetly told Pao to stop his plotting and fundraising 20 years ago. Or 10. Instead he got Operation Tarnished Eagle. The Hmong sacrificed their lives and lost their homeland fighting alongside the Americans. Locking up their aging general is a final, contemptible act of betrayal.[3]

General Vang Pao affirmed during a court hearing that the CIA had known about his activities for decades.[4] Given the agency's long history with the general as a collaborator, as well as its knowledge of his desire and efforts to assist Hmong peoples forsaken by the United States in Laos, the CIA could have simply communicated its concerns to him. The U.S. government, with appalling disregard, instead chose to arrest a longtime associate.

Additionally, a *Hmong Today* article remarked on the make-believe character of the plans, which were more aspirational than realistic: "The talk of plotting to overthrow a foreign government was nothing more than a 'fantasy' egged on by the undercover ATF agent who posed as an arms dealer."[5] It further explained the justice orientation of the group by noting that "whatever transpired was motivated solely by a desire to end the suffering of the Hmong in Laos, who have been persecuted for decades."[6] Another *Hmong Today* article reported the alleged conspirators deemed the plan to have been approved by the U.S. government. A lawyer for one of the accused argued that "the undercover agent working the case and others gave the alleged conspirators the impression they were connected to high levels of the U.S. government," and given "the Hmong's history of working with the CIA [during the secret war], . . . the defendants believed they had the government's unofficial blessing."[7]

Hmong Today contributor Chong Jones similarly pointed out, "Vang Pao for forty years has tried to draw the world's attention to the Hmong's plight but to no avail." Jones underscored the hypocrisy of the charges against the general:

> The recent U.S. policy shift in terror activities by the Bush administration once again will commit another betrayal of its former ally. Ironically, the charges filed against Vang Pao are the same criminal acts exercised by the U.S. that started this atrocity. Had the U.S. lived up to its promises then perhaps Vang Pao would not feel obligated to help the helpless. Vang Pao is the product of U.S. policies. Now U.S. policies will condemn him for his alleged actions. Only in America does the culprit have the audacity to blame the instrument for a crime . . . such hypocrisy.[8]

The account makes at least three incisive observations about the U.S. government's moral bankruptcies. First, the arrest of General Vang Pao was not the first time the United States betrayed the Hmong peoples. This history of betrayal included abandoning Hmong in Laos in the aftermath of the fall of Saigon, including allowing communist Vietnamese and Lao soldiers to "[hunt] the Hmong down like animals,"[9] accepting the inhumane refugee camp conditions faced by Hmong in Thailand,[10] and permitting normal trade relations with Laos to resume in 2004.[11] Second, General Vang Pao was obligated to try to end the persecution of Hmong in Laos because the United States failed to keep its promise.[12] Last, the charge that General Vang Pao's alleged plans to overthrow a country at peace with the United States violated the U.S. Neutrality Act is stunning hypocrisy since such an act would simply take a cue from U.S. imperialism's violation of the 1962 International Agreement on the Neutrality of Laos when it engaged in the so-called secret war. As Jones put it, "The charges filed against Vang Pao are the same criminal acts exercised by the U.S. that started this atrocity" of the oppression of Hmong peoples.

Writing about European dismembering practices targeting anticolonial indigenous leaders, Ngũgĩ wa Thiong'o stated,

> The British captured King Hintsa of the Xhosa resistance and decapitated him, taking his head to the British Museum, just as they had done with the decapitated head of the Maori King of New Zealand. The relationship between Africa and Europe is well represented by the fate of these figures. A colonial act—indeed, any act in the context of conquest and domination—is both a practice of power, intended to pacify a populace, and a symbolic act, a performance of power intended to produce docile minds.[13]

After putting General Vang Pao and Hmong colleagues through the "sheer agony" of federal criminal investigation for four years and spending millions of taxpayer dollars, the U.S government dropped its charges.[14] They first dropped the case against General Vang Pao because "there was no evidence that Vang Pao had agreed to any plan, much less devised one," and a prosecutor of the other defendants later "got his head handed to him" by the judge thanks to a flimsy case.[15]

The Harriet City Hmong community members believed the outrageous arrest of General Vang Pao was an act of retaliation that came against the backdrop of protests from Hmong Americans and advocates against provisions of the USA Patriot Act[16] and the Real ID Act that categorized Hmong as "terrorists" ineligible for asylum and green cards.[17] Under the two acts, Hmong were classified as terrorists because of their guerrilla activities during the Vietnam War (on behalf of the United States), which led to reverberations against the communist Lao government after they were abandoned by the United States.[18] The baseless arrest of General Vang Pao was both a "practice of power" and a "performance of power" that are part of the ongoing dismemberment of Hmong peoples.[19]

Indeed, the fragmentation of Hmong in the U.S. diaspora was a headline in a *New York Times* article entitled "Arrest Uncovers Divide in Hmong-Americans," which probed whether the arrest of General Vang Pao really mattered to younger generations of Hmong Americans.[20] Writer Monica Davey announced, "But young Hmong people here, those who grew up in the United States, saw Gen. Vang Pao as an outdated chapter from their grandparents' memories." She also quoted a Hmong American as saying, "The majority of young people didn't really care what he was doing about going back to Laos . . . They just ignored him. America is their homeland."[21] While Davey's claim about the divisions between younger and older generations of Hmong Americans resound the concerns of Harriet City's Hmong leaders, staffulty, and students, her narrative problematically substantiates the discourses of Hmong elders as "outdated" and the homeland of their heritage and history as not worth remembering. Its cavalier assertion that the younger generation does not care is an expression of organized ignorance that fails to comprehend the basis and gravity of such lack of caring. Given the information in Davey's story and those circulating at the time of the writing, the lack of care amounts to the following statements. Hmong young people do not care about General Vang Pao, a Hmong leader who was also considered "the biggest hero of the Vietnam War" by William Colby, former director of the CIA (1973–76). Hmong young people do not care about their Hmong kin whom the United States abandoned in Laos, who are still facing violent, even deadly persecution. Hmong young people do not care about the anguished memories and yearnings of grandparents and elders who survived the brutalities of imperial wars, escaped through the jungles of Laos, crossed the Mekong River, and subsisted in refugee camps. Although glossed as news, such an outcome of structured forgetting is a mournful, reprehensible enunciation of empire.

School has contributed to the younger generation's indifference through the coloniality of its provided histories, marked by a Western imperial perspective as well as the omission of Hmong histories, experiences, and worldviews. The predominant focus on white male leaders such as George Washington, Thomas Jefferson, and John F. Kennedy reduced General Vang Pao in the consciousness of U.S.-born Hmong generations (according to the *New York Times*) to an "outdated chapter from their grandparents' memories." Indeed, in tributes by Hmong and non-Hmong people after his death, General Vang Pao's legibility was constructed within comparisons to George Washington.[22] Against the backdrop of the demand to forget, General Vang

Pao's name, contributions, and significance to the Hmong diaspora and U.S. history cannot stand on their own, but only as an echo of the achievements of a white man.

Re-membering Culture's exploration of Hmong refugee lifeworlds illuminates the material struggles that take place within cultural and ideological forms of domination. Its explication of Hmong re-membering culture and identity makes intelligible school's principal role in the structured forgetting essential in U.S. imperial formations. The Western ontology and epistemology of school assault Hmong culture, identity, family, and community. As a primary socialization institution, school undermines the ties and attachments to Hmong family and community by systematically devaluing Hmong history, practices, and perspectives. We saw this in Hmong concerns about the waning relations between Hmong parents and children, growing estrangement between "traditional" and "modern" Hmong students, diminishing cultural knowledge and participation in family events, and increasing identity struggles of children. As Valenzuela cogently stated, "Cultural distance produces social distance, which in turn reinforces cultural distance."[23] Significantly, Hmong leaders rearticulated tropes of immigrant "intergenerational conflict" and "culture clash" to assert the culpability of U.S. cultural imperialism in enacting "deculturalization"[24] that sever Hmong relationships and create conflict between Hmong and hegemonic cultures.

Although the concept of culture is often reified and engaged as a descriptor, as a focus of analysis, culture comes into view as "a terrain of conflict"[25] where practices, customs, values, and knowledge systems signify and clarify identity and community. We saw white supremacy in hegemonic narratives that rebuked large Hmong families, gender relations, teenage marriage, and healing practices, among others. Because domination is never absolute, we also saw Hmong challenges to hegemonic discourses and ideologies through practices of re-membering marked by (re)storytelling, resurgence, and refusal. Hmong Americans pinpointed school's role in the struggles of Hmong parents and families through its privileging of Western knowledge systems. Hmong perspectives and experiences refuted narratives about a patriarchal, oppressive Hmong culture. Hmong community leaders Dia Lee and Kou Vang countered the cultural racism that marked Hmong culture as deviant and requiring it be tamed, dominated, and destroyed. Hmong American students disputed notions of teenage marriage as customary. Hmong students and adults also disrupted the "authorized anticipation" of the status quo at Dayton High by making claim to Hmong culture and identity in the structures of school.[26] The Hmong Culture Club's Hmong New Year celebration was a curricular intervention that instantiated Hmong culture and identity and unsettled the cultural repertoire of Dayton High. The Hmong community insisted on Hmong self-representation in district and school administrators, teachers, and staff.

Hmong American education as a site of social, political, and historical critique makes comprehensible a wider set of problems with culture in education as well as the forms of practice that must ensue. First, school is still a project of settler colonialism whose Western epistemic and ontological assumptions regard Hmong children, parents, and families as objects to be assimilated, modernized, and disciplined to hegemonic values and norms. Two barefaced historical examples of U.S. cultural and ideological oppression within its borders include the forcible abduction and enrollment of Native American children in boarding schools to strip them of language, religion, family, and heritage, and the imprisonment of Japanese Americans in concentration camps during World War II, where "the chief aims of the camp curriculum were to study the democratic ideal" and the "chief curricular goals were to Americanize camp residents" in order to safeguard national security.[27] Significantly, during the incarceration of Japanese Americans, the War Relocation Authority's education section administrator was Lucy W. Adams, who previously worked for the Bureau of Indian Affairs. Plans for the internment camp schools replicated the schools Adams supervised on the Navajo reservation.[28] Both instantiations of white supremacy profoundly fragmented families, identity development, and mental and physical health for generations.[29] Although more covert, contemporary school practices of parent and family engagement (e.g., PTAs, parent–teacher conferences, parent trainings) often enact similar assimilationist—Americanizationist—demands.[30] As Khalifa and Abdi point out, as a project of coloniality, school positions children and families "as empty vessels to be filled with knowledge (intended to civilize them)."[31] Hmong Americans' conception of success requires school to shift from Western cultural logics, where school contributes to the "destruction of intimacy, family and community," toward a vision that intertwines school with familial and ethnic identities and commitments.[32]

Second, school does not adequately include Hmong culture, identity, and heritage in curriculum and pedagogy. School increasingly purports to incorporate into its structures culturally relevant pedagogy,[33] culturally responsive teaching,[34] and culturally sustaining pedagogy.[35] Yet the outcome has been the commodification and appropriation of these culture-centered pedagogies in ways that homogenize and neutralize distinctive cultural, historical, and political experiences, and that lull insurgent pedagogical aims into compliance and silence. Culturally universalist pedagogy becomes a culturally sustaining white pedagogy that renews and reconstitutes white cultural hegemony.[36] David Kirkland observed of a culturally sustaining pedagogy that does not name race: "If it belongs not only to the fugitive but to all, one must question what culturally sustaining pedagogy means to the project of whiteness, as whiteness has so involved itself in pedagogy as a tactic / tool of not only achieving supremacy and domination but also sustaining supremacy and domination."[37] Put another way, curriculum and pedagogy that do not specify race or ethnicity are easily recuperated into coloniality's "universal paradigm of knowledge," leaving intact Western cultural logics and domination.[38]

Whereas Kirkland suggests that naming race matters in pedagogy for Black people, I suggest that Hmong ethnicity matters in Hmong American education. Hmong concerns about school's erasure of their history, language, culture, and identity—"de-ethnicization"[39] or "deculturalization"[40]—cannot be adequately addressed by cultural universalism in curriculum and pedagogy. Moreover, for the Hmong community of Harriet City Public Schools, Hmong representation in leadership, teachers, and staff are requisite for serving Hmong students and families. Indeed, the "tenuous 'we'"[41] of Asian American panethnicity wrought out of the political necessity to respond to anti-Asian violence and discrimination with a singular voice[42] is infrequently accepted by Hmong in the United States.[43]

Last, school enacts cultural and ideological oppression by operating from and reproducing Western knowledge and belief systems. Coloniality manifests in the hegemony of Western ontology and epistemology in teacher education,[44] curriculum, and pedagogy[45] characterized by policies and practices such as "ambitious" standards;[46] English language dominance;[47] foreign language and second language education methods that prioritize white, Western languages;[48] and Eurocentric education research approaches,[49] among other practices. For Hmong Americans of Harriet City Public Schools, the coloniality of school privileges the individual over the family and community; pathologizes Hmong culture and identity; produces the loss of language, history, and heritage; imparts internalized racism; and excludes Hmong perspectives from organizational leadership and policy. The structured forgetting in Hmong American education demonstrates the necessity of fostering a "decolonial ethic" in education[50] that involves divesting from the "white gaze,"[51] engaging in "epistemic disobedience," and refusing "the magic of the Western idea of modernity."[52]

Writing about colonized knowledges, Linda Tuhiwai Smith suggests, "The globalization of knowledge and Western culture constantly reaffirms the West's view of itself as the centre of legitimate knowledge, the arbiter of what counts as knowledge and the source of 'civilized' knowledge."[53] Hmong American award-winning author Kao Kalia Yang's account of "science podcast" RadioLab's treatment of her uncle Eng Yang and her as guests on the show as well as Hmong experience with "yellow rain" is instructive:

> My uncle explained Hmong
> knowledge of the bees in the mountains of Laos, said we had harvested honey for
> centuries, and explained that the chemical attacks were strategic; they
> happened far away from established bee colonies, they happened where there were
> heavy concentrations of Hmong. *Robert*
> *grew increasingly harsh, "Did you, with your own eyes, see the yellow powder*
> *fall from the airplanes?"* My uncle said
> that there were planes flying all the time and bombs being dropped, day and
> night. Hmong people did not wait around
> to look up as bombs fell. We came out in
> the aftermath to survey the damage. He
> said what he saw, "Animals dying, yellow that could eat through leaves, grass, yellow
> that could kill people—the likes of which bee poop has never done."[54]

The podcast's September 2012 episode, "The Fact of the Matter," was hosted by Robert Krulwich and Jad Abumrad and produced by Pat Walters as part of National Public Radio. From the outset, the show denigrated its Hmong guests by introducing two scientists and a former CIA officer by their titles and affiliations, while Eng Yang was presented as "the Hmong guy" and Kao Kalia Yang as "his niece." The production legitimized the knowledge of the three guests invited to represent Western knowledge that refuted "yellow rain" as a chemical weapon while at the same time delegitimizing and disappearing the distinction of Eng Yang's experience as a survivor of yellow rain and work within the Thai government as a documenter of Hmong experience, and Kao Kalia Yang's worth as an award-winning author of the Hmong refugee experience. The show itself was a ruse because Pat Walters already reached a conclusion about yellow rain after spending "several months reviewing nearly 20 years' worth of academic papers and media reports on yellow rain."[55] He chose to exclude scientists whose research refuted the bee dung theory, even though Kao Kalia Yang shared the research.[56] Pat Walters, Robert Krulwich, and Jad Abumrad (among others) were not interested in Hmong knowledge about yellow rain and instead sought to juxtapose their authorized Western science against the "hearsay" of Hmong knowledge under the banner of truth seeking.[57]

Robert Krulwich further asserted that Kao Kalia Yang wanted to "monopolize" the story of yellow rain to tell the story of Hmong genocide:

> It is not fair to ask us to not consider the other stories and the other frames of this story. The fact that the most powerful man in the world, Ronald Reagan, used this story to order the manufacture of chemical weapons for the first time in twenty years. If the United States were to manufacture chemical weapons again and use them, because the Russians supposedly had, then people would have died ugly deaths in the consequence of that. And that is not unimportant. That is hugely important. But that is not important to her. So should that not be important to us? [. . .] Her desire was to monopolize the story. And that we can't allow.

Only "an imperialist white man"[58] can constitute Hmong knowledge as "not fair," "wrong," and an effort to "monopolize" official knowledge despite the power of Robert Krulwich and colleagues to produce official knowledge by framing the segment, asking questions, and editing the interviews. As Kao Kalia Yang observed of RadioLab's editing, "Radiolab had simply re-contextualized their position, taken out the laughter at the end, and 'cleaned' away incriminating evidence."[59] Hmong knowledge of *actual* Hmong massacre is unallowable to safeguard the *potential* of (another) immoral U.S. executive action and the potential of other "ugly deaths" as a "consequence" of its legitimacy. In defense of hypothetical human suffering, imperial truth telling effaces Hmong humanity.

The institutions, scenes, and everydayness of Hmong refugee lifeworlds are enunciated with imperial knowledge production that consists of violent affirmation of Western knowledge systems, requiring Hmong (re)storytelling, resurgence, and refusal. School as part of U.S. imperial architectures has as its foundation the "coloniality of knowledge."[60] In the end, onto-epistemic justice in education summons us to sever colonized knowledge from school, and from its ruins conceive school as a project of re-membering.

Acknowledgments

Much of this book is about family and community, and much of it is possible because of family and community. My work as an educational ethnographer depends on being allowed to immerse myself in communities. I cannot fully express my gratitude to the staff, teachers, and students who opened their school, classrooms, and lives to me. They took a leap of faith with me toward a better conception of culture in Hmong American education. I am especially indebted to Hmong American leaders, parents, teachers, staff, and high school students, whose concerns and insights I foreground in this book. I am humbled by their courage, generosity, acuity, and persistence in the face of white cultural hegemony. While I endeavored to stay true to the perspectives they shared with me, I take all responsibility for the interpretations and representations. I deeply hope the stories I carry forward in this book will contribute to a resonant understanding of Hmong refugee lifeworlds and the ontoepistemic change needed in education.

I stand on the shoulders of giants. Stacey J. Lee and Gloria Ladson-Billings, my mentors from the University of Wisconsin–Madison, continue to influence my work. They serve as guideposts in my endeavors as a critical ethnographer and scholar. Stacey's contribution to the knowledge base on Asian American education and Gloria's pivotal theory of culturally relevant pedagogy seeded my development as a researcher. In this project I bring these ideas together with those inspired by the scholarship of Ngũgĩ wa Thiong'o, Richard Delgado, Jean Stefancic, Jeff Corntassel, Glen Coulthard, Audra Simpson, Carol McGranahan, and Yen Le Espiritu, among others I note in the book.

Thank you to colleagues and friends, old and new, who move me not only with their humanity and brilliance but also with their resolve to better understand and rupture white supremacy, including Timothy Lensmire, Vichet Chhuon, Mary Hermes, Nina Asher, Blanca Caldas Chumbes, Amanda Sullivan, Abby Rombalski, Cynthia Lewis, Nimo Abdi, Sabina Vaught, Roland Sintos Coloma, Betina Hsieh, Ming Fang He, and Lin Wu. I am lucky to have among these colleagues those whom Vichet Chhuon would suggest are my "ride or die" friends. Thank you also to my students, who were interlocutors and writing partners during our #SUAW sessions, including Emina Buzinkic, Diana Chandara, Carol Cousins, Bao Diep, Denise Hanh Huynh, Shakita Thomas Kpetay, Thong Vang, Bisola Wald, Verna Wong, and Ariana Yang.

I owe much to individuals who worked behind the scenes with various components that make this book possible. Louise Covert supported some of the data collection and organization as my graduate research assistant. Pieter Martin, my editor at the University of Minnesota Press, offered me gracious patience as life and family took precedence over the book. Anne Carter, University of Minnesota Press editorial assistant, helped with the critical aspects of formatting and logistics. I am grateful to the reviewers who took time to give me thoughtful and constructive feedback. I am also obliged to the publishers of select journals for allocating rights for me to extend my earlier thinking and writing in this book. Early iterations of parts of chapters of this book first appeared in *American Educational Research Journal; Diaspora, Indigenous, and Minority Education; Educational Studies; Journal of Language, Identity, and Education;* and *Journal of Southeast Asian American Education and Advancement.*

When I started this writing project, my household consisted of a three-person nuclear family. By the delivery of the manuscript, my household grew to a six-person multigenerational family indelibly transformed by the Covid-19 pandemic, caregiving commitments, and re-membered obligations to reciprocity, kinship, and care of family. The tensions between Western cultural logics' esteem for individual success and Hmong concerns for collective well-being that study participants shared with me reverberate in my own life. Within academia, it is too easy to feel that work is life, and family is a disruption to this work life. What we must re-member, as one of the students whom I spotlight in this book affirmed, is that "family is [. . .] worth more than anything in the world." Thank you to my parents, siblings, and immediate and extended families for your care and need for care. You ground me and remind me to hold on to and live out the primacy of family and mutual relations of care.

I want to especially extend my gratitude to Chris, Isko, and Mia, who are my joy, heart, and compass. Chris, the depth and breadth of your love and support for me are the stuff of dreams. You are the best possible partner and parent. Isko, my grade-school-age in-house editor, thank you for caring about this project and keeping tabs on me with questions and comments: "How's your book going?" "Are you done with your book yet?" "I can't wait to hear back from your editor." You amaze me with your curiosity, creativity, and intellect. Here's to Oreo and Bamboo! Mia, my precocious, independent "all by myself" little one, the way you experience the world with wonder and delight is a beacon for my every day. I see your wings. I know you will soar. Chris, Isko, and Mia, this book is for you. Everything is for you.

Notes

INTRODUCTION

1. The names of people and places in the study are pseudonyms.

2. Jung (2022), Lowe (2015), Okihiro (2016), Stoler (2006). See Stoler (2006) for an explication of U.S. empire, imperialism, and (internal) colonialism.

3. I focus on school rather than education to underscore the actualities of teaching and learning—contestations that take place within buildings and sites of interactions. See also Valenzuela (1999), Khalifa and Abdi (2023).

4. King (1967), 7. From "Beyond Vietnam," a speech Dr. King delivered on April 4, 1967, at Riverside Church, New York City, at the invitation of Clergy and Laymen Concerned about Vietnam—exactly one year before his assassination.

5. King (1967), 6.

6. Hamilton-Merritt (1993), Vang (2021).

7. Hamilton-Merritt (1993).

8. Hamilton-Merritt (1993), Hillmer (2010).

9. Hamilton-Merritt (1993), 113.

10. Hillmer (2010), 101.

11. President Barack Obama (2016) acknowledged, "Over nine years—from 1964 to 1973—the United States dropped more than two million tons of bombs here in Laos—more than we dropped on Germany and Japan combined during all of World War II."

12. Hamilton-Merritt (1993), Vang (2021).

13. Vang (2021).

14. Jacobs (1996).

15. Hamilton-Merritt (1993), Hillmer (2010).

16. Hamilton-Merritt (1993), Hillmer (2010), Jacobs (1996).

17. King (1967), 6.

18. Rumbaut (1996).

19. Espiritu (2021), 3.

20. Espiritu (2006, 2021), Schlund-Vials (2016).
21. Espiritu (2021), Schlund-Vials (2016).
22. Espiritu (2021), 5; see also Tang (2015).
23. Wisconsin Historical Society (1991).
24. Wisconsin Historical Society (1991).
25. Schein and Thoj (2007).
26. Associated Press (2004), Baldillo, Mendy, and Eng (2005).
27. Miner (2007 January 9), Saulny (2007 January 14).
28. Lyons (2015).
29. Williams (2009), Xiong (2006).
30. Williams (2009), Xiong (2006).
31. Faircloth and Libor (2019 December 18), Jany (2020).
32. Chan (2021).
33. Xiong (2021).
34. Crann, Bui, and Stroozas (2023).
35. Associated Press (2023).
36. Mueller (2017).
37. Rivas (2011).
38. Buffamonte (2017).
39. Anguiano (2021), Associated Press (2021).
40. From the inscription on the Statue of Liberty's tablet: "Give me your tired, your poor, your huddled masses yearning to breathe free, the wretched refuse of your teeming shore." These lines are from Emma Lazarus's 1883 poem "The New Colossus."
41. Schlund-Vials (2016), 201.
42. Adichie (2009).
43. Espiritu (2006), 422.
44. Hmong activist Zurg Xiong was on day 12 of a hunger strike to demand an external review of the killing of farmer Sooblej Kaub Hawj when he made this statement before a march to protest the actions of Siskiyou County law enforcement. See Chan (2021).
45. wa Thiong'o (2009), 6.
46. wa Thiong'o (2009), 6.
47. wamwa Mwanga (2022), 85.
48. wa Thiong'o (2009), 28.
49. wa Thiong'o (2009).
50. wamwa Mwanga (2022), 83.
51. wamwa Mwanga (2022).
52. Hall ([1990] 1994), 394.
53. Maldonado-Torres (2007), 243; see also Quijano (2007).
54. Maldonado-Torres (2007), 243.
55. Maldonado-Torres (2007), 243.
56. Dillard (2008, 2020), Gardner et al. (2020), King and Swartz (2014, 2015).
57. Dillard (2008), 91.

58. Dillard (2008), 91.
59. King and Swartz (2014), 1.
60. King and Swartz (2015), 1.
61. wa Thiong'o (2009, 2012).
62. Said (1994), xiii.
63. Delgado (1989), 2414.
64. Vizenor (2008).
65. For this reason, I use (re)storytelling rather than counterstorytelling or counternarrative.
66. Delgado (1989), Delgado and Stefanic (2001).
67. Delgado (1989), 2436.
68. This remark was made in response to Derrick Bell's Space Traders chronicles; Fan (1997), 1216.
69. Delgado (1989), Delgado and Stefanic (2001).
70. DeCuir and Dixson (2004), Solórzano and Yosso (2002). A few studies focusing on indigenous education have engaged (re)storytelling as a central component of resurgence; see, e.g., Tzou et al. (2019).
71. See Han (2014), Kalano (2016), Solorzanao et al. (2019), Urrieta and Villenas (2013).
72. See An (2017), Cho (2017), Cook and Dixson (2013), Rodriguez (2020).
73. Urrieta and Villenas (2016), 516–17.
74. Cho (2017).
75. Corntassel (2012), 97.
76. Coulthard (2007), 2014.
77. Coulthard (2007), 456.
78. Corntassel (2012), 89.
79. Alfred and Corntassel (2005), Corntassel (2012).
80. Corntassel and Hardbarger (2019), Sumida Huaman (2020), Tzou et al. (2019).
81. Sumida Huaman (2020), 264.
82. Corntassel and Hardbarger (2019).
83. Corntassel and Hardbarger (2019), 113.
84. Corntassel and Hardbarger (2019), 112.
85. Tzou et al. (2019).
86. Tzou et al. (2019), 307.
87. Simpson (2017), 19.
88. Coulthard (2014), McGranahan (2016), Simpson (2014, 2017).
89. Simpson (2017), 29.
90. McGranahan (2016).
91. McGranahan (2016), 322
92. McGranahan (2016), 322.
93. Simpson (2017), 330.
94. McGranahan (2016), 322–23.
95. McGranahan (2016) draws on Zournazi's (2002) understanding of hope.
96. McGranahan (2016), 323.

97. Chandler (2018), Gonzales and Shotton (2022), Grande (2018), Yuan (2021).

98. Grande (2018), 61.

99. Chandler (2018).

100. Yuan (2021).

101. Espiritu (2021), 4.

102. Espiritu (2021), Schlund-Vials (2012).

103. The terminology for the racial groups reflects the ones used by Harriet City Public Schools. The district did not disaggregate by ethnic groups, including distinctions between U.S.-born African Americans and African immigrants (e.g., Ethiopians).

104. The district used data for home language to identify percentage of Hmong students.

105. This percentage is based on district home language data.

106. Only one of the seven high schools achieved adequate yearly progress (AYP) in reading. Six high schools did not make AYP in reading or math.

107. Blum (2022), Davies and Bansel (2007).

108. Lincoln and Guba (1985), 109.

109. Fetterman (1998).

110. Emerson, Fretz, and Shaw (1998).

111. Hmong leaders include school leaders who are teachers and staff members.

112. Delgado and Stefancic (2001), 144.

113. Espiritu (2021), Schlund-Vials (2016).

114. The candidates for the homecoming court included eight Hmong American and one African American female nominees, and five Hmong American and four African American male nominees.

115. Jung (2022), 10.

1. THE DISMEMBERING FORCE OF SCHOOL

1. Erickson and Mohatt (1982).
2. Vogt, Jordan, and Tharp (1987).
3. Ladson-Billings (1995).
4. Paris (2012).
5. Valenzuela (1999).
6. Baumann (1996).
7. Deyhle (1995).
8. Rah, Choi, and Nguyen (2009), 362.
9. DePouw (2012), Lee (2005).
10. Lee and Hawkins (2008).
11. Apple (1996).
12. Hamilton-Merritt (1993), Hillmer (2011).
13. Fuller (2007).
14. Palazzo (2010).
15. Valdes (1996).
16. Rah, Choi, and Nguyen (2009), 362.
17. Apple (1996), 222.

18. Olsen (1997).
19. Bourdieu (1986).
20. Eckes (2015).
21. Wilson (2016).
22. Suárez-Orozco (2001).
23. González, Moll, and Amanti (2005).
24. Hansen (1996).
25. Hansen (1996), 494.
26. See Brah (1987), Ngo (2008b).
27. wamwa Mwanga (2022), 85.
28. Wong-Fillmore (1991).
29. Cho (2000), Fishman (1991), Wong-Fillmore (1991, 2000).
30. El-Haj (2015), Lowe (1996), Maira (2008).
31. Lee (1999), 8.
32. Lee (1999).
33. Tuan (1998).
34. Lowe (1996), 5–6.
35. Tuan (1998), 18.
36. Lowe (1996). This racialization is exemplified by the murder of a second-generation Chinese American, Vincent Chin, who was racialized as Japanese and killed by white Detroit autoworkers in retaliation for the loss of their jobs (Takaki 1989).
37. Fanon ([1952] 2008), 1–2.
38. Gibson (1998), Espiritu (2003), Lee (2005), Sarroub (2005), Waters (1999), Zhou and Bankston (1998).
39. Marroni (2017).
40. Hardy (2014).
41. Ott (2006).
42. Osiagwu (2021).
43. See Yang (2003).
44. Dublin (1996), Qin (2006), Portes and Rumbaut (2006).
45. Dublin (1996).
46. Portes and Rumbaut (2006), 53–54.
47. Qin (2006), Wong (2010).
48. Qin (2006), 171.
49. Lowe (1996), 63, original emphasis.
50. McCarty (2002), Smith-Hefner (1999), Valenzuela (1999).
51. Lee (2005), 51–52.
52. Hernández-Chávez (1988), Valenzuela (1999).
53. Chan (1994), 226.
54. Cummins (1986), Garza and Crawford (2005), Gibson (1993), Valenzuela (1999).
55. Ladson-Billings (2006), 36.
56. Koltyk (1998), Xiong, Deenanath, and Mao (2013).
57. Xiong, Deenanath, and Mao (2013), 93.
58. Dunnigan (1982), Keown-Bomar (2004), Xiong, Deenanath, and Mao (2013).

59. Conquergood and Thao (1989), 44.

60. Koltyk (1998), 38.

61. Dunnigan (1982), Keown-Bomar (2004), Koltyk (1998), Xiong, Deenanath, and Mao (2013).

62. Chan (1994), Donnelly (1994), Faderman and Xiong (1999).

63. Koltyk (1998), 40.

64. Apple (1996).

65. Barth (1969), Lamont (2009).

66. Espiritu (2001), 415.

67. Koltyk (1998), 127.

68. Conquergood and Thao (1989).

69. Bliatout (1982).

70. Conquergood and Thao (1989), 44.

71. Fordham (1996), Valenzuela (1999).

72. Apple (1996), Fordham (1996), Valenzuela (1999).

73. Fordham (1996), Fordham and Ogbu (1986).

74. Cf. Deyhle (1995).

75. Conquergood and Thao (1989).

76. Fordham (1996).

77. Valenzuela (1999).

78. Bourdieu (1986).

79. Valenzuela (1999).

80. Olsen (1997), Valenzuela (1999).

81. Fordham (1996), 52.

82. Lee (2005), Olsen (1997).

2. HMONG PARENTS NAVIGATING EXCLUSION

1. Swartz (1997), 90.

2. Bourdieu (1986).

3. Grenfell and James (1998).

4. Bourdieu and Passeron (1977), Grenfell and James (1998), Lareau and Horvat (1999).

5. Grenfell and James (1998).

6. Bourdieu and Passeron (1977).

7. Calabrese Barton et al. (2004), Delgado-Gaitan (2001), Doucet (2008), Lareau (1989).

8. Yosso (2005).

9. See also Ngo (2008b), Smith-Hefner (1999), Doucet (2008).

10. Lareau and Weininger (2003).

11. Hillmer (2011), Miyares (1997).

12. Koumarn and Barney (1981), Miyares (1997).

13. Hang et al. (2004), Xiong (2005).

14. Green and Reder (1986), Hang et al. (2004), Long (1993), Walter (1994), Xiong (2005), Xiong (2010).

15. Hillmer (2011), 43.
16. Hillmer (2011), 44.
17. Hillmer (2011), 44.
18. Lareau (1987), 79.
19. Lareau (1987), 80.
20. Ruiz-de-Velasco, Fix, and Clewell (2000).
21. Carreón et al. (2005), Cooper (2009), Lightfoot (2004), Lopez (2001).
22. Bourdieu (1977), 494.
23. See also Thao (2003).
24. Lawson (2003), 91.
25. Graue (1993), 467.
26. Carreón et al. (2005), Doucet (2008), Graue (1993), Lawson (2003).
27. Carter, Locks, and Winkle-Wagner (2013), Corrigan (2003). See also Hli's story in chapter 3.
28. Lopez and Stack (2001), 48.
29. Lamont and Lareau (1988), 155.
30. Doucet (2011), 414.
31. Valdes (1996).
32. Delpit (1988).
33. Delgado-Gaitan (1990), Lo (2009), Valdes (1996).
34. See also Lareau and Horvat (1999).
35. Nasir (2004).
36. Nasir (2004), 113.
37. Bourdieu (1977), Lamont and Lareau (1988).
38. Nakagawa (2000).
39. Lareau (1987), Nasir (2004).
40. See also Thao (2003).
41. Stanton-Salazar (1997), 6.
42. Stanton-Salazar (1997), 6.
43. Conchas (2006), Lew (2006).
44. Yosso (2005), 80.
45. Nasir (2004).
46. Graue, Kroeger, and Prager (2001), 489.
47. Graue, Kroeger, and Prager (2001), Lareau and Horvat (1999).
48. Carreón et al. (2005).
49. Yosso (2005).
50. See also Lee and Green (2008), Teranishi (2004).
51. Bourdieu and Passeron (1977).
52. See, e.g., Lewis ([1966] 1981).
53. Yosso (2005), Valenzuela (1999).
54. Lopez and Stack (2001), 49.
55. Lopez and Stack (2001).
56. Stanton-Salazar (1997).
57. Carreón et al. (2005), Fine (1993), Graue (1993).

58. Coulthard (2014), Simpson (2014, 2017).
59. Cooper (2009), Lightfoot (2004).
60. Yosso (2005), 80.
61. Yosso (2005), 80.
62. Yosso (2005), 80.

3. BETWEEN INDIVIDUALISM AND COLLECTIVISM

1. Phelan, Davidson, and Yu (1998).
2. Chan (1994), Dunnigan (1982), Keown-Bomar (2004), Koltyk (1998). See chapter 1.
3. Espiritu (2003), Kibria (1993), Zhou and Bankston (1998).
4. Chhuon et al. (2010), Espiritu (2003), Kang et al. (2010), Kibria (1993), Smith-Hefner (1999).
5. Zhou and Bankston (1998), 151.
6. Kibria (1993).
7. Chhuon et al. (2010), Espiritu (2003), Lopez (2003), Orellana (2001), Suárez-Orozco and Qin-Hilliard (2004), Valenzuela (1999).
8. Valenzuela (1999), Waters (1999).
9. Chhuon et al. (2010), Kibria (1993), Ong (2003), Smith-Hefner (1999).
10. See, e.g., Lopez (2003).
11. See, e.g., Lee (2005), Ngo (2008b).
12. Lutz and Jarayam (2015).
13. Hli was unsure of the specifics of her mother's illness. She reported that it prevented her from cooking because of frequent allergic reactions.
14. Portes and Rumbaut (2006).
15. Chan (1994), 125.
16. Yang (2008), 22.
17. Lamborn and Moua (2008) found that Hmong youth understand that their parents love them, and that they convey their love through hard work and providing children with a good life.
18. Chan (1994), Faderman (1998), Supple and Small (2007).
19. Pyke (2000).
20. Supple, McCoy, and Wang (2010).
21. Cf. Lopez (2003), Sarroub (2005).
22. Espiritu (2003), Gibson (1998), Zhou and Bankston (1998), Qin (2006).
23. Bloom (2007), 351.
24. Similarly, other students like Toua reported his grandmother encouraged him to get a job immediately after high school graduation, particularly because she saw his uncles were able to become financially successful (e.g., own a nice, large home and multiple cars) after doing so.
25. Bozick and DeLuca (2005).
26. Haigler and Nelson (2005).
27. See also Tseng (2004).
28. Kang et al. (2010), Suárez-Orozco and Todorova (2003).

29. See, e.g., Espiritu (2003), Lopez (2003), Valenzuela (1999).
30. See also Chhuon et al. (2010).
31. Chhuon et al. (2010), Lopez (2003).
32. Qin (2006).
33. Lee et al. (2009).
34. Toua's mother died a few months after the school year ended.
35. See also Valenzuela (1999).
36. Valenzuela (1999).
37. Chhuon and Wallace (2014).
38. Dunnigan (1982).
39. See, e.g., Symonds (2004).
40. Cha (2003), Symonds (2004).
41. Hughes et al. (2006), Moua and Lamborn (2010), Thao (2016), Xiong, Deenanath, and Mao (2013).
42. Koltyk (1998), Symonds (2004).
43. Koltyk (1998), 86.
44. Koltyk (1998), 52.
45. Koltyk (1998), 52.
46. Conquergood and Thao (1989), 7. See also Cha (2003).
47. Xiong, Deenanath, and Mao (2013).
48. Cha (2003), Symonds (2004).
49. Conquergood and Thao (1989), 45.
50. Conquergood and Thao (1989), 44.
51. Phelan, Davidson, and Yu (1998).
52. Noddings (2005), 69.
53. Noddings (2005).
54. Pang (2005), Valenzuela (1999).
55. Chhuon and Wallace (2014).
56. Ngo (2008a).

4. (RE)STORYTELLING GENDER REPRESENTATIONS

1. Browning and Louwagie (2005), Louwagie and Browning (2005a, 2005b).
2. Anthias and Yuval-Davis (1992), Donald and Rattansi (1994).
3. Espiritu (2006), 422.
4. Coulter (2018).
5. Nelson (2005).
6. Berry (2000), Keenan (2013), Terry et al. (2011).
7. Johnson et al. (2021).
8. Gylys and McNamara (1996), Payne, Lonsway, and Fitzgerald (1999), Stubbs-Richardson, Rader, and Cosby (2018).
9. Campbell et al. (2001), Logan et al. (2005), Maier (2008).
10. Dias and Horowitz (2019).
11. Mettier (2019).
12. Brice-Saddler (2019).

13. Macur (2013).
14. Solomos and Back (1995).
15. Anthias and Yuval-Davis (1992), Blackledge (2003), Donald and Rattansi (1994), Macleod and Durrheim (2002).
16. Blackledge (2003), Donald and Rattansi (1994), Macleod and Durrheim (2002), Solomos and Back (1995).
17. Lowe (1996).
18. Delgado (1989), 240.
19. Browning and Louwagie (2005).
20. See, e.g., K. Yang (2007).
21. Browning and Louwagie (2005).
22. Macleod and Durrheim (2002).
23. Vang, Nibbs, and Vang (2016).
24. Vang, Nibbs, and Vang (2016).
25. I have explored internalized racism among Hmong American youth elsewhere (Ngo 2017).
26. Xiong and Detzner (2005).
27. See, e.g., Koumarn and Barney (1981), Schein (2016).
28. Schein (2016), 253; cf. Lee (2016).
29. "Steve-O" LaTart, "Hmong Parody Song," as reported on MPR (2011).
30. Tang (2015).
31. Hmong National Development Inc. (2011).
32. Driscoll et al. (2017).
33. See, e.g., Louwagie and Browning (2005a, 2005b).
34. Meredith and Rowe (1986).
35. Ngo (2002).
36. Lee, Xiong, and Yuen (2006).
37. See also Donnelly (1994), Evans-Pritchard and Renteln (1994).
38. Ngo (2002).
39. See, e.g., Louwagie and Browning (2005a, 2005).
40. Hutchison and McNall (1994), Lee, Xiong, and Yuen (2006), Meredith and Rowe (1986), Vang and Her (2014).
41. Lee, Xiong, and Yuen (2006).
42. Hutchison and McNall (1994), 588.
43. Evans-Pritchard and Renteln (1994), 14.
44. Evans-Pritchard and Renteln (1994), 15. Evans-Pritchard and Renteln also note that scholars assert that Hmong marriage rituals, such as the tradition of elopement or marriage by capture, have been misinterpreted by the press as kidnapping; see, e.g., Mitchell (1992).
45. Lee, Xiong, and Yuen (2006).
46. Lee, Xiong, and Yuen (2006), 30.
47. Dunnigan (1982), Lee, Xiong, and Yuen (2006), Xiong et al. (2006).
48. Lee, Xiong, and Yuen (2006), Dunnigan (1982).
49. Lee, Xiong, and Yuen (2006), 30.

50. See also Ngo (2002).

51. Hmong staffulty pointed out that the second way Hmong female adolescents leave the restrictive family households is through the pursuit of higher education. See Hli's story in chapter 3.

52. Lee, Xiong, and Yuen (2006), Ngo (2002), Vang and Her (2014).

53. Lee, Xiong, and Yuen (2006), 32. See also Edinburgh, Garcia, and Saewyc (2013), Vang and Her (2014).

54. Scott (1992), 37.

55. Lee, Xiong, and Yuen (2006), Xiong et al. (2006).

56. Donnelly (1994), Dunnigan (1982).

57. Billson (1995), 168. See also Gibson (1998), Kurien (1999), Orsi (1985), Smith-Hefner (1999).

58. Billson (1995), Orsi (1985).

59. Espiritu (2003), 167–68. See also Gibson (1998), Orsi (1985).

60. See also Lee (2001b).

61. Evans-Pritchard and Renteln (1994), Mitchell (1992).

62. Ngo (2002), Vang and Her (2014).

63. Ngo (2002).

64. Espiritu (2003), Lopez (2003), Raffaelli and Ontai (2004), Sarroub (2005), Valenzuela (1999), Waters (1999), Zhou and Bankston (2001).

65. Lee et al. (2009), 551.

66. Coulter (2018).

67. See also Lee (2001b), Xiong, Detzner, and Cleveland (2004–5).

68. Faderman (1998), Xiong and Detzner (2005).

69. Xiong, Detzner, and Cleveland (2004–5).

70. At a Hmong PTO meeting where Dayton High staffulty invited a Harriet City police officer to provide a presentation on youth gangs to Hmong parents, a non-Hmong staffulty announced the presentation was "not meant to scare parents." A Hmong student turned to me and reported that "parents are afraid their children may get killed," so they become "more strict" because "they don't want anything to happen to their children."

71. Sarroub (2005), 26.

72. See also Espiritu (2001), Qin (2006).

73. See, e.g., Espiritu (2003), Gibson (1998), Zhou and Bankston (1998).

74. Donnelly (1994), Lee (2001a).

75. Donnelly (1994), Dunnigan (1982), Lee, Xiong, and Yuen (2006).

76. I suggest Kajua's use of "traditional" and "modern" to describe Hmong parents draws on hegemonic discourses.

77. Lee (1997).

78. Vang and Her (2014), 139; see also Lee, Xiong, and Yuen (2006).

79. See, e.g., Browning and Louwagie (2005), Louwagie and Browning (2005a, 2005b).

80. Blackledge (2003).

81. Uecker and Stokes (2008).

82. Axinn and Thornton (1992).
83. Thornton (1991).
84. Glick et al. (2006), Teachman, Tedrow, and Crowder (2000).
85. Driscoll et al. (2017).
86. Lee, Xiong, and Yuen (2006).
87. Xiong, Detzner, and Cleveland (2004–5).
88. Ngo (2002), Vang and Her (2014).

5. RE-MEMBERING CULTURE IN HMONG CLUB

1. Auer (2010, 2013).
2. Fishman (1991), Portes and Hao (1998).
3. Shannon (1995), 175.
4. Portes and Hao (1998).
5. Fishman (1966, 1981).
6. Fishman (1991).
7. Wiley (2001).
8. The joke parodied the pronunciation of "oil" as "oy" by a Hmong mother.
9. Hmong students referred to white students as Americans.
10. Corntassel (2012), Coulthard (2007).
11. Hall ([1990] 1994), 200.
12. Hall ([1990] 1994), 200. See also Gilroy (1994).
13. See Ngo and Lee (2007).
14. Gutmann (1994).
15. Taylor ([1992] 1997), 26.
16. Fraser and Honneth (2003), 29.
17. Fraser and Honneth (2003), 29.
18. Huttunen (2007).
19. Fraser and Honneth (2003), 29.
20. Lee (2005), 54.
21. Pyke and Dang (2003), Trieu and Lee (2018).
22. Du Bois ([1903] 1989), 3.
23. Fanon ([1952] 2008).
24. Fanon ([1952] 2008).
25. Osajima (1993).
26. Osajima (1993), Pyke and Dang (2003), Trieu and Lee (2018).
27. The English alphabet spelling of "Hmong" represented the Americanized Hmong community, while the Romananized Popular Alphabet spelling "Hmoob" represented the traditional Hmong community.
28. Cha (2003), Conquergood (1989), Mottin (1984).
29. Cha (2003), Conquergood (1989), Mottin (1984), Tapp (1989).
30. Mottin (1984).
31. Cha (2003), Conquergood (1989), Mottin (1984), Tapp (1989).
32. Tapp (1989), 73.
33. Pyke and Dang (2003).

34. Phenice, Martinez, and Grant (1986), 122.
35. Yang (1998), which reviews Fadiman (1997).
36. Yang (1998), 6.
37. Conquergood (1989), 7. See also Cha (2003).
38. Conquergood (1989), 7.
39. Goodwin (2010).
40. Fanon ([1952] 2008).
41. Perry (2001).
42. Conquergood (1989), 8.
43. Dixson and Rousseau (2005), Ngo (2010), Park (2011).
44. Banks (2001).
45. Dayton High School's multicultural festival was viewed as an exemplar of multiculturalism within the district. During the time of the study, at least one student and staffulty group from another high school attended the festival to learn about it so that they might replicate it.
46. Ladson-Billings (2004).
47. Banks (2001), Mohanty (1984).
48. Banks (2001), Dixson and Rousseau (2005), Meyer and Rhoades (2006), Park (2011).
49. Dao (1992), 300.
50. Yang (2007).
51. Dao (1992), 301.
52. Dao (1992), Hillmer (2010), Yang (2007).
53. Moua and Lamborn (2010).
54. G. Y. Lee (2008).
55. Lynch, Detzner, and Eicher (1996), 116–17.
56. G. Y. Lee (2008), Lynch, Detzner, and Eicher (1996).
57. Dao (1992), 300.
58. See also G. Y. Lee (2008).
59. Kumashiro (2000), 31.
60. Ladson-Billings (1995, 2006).
61. See, e.g., Park (2011).
62. Corntassel (2012), Coultard (2007, 2014).
63. Chang and Aoki (1997), 1399.
64. See, e.g., Chang and Aoki (1997), Lee (1999), Tuan (1998).
65. El-Haj (2015), Tang (2015).
66. Chang and Aoki (1997), Lee (1999), Lowe (1996), Takaki (1989).
67. Barth (1969), Lamont (2009).
68. Carter (2007), Warikoo (2007).
69. Corntassel (2012), Coultard (2007, 2014).
70. Hall (1995), 200.
71. Espiritu (1992).
72. Rose (1995).
73. Hall (1995), 182, original emphasis.

74. Massey and Jess (1995), 233.
75. Hall (1995), 200.
76. Barth (1969), Gilroy (1994), Hall (1995).
77. See, e.g., Jaret (1999), Maira (2008), Ngo (2017).
78. González, Moll, and Amanti (2005), Valenzuela (1999).
79. Fraser and Honneth (2003).
80. Hall (1986), 26.
81. hooks (1990), 42.
82. Fraser and Honneth (2003).
83. Trask (1999), 142.
84. wa Thiong'o (2012).

6. REFUSING THE NEUTRALITY OF SCHOOL

1. This study commenced at the beginning of this new academic year, the first year of Deborah Finch's superintendency.
2. Barth (1969), 14–15.
3. Nagel (1994), Olzak (1983).
4. S. S. Lee (2008), Takagi (1992).
5. Cabrera et al. (2013), Otero and Cammarota (2011).
6. Canon and Posner (1999), Lublin (1999).
7. Lee (1993).
8. Spivak ([1985] 1996).
9. In addition to the Hmong community forum, Superintendent Finch met with various groups, including the African American and Latinx American communities as well as teacher educators.
10. The opportunity for a Q&A with Superintendent Finch was significant because the Latinx American community was not given the chance to ask her questions.
11. At the end of the meeting, twenty index cards were handed in to Shoua Her.
12. Johnson (2007), 50. See also Khalifa et al. (2016).
13. Ainscow (2005), Khalifa (2013), Johnson (2006, 2007).
14. Superintendent Finch planned to name two additional senior leadership team members: a chief accountability officer and a special assistant.
15. KaBao, Hmong student leader's presentation of the petition to the Harriet City Public Schools Board of Education.
16. See, e.g., Browning and Louwagie (2005), Coulter (2018), Louwagie and Browning (2005a, 2005b).
17. See Milner (2006), Philip (2011, 2014).
18. See Gay (2018), Johnson (2006, 2007), Khalifa et al. (2016), Ladson-Billings (1995).
19. Cf. Dee (2004).
20. Bower-Phipps et al. (2013), Cabrera-Duran (2016), Kelly and McCann (2014).
21. Dayton High School's white male principal was leaving the district for a position as principal at a middle school in a suburban school district.
22. Deal and Peterson (1999), Murakami-Ramalho (2010).
23. Cole (2008), Davis and Martinez (1994), Matsuda (1990).

24. Sautman (2014).
25. Simpson (2017), 26.
26. Simpson (2017), 26.
27. Fraser and Honneth (2003).
28. Cf. Deyhle (1995).
29. Khalifa et al. (2016), 1290.

CONCLUSION

1. Moua (2007a).
2. Binkley (2011), Moua (2007b).
3. Brody (2007).
4. Rauhala (2011).
5. Moua (2007b).
6. Moua (2007b).
7. Moua (2007b).
8. Jones (2007).
9. Hamilton-Merritt (1993), xviii.
10. For example, Hamilton-Merritt witnessed at Ban Vinai camp "bulldozers [climbing] the hill behind the refugee huts to the Hmong burial grounds, ripping out fresh bodies of the dead, children bloating and crying from starvation, and Hmong forced to grow vegetables on top of graves." Hamilton-Merritt (1993), 473–74.
11. Jones (2007), Vang (2021).
12. See also Hamilton-Merritt (1993), Hillmer (2011).
13. wa Thiong'o (2009), 3–4.
14. Frank (2011). Frank also reported the federal government dropped its case against General Vang Pao in September 2009, and all other cases were dropped in January 2011.
15. Frank (2011).
16. The U.S. Patriot Act was authored by Viet D. Dinh, a Vietnamese refugee born in Saigon, South Vietnam.
17. Vezner (2007), VOA (2007).
18. Vezner (2007), VOA (2007).
19. wa Thiong'o (2009).
20. Davey (2007).
21. In contrast, one publication reported, "Xang Vang (no relation), one of the General's closest advisors, was encouraged by the show of support [at a courthouse rally], 'especially among the youth who have never shown much interest for General Vang Pao in the past.'" Moua (2007a).
22. See, e.g., Binkley (2011), Fontana and Tavlian (2011), Memmott (2011), MPR (2011).
23. Valenzuela (1999), 20.
24. Spring (2016).
25. Deyhle (1995), 409.
26. McGranahan (2016), 323.

27. Wu (2007), 234. See also James (1987).
28. James (1987).
29. Bear et al. (2019), Haag (2007), Nagata, Trierweiler, and Talbot (1999).
30. Ishimaru and Takahashi (2017), Khalifa and Abdi (2023).
31. Khalifa and Abdi (2023), 118.
32. Fishman (1991), 4.
33. Ladson-Billings (1995).
34. Gay (2018).
35. Paris and Alim (2014).
36. Kirkland (2021); see also Vasquez (2021).
37. Kirkland (2021), 65–66.
38. Quijano (2007), 172.
39. Lopez (1976), 237.
40. Spring (2016).
41. Butler (2004), 20.
42. Espiritu (1992).
43. Kwan (2020), Lamborn and Moua (2008), Ng (1993).
44. Domínguez (2019, 2021), Kerr (2014).
45. Grande (2015), Paraskeva (2016).
46. Domínguez (2021).
47. Macedo, Dendrinos, and Gounari (2015).
48. Macedo (2019).
49. Kana'iaupuni (2005), Patel (2014), Scheurich and Young (1997).
50. Bang (2017), 117.
51. Morrison (1998).
52. Mignolo (2009), 161; see also Mignolo (2000, 2007), Quijano (2000, 2007).
53. Smith (2012), 66.
54. Yang (2012), emphasis added.
55. Lapin (2012b). Dean Cappello, NPR's (WNYC) senior vice president of programming, made this statement in response to Kao Kalia Yang.
56. Hillmer and Yang (2017), Yang (2012).
57. In Krulwich's nonapology to Kao Kalia Yang and Eng Yang, he maintained that the truth was of utmost importance to him. See Lapin (2012a).
58. Yang (2012).
59. Yang (2012).
60. Quijano (2000).

Bibliography

Adichie, C. N. 2009. "The Danger of a Single Story." TED Talk, July 2009. https://www.ted.com/talks/chimamanda_ngozi_adichie_the_danger_of_a_single_story/c/transcript.

Ainscow, M. 2005. "Developing Inclusive Education Systems: What Are the Levers for Change?" *Journal of Educational Change* 6:109–24. https://doi.org/10.1007/s10833-005-1298-4.

Alfred, T., and J. Corntassel. 2005. "Being Indigenous: Resurgences against Contemporary Colonialism." *Government and Opposition* 40 (4): 597–614.

An, S. 2017. "Teaching Race through AsianCrit-Informed Counterstories of School Segregation." *Social Studies Research and Practice* 12 (2): 210–31. https://doi.org/10.1108/SSRP-05-2017-0023.

Anguiano, D. 2021. "'I Don't Believe Anyone Is Safe': Drought Rules Spark Accusations of Racism in California Outpost." *Guardian*, August 21, 2021. https://www.theguardian.com/us-news/2021/aug/21/california-drought-hmong-americans-race-water.

Anthias, F., and N. Yuval-Davis. 1992. *Racialized Boundaries: Race, Nation, Gender, Colour and Class and the Anti-racist Struggle.* New York: Routledge.

Appiah, K. A. 2007. *The Ethics of Identity.* Princeton, N.J.: Princeton University Press.

Apple, M. W. 1996. *Cultural Politics and Education.* New York: Routledge.

Associated Press. 2004. "Bumper Sticker Advocates Anti-Hmong Violence." *NBC News*, December 14, 2004. https://www.nbcnews.com/id/wbna6709956#.XqsWOC2ZPUp.

Associated Press. 2021. "Judge: California County Can't Ban Water Delivery to Hmong Pot Farmer." *Business Journal*, September 9, 2021. https://thebusinessjournal.com/judge-county-cant-ban-water-delivery-to-hmong-pot-farmers/.

Associated Press. 2023. "Family: Man Shot by Police Couldn't Hear, Speak English." *U.S. News and World Report*, February 18, 2023. https://www.usnews.com/news/best-states/minnesota/articles/2023-02-18/family-man-shot-by-police-couldnt-hear-speak-english.

Auer, P. 2010. "Code-Switching/Mixing." In *The Sage Handbook of Sociolinguistics,* edited by R. Wodak, B. Johnstone, and P. E. Kerswill, 460–78. Thousand Oaks, Calif.: Sage.

Auer, P., ed. 2013. *Code-Switching in Conversation: Language, Interaction, and Identity.* New York: Routledge.

Axinn, W. G., and A. Thornton. 1992. "The Influence of Parental Resources on the Timing of the Transition to Marriage." *Social Science Research* 21 (3): 261–85.

Baldillo, A. J., J. Mendy, and V. A. Eng. 2005. "Save a Hunter, Shoot a Hmong." *Modern American* 1 (1): 2.

Bang, M. 2017. "Towards an Ethic of Decolonial Trans-ontologies in Sociocultural Theories of Learning and Development." In *Power and Privilege in the Learning Sciences: Critical and Sociocultural Theories of Learning,* edited by I. Esmonde and A. N. Booker, 115–38. New York: Routledge.

Banks, J. A. 2001. "Multicultural Education: Characteristics and Goals." In *Multicultural Education,* 4th ed., edited by J. Banks and C. McGee Banks, 3–30. New York: Wiley.

Barth, F., ed. 1969. Introduction to *Ethnic Groups and Boundaries: The Social Organization of Culture Difference,* 9–38. Long Grove, Ill.: Waveland.

Baumann, G. 1996. *Contesting Culture: Discourses of Identity in Multi-ethnic London.* Cambridge: Cambridge University Press.

Bear, U. R., Z. M. Thayer, C. D. Croy, C. E. Kaufman, S. M. Manson, and the AI-SUPERPFP Team. 2019. "The Impact of Individual and Parental American Indian Boarding School Attendance on Chronic Physical Health of Northern Plains Tribes." *Family and Community Health* 42 (1): 1–7. https://doi.org/10.1097/fch.0000000000000205.

Bell, D. 1990. *Rutgers Louis Law Review* 1.

Bernstein, M. 2005. "Identity Politics." *Annual Review of Sociology* 31:47–74.

Berry, J. 2000. *Lead Us Not into Temptation: Catholic Priests and the Sexual Abuse of Children.* Champaign: University of Illinois Press.

Bhabha, H. 1990. "The Third Space: Interview with Homi Bhabha." In *Identity: Community, Culture, Difference,* edited by J. Rutherford, 207–21. London: Lawrence & Wishart.

Bhabha, H. 1999. "Staging the Politics of Difference." In *Race, Rhetoric, and the Postcolonial,* edited by G. Olson and L. Worsham, 3–39. Albany, N.Y.: SUNY Press.

Billson, J. M. 1995. *Keepers of the Culture: The Power of Tradition in Women's Lives.* San Francisco: Jossey-Bass.

Binkley, M. 2011. "Minn. Hmong Community Mourns General's Death." *CBS News,* January 11, 2011. https://www.cbsnews.com/minnesota/news/minn-hmong-community-mourns-generals-death/.

Blackledge, A. 2003. "Imagining a Monocultural Community: Racialization of Cultural Practice in Educational Discourse." *Journal of Language, Identity, and Education* 2 (4): 331–47.

Bliatout, B. 1982. *Hmong Sudden Unexpected Nocturnal Death Syndrome.* Portland, Ore.: Sparkle.

Bliatout, B. T., B. Downing, J. Lewis, and D. Yang. 1988. *Handbook for Teaching Hmong-Speaking Students.* Folsom, Calif.: Folsom Cordova Unified School District, Southeast Asia Community Resource Center.

Bloom, J. L. 2007. "(Mis)reading Social Class in the Journey towards College: Youth Development in Urban America." *Teachers College Record* 109:343–68.

Blum, L. 2022. "Neoliberalism and Education." In *Handbook of Philosophy of Education,* edited by R. Curren, 257–69. New York: Routledge.

Bourdieu, P. 1977. "Cultural Reproduction and Social Reproduction." In *Power and Ideology in Education,* edited by I. Karabel and A. H. Halsey, 487–511. Oxford: Oxford University Press.

Bourdieu, P. 1986. "The Forms of Capital." In *The Handbook of Theory and Research in the Sociology of Education,* edited by J. Richardson, 241–58. Westport, Conn.: Greenwood Press.

Bourdieu, P., and J.-C. Passeron. 1977. *Reproduction in Education and Society.* Thousand Oaks, Calif.: Sage.

Bower-Phipps, L., R. W. Tate, S. Mehta, and A. L. Sature. 2013. "Everyone Has a Story: A Collaborative Inquiry Project by Five Teacher Candidates of Color and One White Professor." *Current Issues in Education* 16 (1). https://cie.asu.edu/ojs/index.php/cieatasu/article/view/1074.

Bozick, R., and S. DeLuca. 2005. "Better Late than Never? Delayed Enrollment in the High School to College Transition." *Social Forces* 84:527–50.

Brah, A. 1987. "Women of South Asian Origin in Britain." *South Asia Research* 7 (1): 39–54.

Brice-Saddler, M. 2019. "'Close Your Legs'? Judge May Be Suspended over Questions He Asked an Alleged Rape Survivor." *Washington Post,* April 4, 2019. https://www.washingtonpost.com/nation/2019/04/05/close-your-legs-judge-may-be-suspended-over-questions-he-asked-an-alleged-rape-victim/.

Brody, J. 2007. "Betraying an Old Friend." *Los Angeles Times,* June 18, 2007.

Browning, D., and P. Louwagie. 2005. "Shamed into Silence: In This World, There Are No Easy Cases." *Star Tribune.*

Buffamonte, S. 2017. "Speaking Out against Hate toward the Hmong Community." *WSAW-TV,* March 13, 2017. https://www.wsaw.com/content/news/Speaking-out-against-hate-toward-the-Hmong-Community--416087443.html.

Bustamante, R. M., J. A. Nelson, and A. J. Onwuegbuzie. 2009. "Assessing Schoolwide Cultural Competence: Implications for School Leadership Preparation." *Educational Administration Quarterly* 45 (5): 793–827.

Butler, J. 2004. *Precarious Life: The Powers of Mourning and Violence.* London: Verso.

Cabrera, N. L., E. L. Meza, A. J. Romero, and R. C. Rodríguez. 2013. "'If There Is No Struggle, There Is No Progress': Transformative Youth Activism and the School of Ethnic Studies." *Urban Review* 45 (1): 7–22.

Cabrera-Duran, E. 2016. "More than Numbers: Recruitment and Retention of Teachers of Color in U.S. Public Schools." *CritEdPol: Journal of Critical Education Policy Studies at Swarthmore College* 1 (1): 39–52.

Calabrese Barton, A., C. Drake, J. G. Perez, K. St. Louis, and M. George. 2004. "Ecologies of Parental Engagement in Urban Education." *Educational Researcher* 33 (4): 3–12.

Campbell, R., S. M. Wasco, C. E. Ahrens, T. Sefl, and H. E. Barnes. 2001. "Preventing the 'Second Rape' Rape Survivors' Experiences with Community Service Providers." *Journal of Interpersonal Violence* 16 (12): 1239–59.

Canon, D. T., and R. A. Posner. 1999. *Race, Redistricting, and Representation: The Unintended Consequences of Black Majority Districts.* Chicago: University of Chicago Press.

Carreón, G. P., C. Drake, and A. C. Barton. 2005. "The Importance of Presence: Immigrant Parents' School Engagement Experiences." *American Educational Research Journal* 42 (3): 465–98.

Carter, D. F., A. M. Locks, and R. Winkle-Wagner. 2013. "From When and Where I Enter: Theoretical and Empirical Considerations of Minority Students' Transition to College." In *Higher Education: Handbook of Theory and Research,* 93–149. Dordrecht: Springer.

Carter, P. 2003. "'Black' Cultural Capital, Status Positioning, and Schooling Conflicts." *Social Problems* 50 (1): 136–55.

Carter, P. 2007. "Straddling Boundaries: Identity, Culture, and School." *Sociology of Education* 79 (4): 304–28.

Cha, D. 2003. *Hmong American Concepts of Health.* New York: Routledge.

Chan, L. 2021. "Hmong Americans Protest Deputy Shooting Death of Farmer." *AsAmNews,* July 17, 2021. https://asamnews.com/2021/07/17/hmong-farmers-say-firefighters-left-their-properties-largely-unprotected-during-the-recent-lava-fire/.

Chan, S., ed. 1994. *Hmong Means Free: Life in Laos and America.* Philadelphia: Temple University Press.

Chandler, K. L. 2018. "I ulu no ka lālā i ke kumu, the Branches Grow Because of the Trunk: Ancestral Knowledge as Refusal." *International Journal of Qualitative Studies in Education* 31 (3): 177–87. https://doi.org/10.1080/09518398.2017.1401146.

Chang, R. S., and K. Aoki. 1997. "Centering the Immigrant in the Inter/national Imagination." *California Law Review* 85:1395–447.

Chhuon, V., C. Hudley, M. E. Brenner, and R. Macias. 2010. "The Multiple Worlds of Successful Cambodian American Students." *Urban Education* 45 (1): 30–35.

Chhuon, V., and T. L. Wallace. 2014. "Creating Connectedness through Being Known: Fulfilling the Need to Belong in U.S. High Schools." *Youth and Society* 46 (3): 379–401.

Chiu, M. 2004. "Medical, Racist, and Colonial Constructions of Power: Creating the Asian American Patient and the Cultural Citizen in Anne Fadiman's *The Spirit Catches You and You Fall Down.*" *Hmong Studies Journal* 5:1–36.

Cho, G. 2000. "The Role of Heritage Language in Social Interactions and Relationships: Reflections from a Language Minority Group." *Bilingual Research Journal* 24 (4): 369–84.

Cho, H. 2017. "Racism and Linguicism: Engaging Language Minority Pre-service Teachers in Counter-storytelling." *Race, Ethnicity, and Education* 20 (5): 666–80.

Cocca, C. E. 2002. "From 'Welfare Queen' to 'Exploited Teen': Welfare Dependency, Statutory Rape, and Moral Panic." *NWSA Journal* 14 (2): 56–79.

Cole, E. R. 2008. "Coalitions as a Model for Intersectionality: From Practice to Theory." *Sex Roles* 59 (5–6): 443–53.

Collins, B. 2011. "Radio Stations Hmong Parody Sparks Backlash." *MPR News,* March 30, 2011. https://blogs.mprnews.org/newscut/2011/03/radio_station_hmong_parody_spa/.

Conchas, G. Q. 2006. *The Color of Success: Race and High-Achieving Urban Youth.* New York: Teachers College Press.

Conquergood, D. 1989. "Establishing the World: Hmong Shamans." *CURA Reporter* 19:5–9.

Conquergood, D., and P. Thao. 1989. *I Am a Shaman: A Hmong Life Story with Ethnographic Commentary.* Minneapolis: Southeast Asian Refugee Studies.

Cook, D. A., and A. D. Dixson. 2013. "Writing Critical Race Theory and Method: A Composite Counterstory on the Experiences of Black Teachers in New Orleans Post-Katrina." *International Journal of Qualitative Studies in Education* 26 (10): 1238–58.

Cooper, C. W. 2009. "Parent Involvement, African American Mothers, and the Politics of Educational Care." *Equity and Excellence in Education* 42 (4): 379–94.

Corntassel, J. 2012. "Re-envisioning Resurgence: Indigenous Pathways to Decolonization and Sustainable Self-Determination." *Decolonization* 1 (1): 86–101.

Corntassel, J., and T. Hardbarger. 2019. "Educate to Perpetuate: Land-Based Pedagogies and Community Resurgence." *International Review of Education* 65 (1): 87–116.

Corrigan, M. E. 2003. "Beyond Access: Persistence Challenges and the Diversity of Low-Income Students." *New Directions for Higher Education* 121:25–34.

Coulter, A. 2018. "Country Overboard! Women and Children Last!" Ann Coulter (blog), June 27, 2018. https://anncoulter.com/.

Coulthard, G. S. 2007. "Subjects of Empire: Indigenous Peoples and the 'Politics of Recognition' in Canada." *Contemporary Political Theory* 6:437–60.

Coulthard, G. S. 2014. *Red Skin, White Masks: Rejecting the Colonial Politics of Recognition.* Minneapolis: University of Minnesota Press.

Crann, T., N. Bui, and S. Stroozas. 2023. "Weeks after St. Paul Police Shot and Killed Yia Xiong, Community Members Ask for More Action." *MPR News,* March 7, 2023. https://www.mprnews.org/story/2023/03/07/weeks-after-st-paul-police-shot-and-killed-yia-xiong-community-members-ask-for-more-action.

Cummins, J. 1986. "Empowering Minority Students: A Framework for Intervention." *Harvard Educational Review* 56:18–36.

Dao, Y. 1992. "The Hmong: Enduring Traditions." In *Minority Cultures of Laos: Kammu, Lua, Hmong, and Iu-Mien,* edited by J. Lewis, 249–327. Rancho Cordova, Calif.: Southeast Asia Community Resource Center–Folsom Cordova Unified School District.

Davey, M. 2007. "Arrest Uncovers Divide in Hmong-Americans." *New York Times,* June 14, 2007. https://www.nytimes.com/2007/06/14/us/14hmong.html.

Davies, B., and P. Bansel. 2007. "Neoliberalism and Education." *International Journal of Qualitative Studies in Education* 20 (3): 247–59.

Davis, A., and E. Martinez. 1994. "Coalition Building among People of Color." *Inscriptions* 7:42–53.

Deal, T. E., and K. D. Peterson. 1999. *Shaping School Culture: The Heart of Leadership.* San Francisco: Jossey-Bass.

DeCuir, J. T., and A. D. Dixson. 2004. "'So When It Comes Out, They Aren't That Surprised that It Is There': Using Critical Race Theory as a Tool of Analysis of Race and Racism in Education." *Educational Researcher* 33 (5): 26–31.

Dee, T. S. 2004. "The Race Connection: Are Teachers More Effective with Students Who Share Their Ethnicity?" *Education Next* 4 (2): 52–59.

Delgado, R. 1989. "Storytelling for Oppositionists and Others: A Plea for Narrative." *Michigan Law Review* 87 (8): 2411–41.

Delgado, R., and J. Stefancic. 2001. *Critical Race Theory: An Introduction.* New York: New York University Press.

Delgado-Gaitan, C. 1990. *Literacy for Empowerment: The Role of Parents in Children's Education.* New York: Routledge.

Delgado-Gaitan, C. 1992. "School Matters in the Mexican-American Home: Socializing Children to Education." *American Educational Research Journal* 29 (3): 495–513.

Delgado-Gaitan, C. 2001. *The Power of Community: Mobilizing for Family and Schooling—Immigration and the Transnational Experience.* Lanham, Md.: Rowman & Littlefield.

Delpit, L. 1988. "The Silenced Dialogue: Power and Pedagogy in Educating Other People's Children." *Harvard Educational Review* 58 (3): 280–99. https://doi.org/10.17763/haer.58.3.c43481778r528qw4.

Denzin, N., and Y. Lincoln, eds. 2000. *The Handbook of Qualitative Research.* 3rd ed. Thousand Oaks, Calif.: Sage.

DePouw, C. 2012. "When Culture Implies Deficit: Placing Race at the Center of Hmong American Education." *Race Ethnicity and Education* 15 (2): 223–39.

Deyhle, D. 1995. "Navajo Youth and Anglo Racism: Cultural Integrity and Resistance." *Harvard Educational Review* 65:403–44.

Dias, E., and J. Horowitz. 2019. "Pope Defrocks Theodore McCarrick, Ex-Cardinal Accused of Sexual Abuse." *New York Times,* February 16, 2019. https://www.nytimes.com/2019/02/16/us/mccarrick-defrocked-vatican.html.

Dillard, C. B. 2008. "Re-membering Culture: Bearing Witness to the Spirit of Identity in Research." *Race, Ethnicity, and Education* 11 (1): 87–93.

Dillard, C. B. 2020. "(Re)membering Blackness, (Re)membering Home: Lessons for Teachers from a Primary School in Ghana, West Africa." *International Journal of Qualitative Studies in Education* 33 (7): 698–708.

DiMaggio, P. 1982. "Cultural Capital and School Success: The Impact of Status Culture Participation on the Grades of U.S. High School Students." *American Sociological Review* 9 (1): 189–201. https://doi.org/10.1177/1097184X04271387.

Dixson, A. D., and C. K. Rousseau. 2005. "And We Are Still Not Saved: Critical Race Theory in Education Ten Years Later." *Race, Ethnicity, and Education* 8 (1): 7–27.

Domínguez, M. 2019. "Decolonial Innovation in Teacher Development: Praxis beyond the Colonial Zero-Point." *Journal of Education for Teaching* 45 (1): 47–62.

Domínguez, M. 2021. "Cultivating Epistemic Disobedience: Exploring the Possibilities of a Decolonial Practice-Based Teacher Education." *Journal of Teacher Education* 72 (5): 551–63. https://doi.org/10.1177/0022487120978152.

Donald, J., and A. Rattansi. 1994. *"Race," Culture, and Difference*. Thousand Oaks, Calif.: Sage.

Donnelly, N. 1994. *Changing Lives of Refugee Hmong Women*. Seattle: University of Washington Press.

Doucet, F. 2008. "How African American Parents Understand Their and Teachers' Roles in Children's Schooling and What This Means for Preparing Preservice Teachers." *Journal of Early Childhood Teacher Education* 29 (2): 108–39.

Doucet, F. 2011. "Parent Involvement as Ritualized Practice." *Anthropology and Education Quarterly* 42 (4): 404–21.

Driscoll A. K., B. E. Hamilton, S. C. Curtin, et al. 2017. "Births and Birth Rates for Unmarried Women: United States, Selected Years, 1940–2015." Hyattesville, Md.: National Center for Health Statistics.

Du Bois, W. E. B. (1903) 1989. *The Souls of Black Folk*. New York: Penguin.

Dublin, T. 1996. *Becoming American, Becoming Ethnic: College Students Explore Their Roots*. Philadelphia, Pa.: Temple University Press.

Dunnigan, T. 1982. "Segmentary Kinship in an Urban Society: The Hmong of St. Paul–Minneapolis." *Anthropological Quarterly* 55 (3): 126–34. https://doi.org/10.2307/3318022.

Eckes, S. 2015. "Haven Charter Schools: Separate by Design and Legally Questionable." *Equity and Excellence in Education* 48 (1): 49–70.

Edinburgh, L. D., C. M. Garcia, and E. M. Saewyc. 2013. "It's Called 'Going Out to Play': A Video Diary Study of Hmong Girls' Perspectives on Running Away." *Health Care for Women International* 34 (2): 150–68.

El-Haj, Thea Renda Abu. 2015. *Unsettled Belonging: Educating Palestinian American Youth after 9/11*. Chicago: University of Chicago Press.

Emerson, R., R. Fretz, and L. Shaw. 1998. *Writing Ethnographic Fieldnotes*. Chicago: University of Chicago Press.

Erickson, F. D. 1987. "Transformation and School Success: The Politics and Culture of Educational Achievement." *Anthropology and Education Quarterly* 18 (4): 335–56.

Erickson, F. D., and Mohatt, G. 1982. "Cultural Organization of Participation Structures in Two Classrooms of Indian Students." In *Doing the Ethnography of Schooling*, edited by G. D. Spindler, 32–175. New York: Holt, Rinehart and Winston.

Espiritu, Y. L. 2003. *Home Bound: Filipino American Lives across Cultures, Communities, and Countries*. Berkeley: University of California Press.

Espiritu, Y. L. 2006. "Toward a Critical Refugee Study: The Vietnamese Refugee Subject in U.S. Scholarship." *Journal of Vietnamese Studies* 1 (1–2): 410–33.

Espiritu, Y. L. 2021. "Introduction: Critical Refugee Studies and Asian American Studies." *Amerasia Journal* 47 (1): 2–7.

Evans-Pritchard, D., and A. Renteln. 1994. "The Interpretation and Distortion of Culture: Hmong Marriage by Capture Case in Fresno, California." *Southern California Interdisciplinary Law Journal* 4 (1): 1–48.

Faderman, L., with G. Xiong. 1999. *I Begin My Life All Over: The Hmong and the American Immigrant Experience.* Boston: Beacon.

Fadiman, A. 1997. *The Spirit Catches You and You Fall Down: A Hmong Child, Her American Doctors, and the Collision of Two Cultures.* New York: Farrar, Straus & Giroux.

Faircloth, R., and J. Libor. 2022. "Family, Community Leaders Question Why Police Fired So Many Shots, Killing Man during Confrontation." *Star Tribune,* December 18, 2019. https://www.startribune.com/family-community-leaders-question-why-police-fired-so-many-shots-killing-man-during-confrontation/566275072/.

Fan, S. S.-W. 1997. "Immigration Law and the Promise of Critical Race Theory: Opening the Academy to the Voices of Aliens and Immigrants." *Columbia Law Review* 97 (4): 1202–40.

Frank, T. A. 2011. "A Strange Hmong Terrorism Trial." *New Republic,* February 9, 2011. https://newrepublic.com/article/83133/hmong-terrorism-trial.

Fanon, F. (1952) 2008. *Black Skin, White Masks.* New York: Grove.

Fetterman, D. 1998. *Ethnography: Step-by-Step.* 2nd ed. Thousand Oaks, Calif.: Sage.

Fine, M. 1993. "[Ap]parent Involvement: Reflections on Parents, Power, and Urban Public Schools." *Teachers College Record* 94 (4): 1–19. https://doi.org/10.1177/016146819309400402.

Fishman, J. A. 1966. "Language Maintenance and Language Shift: The American Immigrant Case within a General Theoretical Perspective." *Sociologus* 16:19–39.

Fishman, J. A. 1991. *Reversing Language Shift: Theoretical and Empirical Foundations of Assistance to Threatened Languages.* Philadelphia: Multilingual Matters.

Fontana, C., and A. Tavlian. 2011. "Gen. Vang Pao Led Hmong as 'Great Man, True Warrior.'" *Fresno (Calif.) Bee,* January 6, 2011. https://www.fresnobee.com/news/local/community/clovis-news/article19508718.html.

Fordham, S. 1996. *Blacked Out.* Chicago: University of Chicago Press.

Fordham, S., and J. Ogbu. 1986. "Black Students' School Success: Coping with the 'Burden of Acting White.'" *Urban Review* 18:176–206.

Fraise, N. J., and J. S. Brooks. 2015. "Toward a Theory of Culturally Relevant Leadership for School–Community Culture." *International Journal of Multicultural Education* 17 (1): 6–21.

Fraser, N., and A. Honneth. 2003. *Redistribution or Recognition? A Political-Philosophical Exchange.* London: Verso.

Fuller, T. 2007. "A Desperate Life for Survivors of the Secret War in Laos." *New York Times,* December 16, 2007. https://www.nytimes.com/2007/12/16/world/asia/16iht-laos.1.8763976.html.

Gardner, R. P., S. L. Osorio, S. Carrillo, and R. Gilmore. 2020. "(Re)membering in the Pedagogical Work of Black and Brown Teachers: Reclaiming Stories as Culturally Sustaining Practice." *Urban Education* 55 (6): 838–64.

Garza, A. V., and L. Crawford. 2005. "Hegemonic Multiculturalism: English Immersion, Ideology, and Subtractive Schooling." *Bilingual Research Journal* 29 (3): 599–619.

Gay, G. 2018. *Culturally Responsive Teaching: Theory, Research, and Practice.* New York: Teachers College Press.

Gibson, M. 1993. "The School Performance of Immigrant Minorities: A Comparative View." In *Minority Education: Anthropological Perspectives,* edited by E. Jacob and C. Jordan. New York: Ablex.

Gibson, M. A. 1998. "Promoting Academic Success among Immigrant Students: Is Acculturation the Issue?" *Educational Policy* 12 (6): 615–33.

Gilroy, P. 1994. *The Black Atlantic: Modernity and Double Consciousness.* London: Verso.

Giroux, H. A. 1993. "Living Dangerously: Identity Politics and the New Cultural Racism: Towards a Critical Pedagogy of Representation." *Cultural Studies* 7 (1): 1–27.

Glick, J. E., S. D. Ruf, M. J. White, and F. Goldscheider. 2006. "Educational Engagement and Early Family Formation: Differences by Ethnicity and Generation." *Social Forces* 84 (3): 1391–415.

Goldstein, B. L. 1988. "In Search of Survival: The Education and Integration of Hmong Refugee Girls." *Journal of Ethnic Studies* 16 (2): 1–28.

Gonzales, L. D., and H. Shotton. 2022. "Coalitional Refusal in a Neoliberal Academy." *International Journal of Qualitative Studies in Education* 35 (5): 540–52.

González, N., L. Moll, and C. Amanti. 2005. *Funds of Knowledge.* Mahwah, N.J.: Lawrence Erlbaum.

Goodwin, A. L. 2010. "Curriculum as Colonizer: (Asian) American Education in the Current U.S. Context." *Teachers College Record* 112 (12): 3102–38.

Grande, S. 2015. *Red Pedagogy: Native American Social and Political Thought.* Lanham, Md.: Rowman & Littlefield.

Grande, S. 2018. "Refusing the University." In *Toward What Justice? Describing Diverse Dreams of Justice in Education,* edited by E. Tuck and K. W. Yang, 47–65. New York: Routledge.

Graue, M. E. 1993. "Social Networks and Home–School Relations." *Educational Policy* 7 (4): 466–90.

Graue, M. E., J. Kroeger, and D. Prager. 2001. "A Bakhtinian Analysis of Particular Home–School Relations." *American Educational Research Journal* 38 (3): 467–98.

Green, K. R., and S. Reder. 1986. "Factors in Individual Acquisition of English: A Longitudinal Study of Hmong Adults." *Psychological Reports* 79:15–18.

Grenfell, M., and D. James. 1998. *Bourdieu and Education: Acts of Practical Theory.* Bristol, Pa.: Falmer.

Gutmann, A., ed. 1994. *Multiculturalism: Examining "The Politics of Recognition."* Princeton, N.J.: Princeton University Press.

Gylys, J. A., and J. R. McNamara. 1996. "Acceptance of Rape Myths among Prosecuting Attorneys." *Psychological Reports* 79 (1): 15–18. https://doi.org/10.2466/pro.1996.79.1.15.

Haag, A. M. 2007. "The Indian Boarding School Era and Its Continuing Impact on Tribal Families and the Provision of Government Services." *Tulsa Law Review* 43:149.

Haga, R. 2014. "'Freedom Has Destroyed the Somali Family': Somali Parents' Experiences of Epistemic Injustice and Its Influence on their Raising of Swedish Muslims." In *Making European Muslims,* 39–55. New York: Routledge.

Haigler, K., and R. Nelson. 2005. *The Gap-Year Advantage.* New York: Macmillan.

Hall, K. 1995. "'There's a Time to Act English and a Time to Act Indian': The Politics of Identity among British-Sikh Teenagers." In *Children and the Politics of Culture,* edited by S. Stephens, 243–64. Princeton, N.J.: Princeton University Press.

Hall, S. 1986. "Gramsci's Relevance for the Study of Race and Ethnicity." *Journal of Communication Inquirty* 10 (2): 5–27.

Hall, S. (1990) 1994. "Cultural Identity and Diaspora." In *Colonial Discourse and Post-colonial Theory: A Reader,* edited by P. Williams and L. Chrisman. London: Harvester Wheatsheaf.

Hall, S. 1995. "New Cultures for Old." In *A Place in the World?,* edited by D. Massey and P. Jess, 175–213. Oxford: Oxford University Press.

Hamilton-Merritt, J. 1993. *Tragic Mountains: The Hmong, the Americans, and the Secret Wars for Laos.* Bloomington: Indiana University Press.

Han, K. T. 2014. "Moving Racial Discussion Forward: A Counterstory of Racialized Dynamics between an Asian-Woman Faculty and White Preservice Teachers in Traditional Rural America." *Journal of Diversity in Higher Education* 7 (2): 126.

Hang, M., et al. 2004. "American Paj Ntaub: Wat Tham Krabok Assessment Team Report." St. Paul, Minn. https://brycs.org/clearinghouse/0840/.

Hanh, T. N., and D. Berrigan. 2009. *The Raft Is Not the Shore: Conversations toward a Buddhist–Christian Awareness.* Maryknoll, N.Y.: Orbis.

Hansen, M. L. 1996. "The Problem of the Third Generation Immigrant." In *Theories of Ethnicity,* edited by W. Sollors, 201–15. New York: New York University Press.

Hardy, E. 2014. "*The Good Lie* Tracks Sudanese Immigrants to America and Explores a Culture Clash." *Village Voice,* October 1, 2014.

Hernández-Chávez, E. 1988. "Language Policy and Language Rights in the United States." In *Minority Education: From Shame to Struggle,* edited by T. Skutnabb-Kangas and J. Cummins, 45–56. Clevedon, U.K.: Multilingual Matters.

Hill-Collins, P. 2006. *From Black Power to Hip Hop.* Philadelphia: Temple University Press.

Hillmer, P. 2010. *A People's History of the Hmong.* St. Paul: Minnesota Historical Society.

Hillmer, P., and M. A. Yang. 2017. "Commentary: Ignorance as Bias: Radiolab, Yellow Rain, and 'The Fact of the Matter.'" *Hmong Studies Journal* 18:1–13.

Hmong National Development to Clear Channel/KDWB, April 20, 2011. https://hndinc.org/.

hooks, b. 1990. "Homeplace (A Site of Resistance)." In *Yearning: Race, Gender, and Cultural Politics,* 41–50. Boston: South End.

Horsford, S. D., T. Grosland, and K. M. Gunn. 2011. "Pedagogy of the Personal and Professional: Toward a Framework for Culturally Relevant Leadership." *Journal of School Leadership* 21 (4): 582–606.

Hughes, D., J. Rodriguez, E. P. Smith, D. J. Johnson, H. C. Stevenson, and P. Spicer. 2006. "Parents' Ethnic-Racial Socialization Practices: A Review of Research and Directions for Future Study." *Developmental Psychology* 42 (5): 747–70.

Hutchison, R., and M. McNall. 1994. "Early Marriage in a Hmong Cohort." *Journal of Marriage and Family* 56 (93): 579–90.

Huttunen, R. 2007. "Critical Adult Education and the Political-Philosophical Debate between Nancy Fraser and Axel Honneth." *Educational Theory* 57 (4): 423–33.

Hvitfeldt, C. 1986. "Traditional Culture, Perceptual Style, and Learning: The Classroom Behavior of Hmong Adults." *Adult Education Quarterly* 36 (2): 65–77.

Ishimaru, A. M., and S. Takahashi. 2017. "Disrupting Racialized Institutional Scripts: Toward Parent–Teacher Transformative Agency for Educational Justice." *Peabody Journal of Education* 92 (3): 343–62.

Jacobs, B. W. 1996. "No-Win Situation: The Plight of the Hmong—America's Former Ally." *Boston College Third World Law Journal* 16:139.

James, T. 1987. *Exile Within: The Schooling of Japanese Americans, 1942–1945*. Cambridge, Mass.: Harvard University Press.

Jany, L. 2020. "Prosecutors: No Charges against Officers in Chiasher Vue Shooting in North Minneapolis." *Star Tribune,* December 21, 2020. https://www.startribune.com/prosecutors-no-charges-against-officers-in-chiasher-vueshooting-in-north-minneapolis/573450731/.

Jaret, C. 1999. "Troubled by Newcomers: Anti-immigrant Attitudes and Action during Two Eras of Mass Immigration to the United States." *Journal of American Ethnic History* 18:9–39.

Johnson, L. 2006. "'Making Her Community a Better Place to Live': Culturally Responsive Urban School Leadership in Historical Context." *Leadership and Policy in Schools* 5 (1): 19–36.

Johnson, L. 2007. "Rethinking Successful School Leadership in Challenging U.S. Schools: Culturally Responsive Practices in School–Community Relationships." *International Studies in Educational Administration* 35 (3): 49–57.

Johnson, N. L., G. H. Rocchino, J. A. Wolf, M. H. Gutekunst, C. Paulvin, and J. A. Farrell. 2021. "Rape Culture and Candidate Selection in the 2016 U.S. Presidential Election." *Social Politics: International Studies in Gender, State and Society* 28 (1): 168–92.

Jones, C. 2007. "Vang Pao and the U.S. Government, Marriage, and Betrayal." *Hmong Today* at *Twin Cities Daily Planet,* July 15, 2007. https://www.tcdailyplanet.net/vang-pao-and-u-s-government-marriage-and-betrayal/#.

Jung, M.-H. 2022. *Menace to Empire: Anticolonial Solidarities and the Transpacific Origins of the U.S. Security State.* Berkeley: University of California Press.

Kaestle, C. 1983. "Pillars of the Republic: Common Schools and American Society, 1780–1860." New York: Hill & Wang.

Kana'iaupuni, S. M. 2005. "Ka'akalai ku kanaka: A Call for Strengths-Based Approaches from a Native Hawaiian Perspective." *Educational Researcher* 34 (5): 32–38.

Kang, H., S. Okazaki, N. Abelmann, C. Kim-Prieto, and S. Lan. 2010. "Redeeming Immigrant Parents: How Korean American Emerging Adults Reinterpret Their Childhood." *Journal of Adolescent Research* 25 (3): 441–64.

Karakayali, N. 2005. "Duality and Diversity in the Lives of Immigrant Children." *Canadian Review of Sociology and Anthropology* 42 (3): 325–44.

Keenan, M. 2013. *Child Sexual Abuse and the Catholic Church: Gender, Power, and Organizational Culture.* Oxford: Oxford University Press.

Kelly, B. T., and K. I. McCann. 2014. "Women Faculty of Color: Stories behind the Statistics." *Urban Review* 46 (4): 681–702.

Keown-Bomar, J. 2004. *Kinship Networks among Hmong-American Refugees.* El Paso, Tex.: LFB Scholarly Publishing.

Kerr, J. 2014. "Western Epistemic Dominance and Colonial Structures: Considerations for Thought and Practice in Programs of Teacher Education." *Decolonization: Indigeneity, Education, and Society* 3 (2): 83–144.

Khalifa, M. 2013. "Creating Spaces for Urban Youth: The Emergence of Culturally Responsive (Hip-Hop) School Leadership and Pedagogy." *Multicultural Learning and Teaching* 8:63–93. https://doi.org/10.1515/mlt-2013-0010.

Khalifa, M., and N. M. Abdi. 2023. "Rescue from Coloniality? The Power of Dreaming." *Journal of Family Diversity in Education* 5 (2): 115–26. https://doi.org/10.53956/jfde.2023.189.

Khalifa, M. A., M. A. Gooden, and J. E. Davis. 2016. "Culturally Responsive School Leadership: A Synthesis of the Literature." *Review of Educational Research* 86 (4): 1272–311. https://doi.org/10.3102/0034654316630383.

Kibria, N. 1993. *Family Tightrope: The Changing Lives of Vietnamese Americans.* Princeton, N.J.: Princeton University Press.

Kim, J. 2010. *Ends of Empire: Asian American Critique and the Cold War.* Minneapolis: University of Minnesota Press.

King, J. E., and E. E. Swartz. 2014. *Re-membering History in Student and Teacher Learning: An Afrocentric Culturally Informed Praxis.* New York: Routledge.

King, J. E., and E. E. Swartz. 2015. *The Afrocentric Praxis of Teaching for Freedom: Connecting Culture to Learning.* New York: Routledge.

King Jr., M. L. 1967. "Beyond Vietnam: A Time to Break Silence." Speech delivered at Riverside Church, New York, April 4, 1967. Civil Rights Movement Archive. https://www.crmvet.org/info/mlk_viet.pdf.

Kirkland, David E. 2021. "A Pedagogy for Black People: Why Naming Race Matters." *Equity and Excellence in Education* 54 (1): 60–67. http://dx.doi.org/10.1080/10665684.2020.1867018.

Kolano, L. 2016. "Smartness as Cultural Wealth: An AsianCrit Counterstory." *Race, Ethnicity, and Education* 19 (6): 1149–63.

Koltyk, J. A. 1998. *New Pioneers in the Heartland: Hmong Life in Wisconsin.* Allyn and Bacon.

Koumarn, Y. S., and G. L. Barney. 1981. *Glimpses of Hmong History and Culture.* Washington, D.C.: English Resource Center.

Kumashiro, K. 2000. "Toward a Theory of Anti-oppressive Education." *Review of Educational Research* 70 (1): 25–53.

Kurien, P. 1999. "Gendered Ethnicity: Creating a Hindu Indian Identity in the U.S." *American Behavioral Scientist* 42:648–70.

Kwan, Y. Y. 2015. "Microaggressions and Hmong American Students." *Bilingual Research Journal* 38 (1): 23–44. https://doi.org/10.1080/15235882.2015.1017026.

Kwan, Y. Y. 2020. "Interrogating Trauma: Hmong and Cambodian American Identity and Subjecthood." *New Directions for Higher Education* 2020 (191): 79–89. https://doi.org/10.1002/he.20384.

Ladson-Billings, G. 1995. "Toward a Theory of Culturally Relevant Pedagogy." *American Educational Research Journal* 32 (3): 465–91.

Ladson-Billings, G. 2004. "New Directions in Multicultural Education: Complexities, Boundaries, and Critical Race Theory." In *Handbook of Research on Multicultural Education,* 2nd ed., edited by J. A. Banks and C. A. McGee Banks, 50–65. San Francisco: Jossey-Bass.

Ladson-Billings, G. 2006. "Yes, but How Do We Do It? Practicing Culturally Relevant Pedagogy." In *White Teachers/Diverse Classrooms: A Guide to Building Inclusive Schools, Promoting High Expectations, and Eliminating Racism,* edited by J. Landsman and C. W. Lewis, 29–42. Sterling, Va.: Stylus.

Lamborn, S. D. and M. Moua. 2008. "Normative Family Interactions: Hmong American Adolescents' Perceptions of Their Parents." *Journal of Adolescent Research* 23 (4): 411–37.

Lamont, M. 2009. *The Dignity of Working Men: Morality and the Boundaries of Race, Class, and Immigration.* Cambridge, Mass.: Harvard University Press.

Lamont, M., and A. Lareau. 1988. "Cultural Capital: Allusions, Gaps, and Glissandos in Recent Theoretical Developments." *Sociological Theory* 6:153–68.

Lapin, A. 2012a. "Radiolab Producers Release 'Yellow Rain' Email." *Current,* October 25, 2012. https://current.org/2012/10/radiolab-producers-release-yellow-rain-email/.

Lapin, A. 2012b. "Search for 'Truth' Results in 'Radiolab' Apology." *Current,* October 24, 2012. https://current.org/2012/10/search-for-truth-results-in-radiolab-apology/.

Lareau, A. 1987. "Social Class Differences in Family–School Relationships: The Importance of Cultural Capital." *Sociology of Education* 60 (2): 73–85.

Lareau, A. 1989. *Home Advantage: Social Class and Parental Intervention in Elementary Education.* Bristol, Pa.: Falmer.

Lareau, A., and E. McNamara Horvat. 1999. "Moments of Social Inclusion and Exclusion: Race, Class, and Cultural Capital in Family–School Relationships." *Sociology of Education* 72:37–53.

Lareau, A., and E. B. Weininger. 2003. "Cultural Capital in Educational Research: A Critical Assessment." *Theory and Society* 32 (5–6): 567–606.

Lawson, M. A. 2003. "School–Family Relations in Context: Parent and Teacher Perceptions of Parent Involvement." *Urban Education* 38 (1): 77–133.

Lazarus, E. 1883. "The New Colossus." Poetry Foundation. https://www.poetryfoundation.org/poems/46550/the-new-colossus.

Lee, G. Y. 2008. "Nostalgia and Cultural Re-creation: The Case of the Hmong Diaspora." *Crossroads* 19 (2): 125–54.

Lee, J. K., and K. Green. 2008. "Hmong Parental Involvement and Support: A Comparison between Families of High and Low Achieving High School Seniors." *Hmong Studies Journal* 9:1–26.

Lee, M. N. M. 2016. "The Women of 'Dragon Capital': Marriage Alliances and the Rise of Vang Pao." In *Claiming Place: On the Agency of Hmong Women,* 87–116. Minneapolis: University of Minnesota Press.

Lee, R. G. 1999. *Orientals: Asian Americans in Popular Culture.* Philadelphia: Temple University Press.

Lee, R. M., K. R. Jung, J. C. Su, A. G. Tran, and N. F. Bahrassa. 2009. "The Family Life and Adjustment of Hmong American Sons and Daughters." *Sex Roles* 60 (7–8): 549–58.

Lee, S. 1997. "The Road to College: Hmong American Women's Pursuit of Higher Education." *Harvard Educational Review* 67 (4): 803–28.

Lee, S. C., Z. B. Xiong, and F. K. Yuen. 2006. "Explaining Early Marriage in the Hmong American Community." In *Teen Pregnancy and Parenthood: Global Perspectives, Issues, and Interventions,* edited by H. Holgate, R. Evans, and F. K. Yuen, 25–37. New York: Routledge.

Lee, S. J. 2001a. "Exploring and Transforming the Landscape of Gender and Sexuality: Hmong American Teenaged Girls." *Race, Gender, and Class,* 35–46.

Lee, S. J. 2001b. "More than Model Minorities or Delinquents: Hmong American High School Students." *Harvard Educational Review* 73 (3): 505–28.

Lee, S. J. 2005. *Up Against Whiteness: Race, School, and Immigrant Students.* New York: Teachers College Press.

Lee, S. J., and M. R. Hawkins. 2008. "'Family Is Here': Learning in Community-Based After-School Programs." *Theory into Practice* 47 (1): 51–58.

Lee, S. M. 1993. "Racial Classifications in the U.S. Census: 1890–1990." *Ethnic and Racial Studies* 16 (1): 75–94.

Lee, S. S. 2008. "The De-minoritization of Asian Americans: A Historical Examination of the Representations of Asian Americans in Affirmative Action Admissions Policies at the University of California." *Asian American Law Journal* 15:129–52.

Le Espiritu, Y. 1992. *Asian American Panethnicity: Bridging Institutions and Identities.* Philadelphia: Temple University Press.

Le Espiritu, Y. 2001. "'We Don't Sleep Around Like White Girls Do': Family, Culture, and Gender in Filipina American Lives." *Signs* 26 (2): 415–40.

Lei, J. 2003. "(Un)necessary Toughness? Those 'Loud Black Girls' and Those 'Quiet Asian Boys.'" *Anthropology and Education Quarterly* 34 (2): 158–81.

Lew, J. 2006. *Asian Americans in Class: Charting the Achievement Gap among Korean American Youth.* New York: Teachers College Press.

Lewis, O. (1966) 1981. "The Culture of Poverty." In *Anthropological Realities: Readings in the Science of Culture,* edited by J. Guillemin, 316–20. New Brunswick, N.J.: Transaction.

Lie, G. Y., P. Yang, K. Rai, and P. Y. Vang. 2004. "Hmong Children and Families." *Culturally Competent Practice with Immigrant and Refugee Children and Families,* 122–45.

Lightfoot, D. 2004. "'Some Parents Just Don't Care': Decoding the Meanings of Parental Involvement in Urban Schools." *Urban Education* 39 (1): 91–107.

Lincoln, Y. S., and E. G. Guba. 1985. *Naturalistic Inquiry.* Thousand Oaks, Calif.: Sage.

Linders, A., and C. Bogard. 2014. "Teenage Pregnancy as a Social Problem: A Comparison of Sweden and the United States." In *International Handbook of Adolescent Pregnancy,* edited by A. L. Cherry and M. E. Dillon, 147–57. Springer.

Lipsitz, G. 1998. *The Possessive Investment in Whiteness: How White People Profit from Identity Politics*. Philadelphia: Temple University Press.

Lo, L. 2009. "Perceptions of Asian Immigrant Families of Children with Disabilities towards Parental Involvement." In *New Perspectives on Asian American Parents, Students, and Teacher Recruitment,* edited by C. C. Park, R. C. Endo, and X. L. Rong, 1–24. Charlotte, N.C.: Information Age.

Logan, T. K., L. Evans, E. Stevenson, and C. E. Jordan. 2005. "Barriers to Services for Rural and Urban Survivors of Rape." *Journal of Interpersonal Violence* 20 (5): 591–616.

Long, L. 1993. *Ban Vinai, the Refugee Camp.* New York: Columbia University Press.

Lopez, D. E. 1976. "The Social Consequences of Chicano Home / School Bilingualism." *Social Problems* 24 (2): 234–46.

Lopez, G. 2001. "The Value of Hard Work: Lessons on Parent Involvement from an (Im)migrant Household." *Harvard Educational Review* 71 (3): 416–38.

Lopez, N. 2003. *Hopeful Girls, Troubled Boys: Race and Gender Disparity in Urban Education.* New York: Routledge.

Lopez, M. L., and C. B. Stack. 2001. "Social Capital and the Culture of Power: Lessons from the Field." In *Social Capital and Poor Communities,* edited by S. Saegert and J. P. Thompson, 31–59. New York: Russell Sage Foundation.

Louwagie, P., and D. Browning. 2005a. "Shamed into Silence." *Star Tribune,* October 9, 2005.

Louwagie, P., and D. Browning. 2005b. "Shamed into Silence: Culture Clash Can Stymie Help." *Star Tribune,* October 10, 2005.

Lowe, L. 1996. *Immigrant Acts: On Asian American Cultural Politics.* Durham, N.C.: Duke University Press.

Lowe, L. 1998a. "The International within the National: American Studies and Asian American Critique." *Cultural Critique* 40:29–47.

Lowe, L. 1998b. "The Power of Culture." *Journal of Asian American Studies* 1 (1): 5–29.

Lowe, L. 2015. *The Intimacies of Four Continents.* Durham, N.C.: Duke University Press.

Lublin, D. 1999. *The Paradox of Representation: Racial Gerrymandering and Minority Interests in Congress.* Princeton, N.J.: Princeton University Press.

Lutz, A., and L. Jayaram. 2015. "Getting the Homework Done: Social Class and Parents' Relationship to Homework." *International Journal of Education and Social Science* 2 (6): 73–84.

Lynch, A., D. F. Detzner, and J. B. Eicher. 1996. "Transmission and Reconstruction of Gender through Dress: Hmong American New Year Rituals." *Clothing and Textiles Research Journal* 14 (4): 257–66.

Lyons, B. 2015. "Pepin Man Sentenced for Beating Menomonie Hunter." *Dunn County News,* May 7, 2015. https://chippewa.com/dunnconnect/news/local/pepin-man-sentenced-for-beating-menomoniehunter/article_d699e88b-a95d-54a2-8ba4-ec58c28d640d.html.

Macedo, D., ed. 2019. *Decolonizing Foreign Language Education: The Misteaching of English and Other Colonial Languages.* New York: Routledge.

Macedo, D., B. Dendrinos, and P. Gounari. 2015. *Hegemony of English.* New York: Routledge.

Macleod, C., and K. Durrheim. 2002. "Foucauldian Feminism: the Implications of Governmentality." *Journal for the Theory of Social Behavior* 32 (1): 41–60. https://doi.org/10.1111/1468-5914.00175.

Macur, J. 2013. "In Steubenville Rape Case, a Lesson for Adults." *New York Times,* November 27, 2013. https://www.nytimes.com/2013/11/27/sports/in-steubenville-rape-case-a-lesson-for-adults.html.

Maier, S. L. 2008. "'I Have Heard Horrible Stories . . .': Rape Victim Advocates' Perceptions of the Revictimization of Rape Victims by the Police and Medical System." *Violence against Women* 14 (7): 786–808.

Maira, S. 2008. "Flexible Citizenship/Flexible Empire: South Asian Muslim Youth in Post-9/11 America." *American Quarterly* 60 (3): 697–720.

Maldonado-Torres, N. 2007. "On the Coloniality of Being: Contributions to the Development of a Concept." *Cultural Studies* 21:240–70. https://doi.org/10.1080/09502380601162548.

Marroni, S. 2017. "'People Fear What They Don't Understand': Culture Clash with Immigrants Divides Pa. Town." (Harrisburg, Pa.) *Patriot-News,* July 28, 2017.

Martinez-Cosio, M., and R. M. Iannacone. 2007. "The Tenuous Role of Institutional Agents: Parent Liaisons as Cultural Brokers." *Education and Urban Society* 39 (3): 349–69.

Massey, D., and P. Jess 1995. "Places and Cultures in an Uneven World." In *A Place in the World?,* edited by D. Massey and P. Jess, 216–38. Oxford: Oxford University Press.

Matsuda, M. J. 1987. "Looking to the Bottom: Critical Legal Studies and Reparations." *Harvard Civil Rights–Civil Liberties Law Review* 22:323–99.

Matsuda, M. J. 1990. "Beside My Sister, Facing the Enemy: Legal Theory Out of Coalition." *Stanford Law Review* 43:1183.

McCarthy, C. 1993. "Beyond the Poverty Theory in Race Relations." In *Beyond Silenced Voices,* edited by L. Weis and M. Fine, 325–46. Albany, N.Y.: SUNY Press.

McCarty, T. L. 2002. *A Place to Be Navajo.* Mahwah, N.J.: Lawrence Erlbaum.

McGranahan, C. 2016. "Theorizing Refusal: An Introduction." *Cultural Anthropology* 31 (3): 319–25.

Memmott, M. 2011. "Vang Pao, Hmong Leader and General Who Led Secret War in Laos, Has Died." *NPR,* January 7, 2011. https://www.npr.org/sections/thetwo-way/2011/01/07/132732562/vang-pao-hmong-leader-and-general-who-led-secret-war-in-laos-has-died.

Meredith, W. H., and G. P. Rowe. 1986. "Changes in Lao Hmong Marital Attitudes after Immigrating to the United States." *Journal of Comparative Family Studies* 17 (1): 117–26.

Mettier, K. 2019. "Judge Said a Teen from a 'Good Family' Should Not Be Tried as an Adult in Sexual Assault." *Washington Post,* July 3, 2019. https://www.washingtonpost.com/nation/2019/07/03/judge-says-teen-good-family-should-not-be-tried-sexual-assault-an-adult/.

Meyer, C. F., and E. K. Rhoades. 2006. "Multiculturalism: Beyond Food, Festival, Folklore, and Fashion." *Kappa Delta Pi Record* 42 (2): 82–87.

Mignolo, W. 2000. *Local Histories/Global Designs: Coloniality, Subaltern Knowledges, and Border Thinking.* Princeton, N.J.: Princeton University Press.

Mignolo, W. D. 2007. "Delinking: The Rhetoric of Modernity, the Logic of Coloniality, and the Grammar of De-coloniality." *Cultural Studies* 21 (2–3): 449–514.

Mignolo, W. D. 2009. "Epistemic Disobedience, Independent Thought, and Decolonial Freedom." *Theory, Culture, and Society* 26 (7–8): 159–81.

Milner IV, H. R. 2006. "The Promise of Black Teachers' Success with Black Students." *Educational Foundations* 20:89–104.

Milner, H. R. 2011. "Culturally Relevant Pedagogy in a Diverse Urban Classroom." *Urban Review* 43 (1): 66–89.

Miner, B. 2007. "Killing Stirs Racial Concerns in North Woods of Wisconsin." *New York Times,* January 9, 2007. https://www.nytimes.com/2007/01/09/us/09hmong.html.

Mitchell, R. E. 1992. "Tradition, Change, and Hmong Refugees." In *Creativity and Tradition in Folklore: New Directions,* edited by S. J. Bronner, 263–75. Logan: Utah State University Press.

Miyares, I. M. 1997. "Changing Perceptions of Space and Place as Measures of Hmong Acculturation." *Professional Geographer* 49:214–24. https://doi.org/10.1111/0033-0124.00071.

Mohanty, C. T. 1984. "Under Western Eyes: Feminist Scholarship and Colonial Discourses." *boundary 2* 12–13:333–58.

Morrison, T. 1998. "Toni Morrison Beautifully Answers an 'Illegitimate' Question on Race (Jan. 19, 1998)." Interview with Charlie Rose. Public Broadcasting Service. https://www.youtube.com/watch?v=-Kgq3F8wbYA.

Mottin, J. 1984. "A Hmong Shaman's Seance." *Asian Folklore Studies* 43 (1): 99–108.

Moua, M. Y., and S. D. Lamborn. 2010. "Hmong American Adolescents' Perceptions of Ethnic Socialization Practices." *Journal of Adolescent Research* 25 (3): 416–40.

Moua, W. 2007a. "Leader in Trouble: 77-Year-Old General Vang Pao Arrested." *Hmong Today* at *Twin Cities Daily Planet,* June 20, 2007. https://www.tcdailyplanet.net/leader-trouble-77-year-old-general-vang-pao-arrested/#.

Moua, W. 2007b. "Community Support Continues to Grow." *Hmong Today* at *Twin Cities Daily Planet,* July 17, 2007. https://www.tcdailyplanet.net/community-support-continues-grow/.

MPR (Minnesota Public Radio). 2011. "Remembrances of Gen. Vang Pao." *MPR News,* January 7, 2011. https://www.mprnews.org/story/2011/01/07/vang-pao-remembrance.

Mueller, C. 2017. "Woman in Wisconsin Tells Hmong Shoppers on Black Friday to 'Speak the Language.'" *USA Today,* November 27, 2017. https://www.usatoday.com/story/news/nation-now/2017/11/27/irate-anti-immigrant-holiday-shopper/899693001/.

Murakami-Ramalho, E. 2010. "Educational Leadership in a Changing World: Preparing Students for Internationalization and Globalization through Advocacy

Leadership." In *New Perspectives in Educational Leadership,* edited by S. Douglass Horsford, 197–215. New York: Peter Lang.

Nagata, D. K., S. J. Trierweiler, and R. Talbot. 1999. "Long-Term Effects of Internment during Early Childhood among Third Generation Japanese Americans." *American Journal of Orthopsychiatry* 69:19–29. https://doi.org/10.1037/h0080378.

Nagel, J. 1994. "Constructing Ethnicity: Creating and Recreating Ethnic Identity and Culture." *Social Problems* 41 (1): 152–76.

Nakagawa, K. 2000. "Unthreading the Ties that Bind: Questioning the Discourse of Parent Involvement." *Educational Policy* 14 (4): 443–72.

Narayan, U. 1997. *Dislocating Cultures.* New York: Routledge.

Nasir, N. S. 2004. "When Culture Is Not in the Students, and Learning Is Not in the Head." Review of J. Ogbu with A. Davis, *Black American Students in an Affluent Suburb. Human Development* 47:108–16.

Nelson, L. 2005. "Culture Affects Hmong Attitudes towards Girls." Letter to the editor. *Star Tribune,* October 12, 2005.

Ng, F. 1993. "Towards a Second Generation Hmong History." *Amerasia Journal* 19 (3): 51–70.

Ngo, B. 2002. "Contesting 'Culture': The Perspectives of Hmong American Female Students on Early Marriage." *Anthropology and Education Quarterly* 33 (2): 163–88.

Ngo, B. 2008a. "The Affective Consequences of Cultural Capital: Feelings of Powerlessness, Gratitude, and Faith among Refugee Hmong Parents." *Journal of Southeast Asian American Education and Advancement* 3:1–16.

Ngo, B. 2008b. "Beyond 'Culture Clash' Understandings of Immigrant Experiences." *Theory into Practice* 47 (1): 4–11.

Ngo, B. 2009. "Ambivalent Urban, Immigrant Identities: The Incompleteness of Lao American Student Identities." *Qualitative Studies in Education* 22 (2): 201–20.

Ngo, B. 2010. "Doing 'Diversity' at Dynamic High: Problems and Possibilities of Multicultural Education in Practice." *Education and Urban Society* 42 (4): 473–95.

Ngo, B. 2017. "Naming Their World in a Culturally Responsive Space: Experiences of Hmong Adolescents in an After-School Theatre Program." *Journal of Adolescent Research* 32 (1): 37–63.

Ngo, B., and K. Kumashiro. 2014. *Six Lenses for Anti-oppressive Education.* 2nd ed. New York: Peter Lang.

Ngo, B., and S. Lee. 2007. "Complicating the Image of Model Minority Success: A Review of Southeast Asian American Education." *Review of Educational Research* 77 (4): 415–53.

Ngo, B., and J. Leet-Otley. 2011. "Discourses about Gender among Hmong American Policymakers." *Journal of Language, Identity, and Education* 10 (2): 99–118.

Nguyen, J., and B. B. Brown. 2010. "Making Meanings, Meaning Identity: Hmong Adolescent Perceptions and Use of Language and Style as Identity Symbols." *Journal of Research on Adolescence* 20 (4): 849–68.

Nguyen, V. T. 2012. "Refugee Memories and Asian American Critique." *positions* 20 (3): 911–42.

Noddings, N., ed. 2005. *Educating Citizens for Global Awareness.* New York: Teachers College Press.

Obama, B. 2016. "Remarks of President Obama to the People of Laos, Vientiane, Laos." Delivered September 6, 2016. White House Office of the Press Secretary. https://obamawhitehouse.archives.gov/the-press-office/2016/09/06/remarks-president-obama-people-laos.

Okihiro, G. Y. 2016. *Third World Studies: Theorizing Liberation.* Durham, N.C.: Duke University Press.

Olsen, L. 1997. *Made in America: Immigrant Students in Our Public Schools.* New York: New Press.

Olzak, S. 1983. "Contemporary Ethnic Mobilization." *Annual Review of Sociology* 9 (1): 355–74.

Ong, A. 2003. *Buddha Is Hiding: Refugees, Citizenship, the New America.* Berkeley: University of California Press.

Orellana, M. F. 2001. "The Work Kids Do: Mexican and Central American Immigrant Children's Contributions to Households and Schools in California." *Harvard Educational Review* 71 (3): 366–90.

Orsi, R. A. 1985. *The Madonna of 115th Street: Faith and Community in Italian Harlem, 1880–1950.* New Haven, Conn.: Yale University Press.

Osajima, K. 1993. "The Hidden Injuries of Race." In *Bearing Dreams, Shaping Visions: Asian Pacific American Perspectives,* edited by L. Revilla, G. Nomura, S. Wong, and S. Hune, 81–91. Pullman: Washington State University Press.

Osiagwu, J. 2021. "Immigrant Parents Struggle with Cultural Clashes." *New Canadian Media,* June 9, 2021. https://newcanadianmedia.ca/immigrant-parents-struggle-with-cultural-clashes/.

Otero, L. R., and J. Cammarota. 2011. "Notes from the Ethnic Studies Home Front: Student Protests, Texting, and Subtexts of Oppression." *International Journal of Qualitative Studies in Education* 24 (5): 639–48.

Ott, T. 2006. "Urban Immigrants Bring a Culture Clash to Older Suburbs." (Cleveland, Ohio) *Plain Dealer,* January 2, 2006.

Palazzo, C. 2010. "The Hmong Plight Continues as the U.S. Continues Their Abandonment." *Veterans Today,* February 27, 2010. http://www.veteranstoday.com.

Pang, V. O. 2005. *Multicultural Education: A Caring-Centered, Reflective Approach.* 2nd ed. New York: McGraw-Hill.

Paraskeva, J. M. 2016. *Curriculum Epistemicide: Towards an Itinerant Curriculum Theory.* New York: Routledge.

Paris, D. 2012. "Culturally Sustaining Pedagogy: A Needed Change in Stance, Terminology, and Practice." *Educational Researcher* 41 (3): 93–97. https://doi.org/10.3102/0013189X12441244.

Paris, D., and H. S. Alim. 2014. "What Are We Seeking to Sustain through Culturally Sustaining Pedagogy? A Loving Critique Forward." *Harvard Educational Review* 84 (1): 85–100.

Park, G. C. 2011. "'Are We Real Americans?' Cultural Production of Forever Foreigners at a Diversity Event." *Education and Urban Society* 43 (4): 451–67.

Patel, A. 2014. "Parental Involvement and Child Development." Social Science Research Network (SSRN), August 7, 2014. https://doi.org/10.2139/SSRN.2477253.

Payne, D. L., K. A. Lonsway, and L. F. Fitzgerald. 1999. "Rape Myth Acceptance: Exploration of Its Structure and Its Measurement Using the Illinois Rape Myth Acceptance Scale." *Journal of Research in Personality* 33 (1): 27–68.

Penzenstadler, N. 2007. "Professor Under Fire for Remarks." *Badger Herald,* February 23, 2007. https://badgerherald.com/news/2007/02/23/professor-under-fire/.

Perry, P. 2001. "White Means Never Having to Say You're Ethnic." *Journal of Contemporary Ethnography* 30:56–91.

Phelan, P., A. L. Davidson, and H. Yu. 1998. *Adolescents' Worlds: Negotiating Family, Peers, and School.* New York: Teachers College Press.

Phenice, L., E. Martinez, and G. Grant. 1986. "Minority Family Agendas: The Home–School Interface and Alternative Schooling Models." In *Child Rearing in the Home and School,* 121–56. New York: Springer.

Philip, T. M. 2011. "Moving Beyond Our Progressive Lenses: Recognizing and Building On the Strengths of Teachers of Color." *Journal of Teacher Education* 62 (4): 356–66.

Philip, T. M. 2014. "Asian American as a Political–Racial Identity: Implications for Teacher Education." *Race, Ethnicity, and Education* 17 (2): 219–41.

Portes, A., and L. Hao. 1998. "E Pluribus Unum: Bilingualism and Language Loss in the Second Generation." Levy Economics Institute Working Paper 229. Social Science Research Network (SSRN). http://dx.doi.org/10.2139/ssrn.121374.

Portes, A., and R. G. Rumbaut. 2006. *Immigrant America: A Portrait.* 3rd ed. Berkeley: University of California Press.

Pyke, K. 2000. "'The Normal American Family' as an Interpretive Structure of Family Life among Grown Children of Korean And Vietnamese Immigrants." *Journal of Marriage and Family* 62 (1): 240–55.

Pyke, K., and T. Dang. 2003. "'FOB' and 'Whitewashed': Identity and Internalized Racism among Second Generation Asian Americans." *Qualitative Sociology* 26 (2): 147–72.

Qin, D. B. 2006. "'Our Child Doesn't Talk to Us Anymore': Alienation in Immigrant Chinese Families." *Anthropology and Education Quarterly* 37 (2): 162–79.

Quijano, A. 2000. "Coloniality of Power and Eurocentrism in Latin America." *International Sociology* 15 (2): 215–32.

Quijano, A. 2007. "Coloniality and Modernity/Rationality." *Cultural Studies* 21 (2–3): 168–78.

Quincy, K. 1995. *Hmong: History of a People.* 2nd ed. Cheney, Wash. Eastern Washington University Press.

Raffaelli, M., and L. L. Ontai. 2004. "Gender Socialization in Latino/a Families: Results from Two Retrospective Studies." *Sex Roles* 50:287–99.

Rah, Y., S. Choi, and T. Nguyen. 2009. "Building Bridges between Refugee Parents and Schools." *International Journal of Leadership in Education* 12 (4): 347–65.

Rauhala, E. 2011. "Vang Pao." *Time,* December 14, 2011. https://content.time.com/time/specials/packages/article/0,28804,2101745_2102136_2102247,00.html.

Rivas, J. 2011. "Racist Phone Call for Hmong City Council Candidate in Minnesota." *Colorlines*, November 10, 2011. https://www.colorlines.com/articles/racist-phone-calls-hmong-city-council-candidate-minnesota.

Rodríguez, N. N. 2020. "'This Is Why Nobody Knows Who You Are': (Counter)stories of Southeast Asian Americans in the Midwest." *Review of Education, Pedagogy, and Cultural Studies* 42 (2): 157–74.

Rosaldo, R. 1989. *Culture and Truth: The Remaking of Social Analysis.* Boston: Beacon.

Rose, G. 1995. "Place and Identity: A Sense of Place." In *A Place in the World?*, edited by D. Massey and P. Jess, 87–132. Oxford: Oxford University Press.

Ruiz-de-Velasco, J., M. Fix, and B. C. Clewell. 2000. *Overlooked and Underserved: Immigrant Students in U.S. Secondary Schools.* Washington, D.C.: Urban Institute.

Rumbaut, R. 1989. "Portraits, Patterns, and Predictors of the Refugee Adaptation Process." In *Refugees as Immigrants,* edited by D. W. Haines, 138–90. Lanham, Md.: Rowman & Littlefield.

Rumbaut, R. 1994. "The Crucible Within: Ethnic Identity, Self-Esteem, and Segmented Assimilation among Children of Immigrants." *International Migration Review* 28:748–94.

Rumbaut, R. G. 1996. "A Legacy of War: Refugees from Vietnam, Laos, and Cambodia." In *Origins and Destinies: Immigration, Race, and Ethnicity in America,* edited by S. Pedraza and R. G. Rumbaut, 315–33. Wadsworth.

Sabzalian, L. 2019. *Indigenous Children's Survivance in Public Schools.* New York: Routledge.

Said, E. 1994. *Culture and Imperialism.* New York: Vintage.

Sarroub, L. K. 2005. *All American Yemeni Girls: Being Muslim in a Public School.* Philadelphia: University of Pennsylvania Press.

Saulny, S. 2007. "Hmong, Shaken, Wonder If a Killing Was Retaliation." *New York Times,* January 14, 2007. https://www.nytimes.com/2007/01/14/us/14hmong.html.

Sautman, B. 2014. "Self-Representation and Ethnic Minority Rights in China." *Asian Ethnicity* 15 (2): 174–96.

Schein, L. 2016. "Thinking Diasporic Sex: Cultures, Erotics, and Media across Hmong Worlds." In *Claiming Place: On the Agency of Hmong Women,* edited by C. Y. Vang, F. Nibbs, and M. Vang, 249–79. Minneapolis: University of Minnesota Press.

Schein, L., and V. M. Thoj. 2007. "Occult Racism: The Masking of Race in the Hmong Hunter Incident. A Dialogue between Anthropologist Louisa Schein and Filmmaker/Activist Va-Megn Thoj." *American Quarterly* 59 (4): 1051–95.

Scheurich, J. J., and M. D. Young. 1997. "Coloring Epistemologies: Are Our Research Epistemologies Racially Biased?" *Educational Researcher* 26 (4): 4–16. https://doi.org/10.3102/0013189X026004004.

Schlund-Vials, C. J. 2012. "Cambodian American Memory Work: Justice and the 'Cambodian Syndrome.'" *positions* 20 (3): 805–30.

Schlund-Vials, C. J. 2016. "The Subjects of 1975: Delineating the Necessity of Critical Refugee Studies." *MELUS* 41 (3): 199–203.

Scott, J. 1992. "Experience." In *Feminists Theorize the Political,* edited by J. Butler and J. W. Scott. London: Routledge.

Shannon, S. M. 1995. "The Hegemony of English: A Case Study of One Bilingual Classroom as a Site of Resistance." *Linguistics and Education* 7 (3): 175–200.

Simpson, A. 2014. *Mohawk Interruptus: Political Life across the Borders of Settler States.* Durham, N.C.: Duke University Press.

Simpson, A. 2017. "The Ruse of Consent and the Anatomy of 'Refusal': Cases from Indigenous North America and Australia." *Postcolonial Studies* 20 (1): 18–33.

Smith, L. T. 2012. *Decolonizing Methodologies: Research and Indigenous Peoples.* 2nd ed. London: Zed.

Smith-Hefner, N. J. 1999. *Khmer American.* Berkeley: University of California Press.

Solomos, J., and L. Back. 1995. *Race, Politics, and Social Change.* New York: Routledge.

Solórzano, D. G., and T. J. Yosso. 2002. "Critical Race Methodology: Counter-storytelling as an Analytical Framework for Education Research." *Qualitative Inquiry* 8 (1): 23–44.

Solórzano, D. G., L. Pérez Huber, and L. Huber-Verjan. 2019. "Theorizing Racial Microaffirmations as a Response to Racial Microaggressions: Counterstories across Three Generations of Critical Race Scholars." *Seattle Journal for Social Justice* 18: 185–215.

Spivak, G. (1985) 1996. "Subaltern Studies: Deconstructing Historiography." In *The Spivak Reader: Selected Works of Gayatri Chakravorty Spivak,* edited by D. Landry and G. MacLean, 203–35. London: Routledge.

Spring, Joel. 2016. *Deculturalization and the Struggle for Equality: A Brief History of the Education of Dominated Cultures in the United States.* 8th ed. New York: Routledge.

Stake, R. 1995. *The Art of Case Study Research.* Thousand Oaks, Calif.: Sage.

Stanton-Salazar, R. 1997. "A Social Capital Framework for Understanding the Socialization of Racial Minority Children and Youths." *Harvard Educational Review* 67 (1): 1–41.

Stoler, A. L. 2006. *Haunted by Empire: Geographies of Intimacy in North American History.* Durham, N.C.: Duke University Press.

Stritikus, T., and D. Nguyen. 2007. "Strategic Transformation: Gender Identity Negotiation in First Generation Vietnamese Youth." *American Educational Research Journal* 44 (4): 853–95.

Stubbs-Richardson, M., N. E. Rader, and A. G. Cosby. 2018. "Tweeting Rape Culture: Examining Portrayals of Victim Blaming in Discussions of Sexual Assault Cases on Twitter." *Feminism and Psychology* 28 (1): 90–108.

Suárez-Orozco, C., and I. L. G. Todorova. 2003. "The Social Worlds of Immigrant Youth." In "Understanding the Social Worlds of Immigrant Youth," edited by C. Suárez-Orozco and I. L. G. Todorova, special issue, *New Directions for Youth Development* 100:15–24. https://doi.org/10.1002/yd.60.

Suárez-Orozco, M. 2001. "Global Shifts: U.S. Immigration and the Cultural Impact of Demographic Change." In *Seismic Shifts,* edited by J. S. Little and R. K. Triest, 179–88. Boston: Federal Reserve Bank of Boston Conference Series No. 46.

Suárez-Orozco, M., and D. Qin-Hilliard. 2004. *Globalization: Culture and Education in the New Millennium.* Berkeley: University of California Press.

Sumida Huaman, E. 2020. "Small Indigenous Schools: Indigenous Resurgence and Education in the Americas." *Anthropology and Education Quarterly* 51:262–81. https://doi.org/10.1111/aeq.12335.

Supple, A. J., and S. A. Small. 2006. "The Influence of Parental Support, Knowledge, and Authoritative Parenting on Hmong And European American Adolescent Development." *Journal of Family Issues* 27 (9): 1214–32.

Supple, A. J., S. Z. McCoy, and Y. Wang. 2010. "Parental Influences on Hmong University Students' Success." *Hmong Studies Journal* 11:1–37.

Swartz, D. 1997. *Culture and Power: The Sociology of Pierre Bourdieu*. Chicago: University of Chicago Press.

Symonds, P. V. 2004. *Calling in the Soul: Gender and the Cycle of Life in a Hmong Village*. Seattle: University of Washington Press.

Takagi, D. Y. 1992. *The Retreat from Race: Asian-American Admissions and Racial Politics*. New Brunswick, N.J.: Rutgers University Press.

Takaki, R. 1989. "Who Killed Vincent Chin?" In *A Look Beyond the Model Minority Image*, edited by G. Yun, 23–29. London: Minority Rights Group.

Tang, E. 2015. *Unsettled: Cambodian Refugees in the New York City Hyperghetto*. Philadelphia: Temple University Press.

Tapp, N. 1989. "Hmong Religion." *Asian Folklore Studies*, 59–94.

Taylor, C. (1992) 1997. "The Politics of Recognition." In *New Contexts of Canadian Criticism*, edited by A. Heble, D. P. Pennee, and J. R. Struthers, 25–73. Peterborough, Canada: Broadview.

Teachman, J. D., L. M. Tedrow, and K. D. Crowder. 2000. "The Changing Demography of America's Families." *Journal of Marriage and Family* 62 (4): 1234–46.

Teranishi, R. T. 2004. "Yellow and Brown: Emerging Asian American Immigrant Populations and Residential Segregation." *Equity and Excellence in Education* 37 (3): 255–63.

Terry, K. J., M. L. Smith, K. Schuth, J. R. Kelly, B. Vollman, and C. Massey. 2011. *The Causes and Context of Sexual Abuse of Minors by Catholic Priests in the United States, 1950–2010*. Washington, D.C.: United States Conference of Catholic Bishops.

Thao, C. 2016. *Hmong Refugees in the New World: Culture, Community, and Opportunity*. Jefferson, N.C.: McFarland.

Thao, Y. J. 2003. "Empowering Mong Students: Home and School Factors." *Urban Review* 35 (1): 25–42.

Thornton, A. 1991. "Influence of the Marital History of Parents on the Marital and Cohabitational Experiences of Children." *American Journal of Sociology* 96 (4): 868–94.

Trask, H. K. 1999. *From a Native Daughter: Colonialism and Sovereignty in Hawaii*. Rev. ed. Honolulu: University of Hawai'i Press.

Trieu, M. M. 2019. "Understanding the Use of 'Twinkie,' 'Banana,' and 'FOB': Identifying the Origin, Role, and Consequences of Internalized Racism within Asian America." *Sociology Compass* 13 (5): e12679. https://doi.org/10.1111/soc4.12679.

Trieu, M. M., and H. C. Lee. 2018. "Asian Americans and Internalized Racial Oppression: Identified, Reproduced, and Dismantled." *Sociology of Race and Ethnicity* 4 (1): 67–82.

Trueba, H., L. Jacobs, and E. Kirton. 1990. *Cultural Conflict and Adaptation: The Case of Hmong Children in American Society.* Bristol, Pa.: Falmer.

Tzou, C. T., Meixi, W. Suarez, P. Bell, D. LaBonte, E. Starks, and M. Bang. 2019. "Making, Materiality, and Robotics within Everyday Acts of Indigenous Presence and Resurgence." *Cognition and Instruction* 37 (3): 306–26.

Tseng, V. 2004. "Family Interdependence and Academic Adjustment in College: Youths from Immigrant and U.S. Born Families." *Child Development* 75:966–83.

Tuan, M. 1998. *Forever Foreigners or Honorary Whites?* New Brunswick, N.J.: Rutgers University Press.

Uecker, J. E., and C. E. Stokes. 2008. "Early Marriage in the United States." *Journal of Marriage and Family* 70 (4): 835–46.

Umemoto, K. 1989. "'On Strike!' San Francisco State College Strike, 1968–69: The Role of Asian American Students." *Amerasia Journal* 15 (1): 3–41.

Urrieta Jr., L., and S. A. Villenas. 2013. "The Legacy of Derrick Bell and Latino/a Education: A Critical Race Testimonio." *Race, Ethnicity, and Education* 16 (4): 514–35.

Valdes, G. 1996. *Con Respeto: Bridging the Distances between Culturally Diverse Families and Schools.* New York: Teachers College Press.

Valenzuela, A. 1999. *Subtractive Schooling: U.S. Mexican Youth and the Politics of Caring.* Albany, N.Y.: SUNY Press.

Vang, C. T. 2005. "Hmong-American Students Still Face Multiple Challenges in Public Schools." *Multicultural Education* 13 (1): 27.

Vang, C. Y., F. Nibbs, and M. Vang, eds. 2016. *Claiming Place: On the Agency of Hmong Women.* Minneapolis: University of Minnesota Press.

Vang, M. 2021. *History on the Run: Secrecy, Fugitivity, and Hmong Refugee Epistemologies.* Durham, N.C.: Duke University Press.

Vang, P. D., and P. Her. 2014. "Teenage Marriage among Hmong American Women." *Journal of Human Behavior in the Social Environment* 24 (2): 138–55.

Vasquez, R. 2021. "(Re)inscribing White Cultural Hegemony: The Paradox of Culturally Relevant Pedagogy?" *Educational Studies* 57 (5): 509–23.

Vezner, T. 2007. "Klobuchar, Coleman Protest Restrictions on Hmong." *Pioneer Press,* May 15, 2007. https://www.twincities.com/2007/05/15/washington-klobuchar-coleman-protest-restrictions-on-hmong-2/.

Vizenor, G. 2008. *Survivance: Narratives of Native Presence.* Lincoln: University of Nebraska Press.

VOA (Voice of America). 2007. "Change Sought in Anti-terror Laws to Aid Hmong Refugees from Laos." *VOA News,* March 29, 2007. https://lao.voanews.com/a/a-52-2007-03-29-voa1-90683389/1185920.html.

Vogt, L. A., C. Jordan, and R. G. Tharp. 1987. "Explaining School Failure, Producing School Success." *Anthropology and Education Quarterly* 18 (4): 276–86.

Walker-Moffat, W. 1995. *The Other Side of the Asian American Success Story.* San Francisco: Jossey-Bass.

Walter, P. 1994. "An Assessment of the Educational Needs of Hmong Adults." *Adult Basic Education* 4 (1): 35–49.

wamwa Mwanga, Kaghondi. 2022. "Re-membering the Postcolonial Musical Audience with Indigenous Soundscapes: Mbeyu Njija Music-Video Documentary in Tanzania." *Journal of African Cultural Studies* 34 (1): 80–97.

Warikoo, N. K. 2007. "Racial Authenticity among Second Generation Youth in Multiethnic New York and London." *Poetics* 35:388–408.

Warikoo, N., and P. Carter. 2009. "Cultural Explanations for Racial and Ethnic Stratification in Academic Achievement." *Review of Educational Research* 79 (1): 366–94.

Waters, M. 1999. *West Indian Immigrant Dreams and American Realities.* New York: Russell Sage Foundation.

wa Thiong'o, N. 2009. *Something Torn and New: An African Renaissance.* New York: Basic.

wa Thiong'o, N. 2012. *Globalectics: Theory and the Politics of Knowing.* New York: Columbia University Press.

Wiley, T. G. 2001. "On Defining Heritage Languages and Their Speakers: Heritage Languages in America." In *Heritage Languages in America: Preserving a National Resource,* edited by J. K. Peyton, D. A. Ranard, and S. McGinnis, 29–36. New York: Center for Applied Linguistics and Delta Systems.

Williams, B. 2009. "Fong Lee's Family Angered by Verdict." *MPR News,* May 28, 2009. https://www.mprnews.org/story/2009/05/28/fong-lees-family-angered-by-verdict.

Wilson, T. S. 2016. "Contesting the Public School: Reconsidering Charter Schools as Counterpublics." *American Educational Research Journal* 53 (4): 919–52.

Wisconsin Historical Society. 1991. "Women's Motivational Workshop: Racist Comment/Actions toward Hmong, July 25, 1991." Online facsimile available in John D. Medinger Papers, La Crosse (Wis.) Area Research Center. http://www.wisconsinhistory.org/turningpoints/search.asp?id=1322.

Wong, N.-W. A. 2010. "'Cuz They Care about the People Who Goes There': The Multiple Roles of a Community-Based Youth Center in Providing 'Youth (Comm) unity' for Low-Income Chinese American Youth." *Urban Education* 45 (5): 708–39.

Wong-Fillmore, L. 1991. "When Learning a Second Language Means Losing the First." *Early Childhood Research Quarterly* 6 (3): 323–46.

Wong-Fillmore, L. 2000. "Loss of Family Languages: Should Educators Be Concerned?" *Theory into Practice* 39 (4): 203–10.

Wu, H. 2007. "Writing and Teaching behind Barbed Wire: An Exiled Composition Class in a Japanese-American Internment Camp." *College Composition and Communication* 59:237–62.

Xiong, C. 2006. "Slain Man's Family Demands Answers: Fong Lee Was Shot Multiple Times by a Minneapolis Police Officer Early Saturday Evening." *Star Tribune,* July 27, 2006.

Xiong, G. P. 2010. "Growing Up Hmong in Laos and America: Two Generations of Women through My Eyes." *Amerasia Journal* 36 (1): 55–103.

Xiong, K. 2005. "Wisconsin's Hmong Resettlement Task Force Report." Madison, Wis.: Task Force on Hmong Resettlement. https://www.wistatedocuments.org/digital/api/collection/p267601coll4/id/1341/download.

Xiong, N. 2021. "Southeast Asian Americans Unite in Solidarity and Demand Justice for Soobleej Kaub Hawj." Southeast Asian Resource Action Center, August 3, 2021. https://www.searac.org/california/southeast-asian-americans-unite-in-solidarity-and-demand-justice-for-soobleej-kaub-hawj/.

Xiong, Z. B., V. Deenanath, and D. Mao. 2013. "Parent–Child Relationships in Hmong Immigrant Families in the United States." In *The Other People*, 91–106. London: Palgrave Macmillan.

Xiong, Z. B., and D. F. Detzner. 2005. "Southeast Asian Fathers' Experiences with Adolescents: Challenges and Change." *Hmong Studies Journal* 6:1–23.

Xiong, Z. B., D. F. Detzner, and M. J. Cleveland. 2004–5. "Southeast Asian Adolescents' Perceptions of Immigrant Parenting Practices." *Hmong Studies Journal* 5:1–20.

Xiong, Z. B., A. Tuicomepee, L. LaBlanc, and J. Rainey. 2006. "Hmong Immigrants' Perceptions of Family Secrets and Recipients of Disclosure." *Families in Society* 87 (2): 231–39.

Yang, D. 1992. "The Hmong: Enduring Traditions." In *Minority Cultures of Laos: Kammu, Lua', Lahu, Hmong, and Iu-Mein*, 249–327. Folsum, Calif.: Folsum Cardova Unified School District.

Yang, K. 2003. "Hmong Americans: A Review of Felt Needs, Problems, and Community Development." *Hmong Studies Journal* 4 (1): 1–23.

Yang, K. 2007. "An Assessment of the Hmong American New Year and Its Implications for Hmong-American Culture." *Hmong Studies Journal* 8:1–32.

Yang, K. K. 2008. *The Latehomecomer: A Hmong Family Memoir.* Minneapolis: Coffee House Press.

Yang, K. K. 2012. "The Science of Racism: Radiolab's Treatment of the Hmong Experience." *Hyphen Magazine*, October 22, 2012. https://hyphenmagazine.com/blog/2012/10/22/science-racism-radiolabs-treatment-hmong-experience.

Yang, Y. 1998. "Practicing Modern Medicine: 'A Little Medicine, a Little Neeb.'" *Hmong Studies Journal* 2 (2): 1–7.

Yosso, T. J. 2005. "Whose Culture Has Capital? A Critical Race Theory Discussion of Community Cultural Wealth." *Race, Ethnicity, and Education* 8:69–91. https://doi.org/10.1080/1361332052000341006.

Yuan, X. 2021. "Refusing Educational Desire: Negotiating Faith and Precarity at an Underground Chinese Christian School." *Asian Anthropology* 20 (3): 190–209. https://doi.org/10.1080/1683478X.2021.1930468.

Zhou, M., and C. L. Bankston III. 1998. *Growing Up American: How Vietnamese Children Adapt to Life in the United States.* New York: Russell Sage Foundation.

Zhou, M., and C. L. Bankston III. 2001. "Family Pressure and the Educational Experience of the Daughters of Vietnamese Refugees." *International Migration* 39 (4): 133–51.

Zournazi, M. 2003. *Hope: New Philosophies for Change.* New York: Routledge.

Index

BIC NGO is professor of curriculum and instruction at the University of Minnesota, where she holds the Rodney S. Wallace Professorship for the Advancement of Teaching and Learning. She is author of *Unresolved Identities: Discourse, Ambivalence, and Urban Immigrant Students* and coeditor of *Six Lenses for Anti-oppressive Education: Partial Stories, Improbable Conversations*.